Y0-BYV-291

Personal Quests and Quandaries

Coming of Age in the 21st Century

Written and Compiled by

Carol W. Hotchkiss

Published by Avocus Publishing, 2004

PERSONAL QUESTS AND QUANDARIES

Avocus Publishing, Inc.
4 White Brook Road
Gilsum, NH 03448
Telephone: 800-345-6665
FAX: 603-357-2073
e-mail: info@avocus.com

All rights reserved. No part of this book may be reproduced or transmitted in any form or by any means, electronic or mechanical, including photocopying, recording or by any information storage and retrieval system without the permission of the authors and Avocus Publishing, except for brief quotations.

Disclaimer:
Nothing in this book is intended in any way to be libelous in nature. Neither is it intent of Avocus Publishing, Inc. to publish any accusatory statement, direct or implied, of improper motives or illegal actions by any individual or educational institution. Any other interpretation of our printing is erroneous and therefore misunderstood. We believe that the public interest in general, and education in particular, will be better served by the publication of the author's experience and opinion.

Copyright © 2004 by Avocus Publishing, Inc.

Printed in the United States of America

ISBN 1-890765-01-5 ($19.95) Softcover

Cover design by Michele Newkirk

Acknowledgments

This book has been a labor of love and celebration of the many students I have known in thirty years as a teacher, counselor, and dean. The stories are a composite of many and I thank each student. If you recognize parts of yourself, I hope that I have done justice to your courage and hard work.

Special thanks and affection goes to those who agreed to write their own story—*Greg Lemmons, Kate Hemion, Clara Zurn, Carie Broeker-Ford, Tammy Bynum, Lorenzo Moreno, Aisha Dawson, Kyra Ryan, Meitar Moscovitz, and my wonderful sister-in-law, Anne Hotchkiss.*

Thanks too to the talented artists who illustrated these stories with their wonderful self-portraits—Suki Boynton, Joannie Chiu, Daniela DiGregorio, Landi Guidetti, Mo Higby, Julia Hopkins, Kim Kern, Jiyoung Kim, Claire Min, Katie Mullet, Anna Petry, JungEn (Jennifer) Shim, Balinder Tara Singh, Robin Strumpf, Hana Tsukamoto, Milee Uhm, Drew Walton, Teresa Wan, and Jessica Webb. Their teachers submitted their work with great pride and deserve thanks and recognition as well: Lisa Brody (Kent School), Kristie Higby (Mercersburg Academy), John Hinman (Kent School), Jill Hoefgen (San Domenico School), Susan Hoffer (Emma Willard School), Charlie Sitzer (Viewpoint School), Jay Torson (Newark Academy), and Jessica Watkin (Kent School). Leslie Boran from St. Margaret's School in Virginia and Nina Fleishman at Emma Willard School in New York and their ISU students were very helpful in contributing ideas to the story on being an international student in the United States and I thank them for their careful, honest thoughts.

I would also like to thank *David Crosby,* who has used his hard-won lessons to reach out to young people, *Cher,* for being a triumphant example of the strength and gifts of dyslexia, *Gloria Steinem,* who has forged the way for a generation of young girls, *Joseph Marshall, Jr.,* for his powerful, compassionate work with young black men, and *Harvey Milk,* for his courageous voice for young gay people across this country. And I hope that the story of my good high school friend, *Steven Toney,* will raise the objections that the injustice of his mistaken incarceration demands.

To my son, *Sam,* and to the many friends who listened, read, reviewed, and cheered me on, here it is. Thanks for believing. To the students who shared their hopes, dreams, and fears, I hope that I have heard you well and that my enduring respect and affection comes through in these stories.

Dedication

I *would like to dedicate this book to my fa-ther, Edward T. Wright, for encouraging me to write and to pay attention to my own stories and the stories around me.*

I hope that everyone who reads this book will feel the comfort and companionship of others who have been where you are, and compassion and understanding for those who you may not have known before.

WISDOM'S PATH

as told by Uncle Frank Davis, Fancy Warrior, Pawnee spiritual elder, age 94

My mother was a good woman. I thought she was the wisest person in the whole world. So one day—when I was just a little feller, maybe six or seven—I asked her how I could become wise like her. She just laughed and laughed and said I was awfully young to be asking such questions. But, she said, since I asked, she would tell me.

"Life is like a path," she said, smiling down at me, "and we all have to walk the path. If we lay down, we even lay down on that path. If we live through the night and hard times, we still have to get up and start walking down that path again. As we walk down that path, we'll find experiences like little scraps of paper in front of us along the way. We must pick up those pieces of scrap paper and put them in our pocket.

"Then one day, we will have enough scraps of paper to put together and see what they say. Maybe we'll have enough to make some sense. Read the information and take it to heart. Then put the scraps of paper back in that pocket and go on, because there will be more pieces to pick up. Later we can pull them out and study them and maybe learn a little more. If we do this all through life, we'll know when to pull out those scraps to read more of the message. The more we read, the more we'll learn the meaning of life. We can become wise—at least wiser than we were.

"But if we never pick up those scraps of paper and never read them, we never become wiser. We'll keep wondering about life and never learn the Creator's instructions for us. Remember one thing," she said with her finger pointed straight at me "even if we pick up all those scraps, we'll still be learning. Nobody ever learns all the answers."

I've always tried to pick up the scraps of paper, like my mother said. Missed a few though. After that, some things just never made sense. Still trying to figure out what was on those missing scraps.

—From *Wisdomkeepers: Meetings with Native American
Spiritual Elders*
by Steve Wall and Harvey Arden

INTRODUCTION

Each of us has a story. There are the short stories of summer camp or a friendship made and lost; a first love, or a frightening adventure. And there is our own personal story that weaves all of our short stories together into a unique pattern that gives emphasis and meaning to our life. It is in the recognition and telling of these stories that we come to know our selves and understand others. A classic piece of literature may be the story of an individual in a foreign time, place, and circumstances, but the telling allows us to identify with the common emotions, struggles, and quandaries of the human experience, no matter how different. A good story shows us both how we are like others and how we are different. Our own story chronicles the quests and quandaries that we encounter, how we have confronted them, and what we have gathered from them that has shaped our lives and character.

In today's world, the quests and quandaries we face embody fewer physical challenges and more complicated personal and social questions. Everyone in modern industrial cultures must juggle conflicting demands and opportunities in a fast-paced world of media messages, Internet access, diverse perspectives, and fragile personal connections. The basic questions remain:

- *What kind of person do I want to be?*

- *What are the challenges I will face and how will I measure up?*

- *How will I deal with my failures, disappointments, and losses?*

- *What is extraordinary and unique about me?*

- *What makes me happy?*

- *What is my obligation to myself, to others, and to the world at large?*

The answers to these questions, however, are increasingly complex and uncertain. Each unique collection of thoughts, hopes, fears, mistakes, and experiences shape and change an individual life—sometimes gradually, sometimes abruptly. The problems and challenges that each of us face are our teachers. They give new understanding as we change and come to observe life in a new way. Our own experiences can create empathy with people whose experiences have been very different than our own. Our unexamined fears and injuries can create distance and misunderstanding.

Adolescence defines the character and possibilities of a culture at any given time. The questions facing young men and women are their cultural heritage shaped by the relationships, education, politics, media, and world events of their times. The adolescent experience defines a culture's spirit and moral fiber.

Today's teens live in a global community and are confronted with unique challenges and possibilities. Personal quests and quandaries today demand a level of wisdom, empathy, courage, and responsibility that often place young people in uncharted territory and sometimes at risk. Affluence, the Internet, and advertising offer infinite choices and pressures. Global awareness and diversity require sophisticated levels of empathy and social responsibility. Parents and families can be isolated and uncertain, providing adolescents with less time, fewer boundaries, and vague guidance. The media is omnipresent, creating needs, insecurities, expectations, skepticism, and phantom relationships. Even in a time of AIDS, sex has fewer boundaries, and street drugs fleetingly promise both escape and connection. Heroes and heroines are in short supply and there are few enclaves that offer a certain sanctuary from random violence or unexpected threats. Young people today are forced to be pragmatic realists, questioning the traditional idealism and rebelliousness of previous generations of adolescents.

On the other hand, many young people have risen to this challenge in courageous and extraordinary ways. Insightful young women and men are boldly redefining the ethics of their culture with empathy and integrity. They are disillusioned by the strained relationships, materialism, and alienation they have seen around them. They are examining their own experience with a hard-won shrewdness and sophistication. They are questioning their cultural and personal assumptions, confronting their personal choices and cultural values in new and questioning ways.

The stories in this book are brief self-portraits of young adults responding to their lives and making sense of today's world in wise, funny, poignant, and painful ways. Some of these stories come directly from teens who have shared their experiences, thoughts, and questions through their writing. Some come from literature, history, or autobiographies. Others are composite, but true stories that reflect the questions that confront each of us as we play out our lives. These stories chronicle success and defeat, courage and confusion. It is hoped that each of these stories will enlighten both your own personal journey and your understanding of others.

Ralph Waldo Emerson asserted that *the unexamined life is not worth living*. It is in sharing our stories that we enlarge and examine our own lives—not only for personal reflection, but to understand where and how we fit into the larger picture of human life. The last chapter is some suggestions on how you can write your own stories. In addition to some tips on getting started, this chapter contains questions on each of the earlier stories that are designed for personal reflection, journal writing, or discussion. You can write your own stories in reaction to the stories and issues in this book. If you are keeping a journal of your thoughts, you can use these questions to begin your own writing. These topics and questions may be used in conjunction with the information and exercises provided in *Quests and Quandaries*, a text for human development, life skills, and English classes. Families, seminars, leadership training, and residential life programs can use these stories and questions to address the challenges facing each of us in the twenty-first century.

For parents and teachers who are attempting to understand the many questions and challenges their children and students are facing, these stories will give you a glimpse at the extraordinary character and courage of young adults today.

Contents

Personal Quests and Quandaries

Coming of Age in the 21st Century

Our deepest fear is not that we are inadequate. Our deepest fear is that we are powerful beyond measure. It is our light, not our darkness that most frightens us. We ask ourselves, who am I to be brilliant, gorgeous, talented, and fabulous? Actually, who are you NOT to be? You are a child of God. Your playing small doesn't serve the world. There's nothing enlightened about shrinking so that other people won't feel insecure around you. We were born to make manifest the glory of God that is within us. It's not just in some of us; it's in everyone. And as we let our own light shine, we unconsciously give other people permission to do the same. As we are liberated from our own fear, our presence automatically liberates others.

—From the 1994 inaugural speech by Nelson Mandela

Chapter 1.

Questing: Coming of Age in the World

SELF-ESTEEM

"Appreciating my own worth and importance and having the character to be accountable for my self and to act responsibly toward others." This was the official definition of self-esteem used by the California Task Force to Promote Self-Esteem and Person and Social Responsibility established in 1990. This three-year task force of twenty-five men and women, representing a multicultural assortment of professional and community leaders, set out to determine the connection between self-esteem and the problems of school dropouts, teenage pregnancy, domestic violence, drug and alcohol addiction, crime, and violence. The task force found an inseparable connection between each of these problems and how an individual views and values him or her self. A girl who values herself and her future makes sexual decisions that protect her body and birth-giving potential. On the other hand, a pregnant fifteen-year-old is often faced with decisions and realities that undermine her confidence and sense of worth. Drug use often robs a person of the skills and independence that create a positive sense of self, and individuals with a high sense of self-esteem seem able to resist the attraction of the quick fix that drugs may offer. It is a catch-22: The more self-esteem you have, the more likely you are to take positive risks, reach out to other people, protect yourself from self-destructive activities, and be successful. This, in turn, builds more self-esteem. When you feel insecure, incompetent, or unlovable, you are less likely to take the steps necessary for your own development and protection that will make you feel better about yourself.

Gloria

The mind is its own place, and in itself can make a Heav'n of Hell, a Hell of Heav'n.

—John Milton

As I write this, I'm still the same person who grew up mostly in a Midwestern, factory-working neighborhood where talk about "self-esteem" would have seemed like a luxury. In my memory of those times and that place, men were valued by what they did, women by how they looked and then by what their husbands did, and all of life was arranged (or so we thought) from the outside in.

This experience of living among good people who were made to feel ungood by an economic class system imposed from above—people who often blamed themselves for hard times they had done nothing to deserve—left me with a permanent resistance to any self-help book or religion or psychological theory that tells us we can solve all our problems on our own. . . .

. . . not until sometime in my thirties did I begin to suspect that there might be an internal center of power I was neglecting. Though the way I'd grown up had encouraged me to locate power almost anywhere but within myself, I began to be increasingly aware of its pinpoint of beginning within—my gender and neighborhood training notwithstanding. . . . As wise women and men in every culture tell us: *The art of life is not controlling what happens to us, but using what happens to us.*

. . . When I enter a familiar room or street, I think I see a past self walking toward me. She can't see me in the future, but I can see her very clearly. She runs past me, worried about being late for an appointment she doesn't want to go to. She sits at a restaurant table in tears of anger arguing with the wrong lover. She strides toward me in the jeans and wine-red suede boots she wore for a decade, and I can remember the exact feel of those boots on my feet. She sits in a newspaper boardroom with the sort of powerful men who undermine her confidence the most, trying to persuade them to support a law that women badly need—and fails. She's a ghost in the lobby of an office building that she and all the women of *Ms. Magazine* walked through for so many years. She rushes toward me outside a lecture hall, talking, laughing, full of optimism.

I used to feel impatient with her: Why was she wasting time? Why was she with this man? At that appointment? Forgetting to say the most important thing? Why wasn't she wiser, more productive, happier? But lately, I've begun to feel a tenderness, a welling of tears in the back of my throat, when I see her. I think: *She's doing the best she can. She's survived—and she's trying so hard.* Sometimes, I wish I could go back and put my arms around her. . . .

We are so many selves. It's not just the long-ago child within us who needs tenderness and inclusion, but the person we were last year, wanted to be yesterday, tried to become in one job or in one winter, in one love affair or in one house where even now, we can close our eyes and smell the rooms.

What brings together these ever-shifting selves of infinite reactions and returnings is this: *There is always one true inner voice.*

Trust it.[1]

—From *Revolution from Within* by Gloria Steinem

ADOPTION

Being adopted may create some unique questions in your efforts to establish your own identity during adolescence. A big piece of the puzzle, your genetic makeup, is often missing. Your adoptive family has provided your environment and the love and care you have needed growing up. Your life in this family is a large, important part of who you are, but it doesn't explain your red hair, some physical characteristics, and even some genetically determined elements of your temperament. Some adopted teenagers have little or no interest in knowing more about their birthparents. Others are mildly curious. And some become determined to find out the circumstances of their adoption.

It is quite normal to speculate about what your birthparents look like, what kind of people they are, and why you were put up for adoption. Some states seal adoption records, but there is a lot of nonidentifying information about your adoption that is available to you. Many states are beginning to recognize the rights of adopted individuals to access this information about themselves. If you decide to search for your birthparents, it will help to have the support of your adoptive parents and enough personal confidence to understand what you discover. Some birthparents welcome contact about a child they have put up for adoption; others may have blocked out what was a painful and secretive decision and may not want to deal with it. It is wonderful if your birthparent becomes an added support person in your life, but if she or he cannot handle a relationship with you, that is because of her or his own problems and fears. There can be some very powerful feelings around these issues, so be sure that you have an objective adult to talk to.

The increase in international adoptions may add another dimension to individual identity questions. You may have no memory of your birthplace or culture, but physical or racial differences can make your adoption a visible part of your everyday life. You have been raised as an American child in an American environment, quite different from your birthparent's culture. The influence of heredity and environment is very real for you. If you are genetically Chinese, Russian, or Brazilian, but raised in Wyoming, what part of you is Chinese, Russian, or Brazilian and what part American? Strangers may expect you to be more like their stereotype of your national heritage, when, in fact, that may be very foreign to you. Nationals from your homeland may be offended by your lack of cultural identity or awareness. You are, first and foremost, a unique and distinct individual. Your bicultural makeup can give you a valuable insight into our international common nature as well as the limitation of judging people by appearance or nationality. Celebrate all of the interrelated parts of your identity and don't let others define you by their assumptions. Some international adopted children might feel "less than" either their adopted identity or their birth identity, but, in reality, they are "more than" either part. This awareness can significantly enrich your understanding of yourself and our world.

Kate

Betty Jean Lifton, an author and adoption activist, talks about the "ghost kingdoms" of adoption. All three members of the "adoption triad"—the babies who have been adopted, the birthparents, and the adoptive parents—live with these ghost kingdoms. Adoptees wonder about their "real" mother or father who they do not yet know. Is my mother a fairy queen? No, she must be a homeless bag lady. No. No, I can't make out her face. . . . Birthparents wonder about their lost child who has been relinquished for adoption. My son is six now, just the age to be wearing a striped T-shirt, shorts, and sweet little bangs bleached by the sun. My daughter. She is fourteen; is she menstruating? Does she know I am thinking about her? Does she have braces? I can't reach her. I see a baby's face, but she is now fourteen. Adoptive parents are often left with the ghost of the biological child they might have had, grieving their biological legacy, imagining how their "real" child might perhaps have been easier, prettier, smarter, or less difficult to parent. The sibling rival of the adopted child will always be the biological child that was never born. These ghosts haunt all of us in the triad until we get to know them. There is no way around it . . . adoption is a complicated matter and it gets more complicated with each new discovery. It wasn't always complicated for me. In fact, you may be thinking, "Adoption isn't complicated at all. I am adopted, but that's the end of the story. I am what I am. No different than anyone else." I thought that when I was a kid and people would ask me, "What's it feel like to be adopted?" or "Does it feel weird to be adopted?" I would always answer, "No, why should I feel different . . . my parents are my parents, my brother is my brother."

In some ways, that is still true. My parents are my parents and my brother is still my brother. What I discovered eventually, however, was that I did not just have a mother and a father, but that I have two mothers and two fathers and that IS different—not many people can say that. While I was raised with one brother, I now also have six brothers and sisters—and maybe more that I don't know. One set of parents raised me and the other set of parents gave birth to me. Both sets of parents are very, very, important if very, very different. It's like straddling the nature-nurture divide. The interesting thing is that you can't have one without the other and both made me who I am. If you don't have nature, you aren't born; if you don't have nurture, you die. I've given up trying to prioritize them or to prove that one is more important than the other. I am a product of both. I am all of my parents and having two sets of parents in my life has made me different.

In high school, I was a 99 percent nurture girl. Culture, your environment, your "parents" were everything. People turned out good or bad because of the influences around them. I believed it passionately and without doubt. At that time, my "parents" were my adoptive parents. There was no awareness or room for birthparents yet in my world. I did not need to know my biological mother. Or so I thought. . . .

Fantasies of my mother were always simple and, I think, typical. Sometimes she was very rich. Other times, I would imagine she was a haggard old bag lady. The worst was thinking she was dead. That was the only fantasy that scared me. It made me afraid to look for her. When I was eight or nine years old, my mother was a princess, but she didn't visit very often or I was too busy chasing my brother up the stairs or petting the cat to notice. I don't remember fantasizing about my birthfather at all, but I am sure he must have been a knight.

At fourteen, my birthmother became a faded sepia photograph, creased and tattered at the edges. The picture would float vaguely across my mind or flit in and out of reach. Sometimes, we played tag. I would catch her and hold her for a while in my hands looking at her, trying to see her. The funny thing was . . . she had a face I couldn't bring into focus. As soon as I held the photograph, moved my eyes downward and focused them on the picture and my hands, anticipating what I would see, her face would blur and the photograph would disappear. In my mind, I never knew where that sepia photograph was kept. It seemed to me there ought to have been a special box under my bed or a little drawer I could open when I needed or wanted to see it. But there wasn't. Instead, it would just appear to me from time to time out of nowhere.

My parents were open about my being adopted. I could not remember a time when I didn't know I was adopted. It was not talked about very much, but all of their friends and all of my friends knew my brother and I were adopted. I thought that it made people uncomfortable, and I tried to make them more comfortable by referring to it casually or not at all.

My need to hold the photograph grew and when someone asked if I ever wondered about my biological mother, I would say, "No, I don't need to know her. But I would like a photograph." I would fantasize about finding her and going to her house to watch her open the front door and go to a bus stop. I guess by this time, she was no longer a princess. Princesses don't have to take the bus. I didn't want to meet her. I just wanted to see her.

At fifteen, I asked my adoptive father if he would help me find my birthmother. His answer was a very encouraging, "Well, yes, I'll help you, when you are eighteen." He had not closed the doors, so that was good. He did not have a heart attack, so THAT was good. He did, however, effectively put the entire idea on hold. Eighteen seemed like a long way off, but my father had seemed "supportive" and that was as far as we all knew how to be around adoption. So I heard "yes" and waited while life took on other imperatives. If I had known then what I know now, I would have liked to find her then. I was not sure of my feelings and I had no sense of my RIGHT to find her, to know her. I would have found out that she was not a sepia photograph, but, in reality, was a beautiful fisherwoman who lived in Alaska.

No one knew my mother was a photograph in my mind. I never told anyone. While I told people I would like to have a picture of my biological mother, I never, never told anyone about my ephemeral sepia ghost mother. I dared not ask anyone to help me find that photograph because they might tell me it had been thrown away or was somehow irretrievable. I never dared ask my adoptive mom if I could look for my birthmother or what she knew about her. It was too painful for her and it was too precious to me—she might have destroyed that ghost photograph.

At the time, I thought I knew so much about my birthparents. Now that I write it down, I see I knew only eight words: *My biological parents were in college and unmarried.* Those ghosts must have been visiting me because I was sure I knew more than eight words about them—I had created elaborate fantasies about them—despite the fact that all I was told was that they were in college and unmarried.

At eighteen, I forgot to look for my mother. How can someone forget to look for her mother you might ask? Well, I don't know the answer to that. But I did. In fact, I forgot to look for her for another ten years. I was busy falling in love, applying to colleges, hiking in Kenya, looking for a job, and thinking about moving to Vermont or joining the Peace Corps. I was busy creating a life separate from *all* my parents, so the ghosts only followed at a distance.

Ten years later, I was married and beginning my own family. It wasn't until my daughter, Molly, was born that I wanted all my parents around me. As I held this new baby in my arms, I realized that she was the first human being I had ever known that was unquestionably my blood relative—and I wanted to know where she got her reddish hair.

I knew then that I would begin my search in earnest, but I had no tools and I would quickly find out that my decision was a very important, but very small step. First, my own fears of what I would find made me procrastinate for over a year. I knew I was afraid that it might be too late, that my mother might be dead, but now I also had to face the possibilities that she may not want to know me or that she was some dreadful human being who had bequeathed me terrible physical, mental, or criminal tendencies. What if I didn't like her? What if she didn't like me?

When I finally convinced myself that I could handle rejection or disappointment, I found out that the laws protected my unknown parents much more than they empowered me. True to his word, my adoptive father agreed to help and provided me with the medical records of my birth and parentage. At that time, my only rights were to know if I had inherited some genetic disease or condition. But the records also indicated that I was born in Vermont to a nineteen-year-old coed, a freshman in college. It was 1964 and she had hidden away in a home for "friendless" women. My heart ached to think of her all alone, frightened, and friendless. Abortion was not legal or easy in those days, but why did she go through all this to give birth to me? Was it hard for her to give me up? Was it the social pressures of that time that forced her to abandon me?

Abandon. That is a pretty strong word and I never allowed myself to even think it for a long time. As my search went on in stops and starts, I started to read about adoption and attend some conferences for people in the adoption triad—adoptees, birthparents, and adoptive parents. I learned that I had a right to know who my birthparents are, but the laws and records might not make it easy. I learned that many other adopted people had some of the same fantasies, fears, and feelings that I had. I learned that adopted kids often struggled with seemingly unrelated problems like drug use, depression, delinquency, A.D.D., and unwanted pregnancies of their own. And I learned that most adopted people (at least those who went to conferences), struggled in some way with feelings of abandonment. How could I feel abandoned by someone I never even knew? I was just a baby. I was days old when my adoptive parents lovingly took me home. How could it be a part of my psyche that some nineteen-year-old woman in a home for friendless women had decided that she did not want to be my mother?

This, of course, seemed completely illogical to me. I may find it hard to trust intimacy and I do tend to protect myself from losses at the slightest hint of abandonment. I like to keep everything on a rational, objective level and I have the hardest time ending or finishing things—it has taken me forever to write this damn story. But my friends would probably describe me as sensitive and caring; I cry over telephone commercials, I tenaciously fight for the underdog, and I am fiercely loyal to the friends who have gained my trust. Faced with these contradictions, logic refused to accept any whining about abandonment—I had never been left alone or uncared for. My adoptive parents provided for all of my needs and more. I could completely understand why a young, unmarried girl in 1964 would want a better life for me than she could provide. And yet all the logic I could muster could not satisfactorily answer the illogical, yet haunting question: Why didn't she want me? Why didn't she fight all logic and convention to keep me and take care of me? The question still seems childish and unreasonable, but it won't go away.

When I could reasonably procrastinate no longer, I decided to take a trip to Vermont and personally investigate my birth records. An unsympathetic, unyielding female clerk in the town hall found my records and guardedly let me see only the most restricted version. She seemed to disapprove of my search and stand as the champion of the rights and privacy of Birthmothers of America. The fact that this insufferable woman was sitting there with fundamental information about my life in her hands which she seemed to take great pleasure in withholding from me, made me apoplectic. I left the town hall with my lingering fears well outweighed by my rage.

My birthparents' names had been whited out along with any identifying information, but I did learn that my mother had taken the care to name me—Brianna. I also learned that she had been a student at the University of Massachusetts and that my father probably never knew that she was pregnant. Motivated by my resolve not to let that town clerk or the state of Vermont or the United States of America deny me the right to know my own parents, I returned to LA and began exploring every means I could find. There were detectives and on-line searches and support groups. I couldn't see it at the time, but, for another year, every time I got a promising lead, I pulled back, got busy, lost a phone number, or just decided "now" was not a good time.

I'm not sure what finally clicked. I had been searching for almost four years. I had attended conferences, rallies, and support groups. I was a walking poster child for adoptees who demanded the right to know their heritage. Yet I kept stopping short of really knowing. Then one evening at an adoptee support group, a woman told me that for $1500, she had an illegal, but very legitimate contact that would guarantee to find my mother within a week. I asked my adoptive father for the money and made an excitingly illicit "drop-off" in cash the next evening. In less than twenty-four hours, this contact called me with the name and phone number of my birthmother. Far from Vermont, she lived in a small fishing village in Alaska where her husband owned a fleet of boats.

I stared at the name and number for over twenty-four hours before I could bring myself to call. The voice that answered the phone sounded competent and confident. I asked her if the date of February 1, 1964, my birthdate, meant anything to her. The air of confidence and composure was suspended in the silence on the other end of the phone.

"Yes, it does. Who is this?"

"I believe that I am your daughter, Brianna."

This was the moment that I had hoped for and feared for most of my life. I had heard stories of mothers who had hung up, who denied any relationship, or who angrily told her adopted child that she wanted nothing to do with her. My fears filled in the silence that seemed interminable. When the shock had settled and my mother's composure returned, she finally said, "I am so glad that you have found me."

The relief made me giddy and I forgot the million questions that I wanted to ask—luckily, there would be time for that later. We gave each other a quick outline of our lives, exchanged numbers, and promised to call the next day when the shock had subsided. At eight o'clock the next morning, the phone rang and my birthmother told me her story and my own. Two weeks later, I flew up to meet her in Seattle. I met scores of relatives, some of whom never knew I existed, including my two half brothers. Several weeks later, she came down to meet my family, including her granddaughter, Molly, and my adoptive father. I must say they all did very well. Everyone was a little nervous, but gallant. My birthmother thanked my adoptive parents for taking such good care of me and my adoptive parents thanked her for giving me to them.

Since that time, I have genuinely felt a part of both of my family's lives. I have never found my father—he is still a ghost in my life—but I have come to know my birthmother well. Our similarities are uncanny and she has been happy to rejoin my life. My adoptive parents know and understand how much I love each of them, and they feel lucky and secure in their role as parents since they have known me all my life. Molly, my daughter, has at least eight grandparents and, since my adoptive father remarried, my husband wonders what he ever did to deserve three mothers-in-law.

What I have learned is that every search is different and deeply personal. The fundamental part of the search is coming to terms with yourself— your hopes and fears and your sense of who you are. You will proceed at your own speed and no one can tell you if and when you will begin your search. I was lucky to find my birthmother, lucky that she was ready to reconnect with me, and lucky that my adoptive parents welcomed her into my life. Each search will have its own outcome, some more difficult than others. In each search, the only constant is the discovery of more and more of yourself—your hopes and fears, your fantasies and realities. As I have met my ghosts and finally have an actual picture of all of my family, I now can see my own reflection more clearly.

"JAMIE" *by Jessica Webb*

TO THINE OWN SELF BE TRUE

One of the empowering and occasionally intimidating aspects of adolescence and adulthood is the freedom and obligation to think for yourself. This is actually much more complicated than it sounds. As a young child, you were probably more outspoken—right or wrong—than you are now. You howled when you were hungry, hit someone when she took your toy, and announced what you thought and liked with little regard to what others might think. As you grew older, you learned to think before you spoke, be considerate of other's feelings, and adjust your thoughts and feelings to the circumstances. At the same time, your family, your friends, your religion, your education, and your culture were subtly shaping your thoughts and beliefs. You modeled yourself after respected family members and friends. You were taught values, manners, history, taboos, and expectations. Even the language that you spoke shaped your experience of the world. You became a very different person than you would have been if you had been raised in a different family, social group, or country. Even within your family, personal differences and experiences combined to create your unique personality. That pure genetic embryo that was once your "true self" became shaped and defined by your environment, experiences, and choices.

To be true to yourself is a constantly evolving process. The essence of who you are is often clouded by what other people want you to be or who you think you should be or who the people around you are. It is when that small voice inside of you conflicts with any of these three voices that you are challenged to think carefully and be true to something most fundamentally yourself. Your parents want you to attend a certain college, but you believe you would be much better suited to a different school. Your friends are doing certain things that you think are wrong or distasteful. Your boyfriend thinks that sex should be an important part of your relationship, but you are not really ready for that. You feel awkward and uncomfortable when people around you make racist or sexist jokes. You find yourself attracted to members of your own gender in a culture that harshly judges homosexuality. You have an interest or passion that other people find odd or dorky. Everyone has always assumed that you would become a doctor, but you really want to become a fashion designer. Your culture expects men or women to behave in certain ways which seem limiting or unnatural to you. You question your parent's religious or political beliefs. You find yourself part of a group that is making fun of someone that you like. Subtle and obvious demands pressure you to behave in ways that don't seem true to who you are and what you believe. It is at these junctures that you struggle to define who you truly are and assert your individuality.

Even after you uncover your true feelings and nature, "being true" can require courage and determination. While none of us wants to become a submissive, mindless clone, neither do we want to become totally alienated or disconnected. Even the most inclusive group encourages some level of conformity and ostracizes deviant behavior. Civilization survives on common agreements about what is acceptable. When you find yourself at odds with the expectations of your social or family group, it will require courage and careful thought to express yourself and respect your inner voice. Whether you are resisting some social injustice, articulating an unpopular opinion, or deciding to follow a personal dream, you will most likely encounter resistance, self-doubt, and trepidation. Your discovery and perseverance is the core of who you are and what your life is about.

Melinda

The first time that I noticed Tyrone was probably seventh grade. We had all merged from several different elementary schools and it was the first time I had black students in my class. It was still a pretty rural, homogenous community, so the few black students in the school stood out. There wasn't any problem as far as I could tell, only curiosity. The reason I remember seventh grade is because one day someone had put a tack on Tyrone's chair and that created quite a scene when he sat down. It was a typical, dumb seventh-grade-boy joke, but I remember the awkward giggling and an apprehensive, guarded look on Ty's face. In spite of my segregated life, I had been raised in a family that taught me not to judge or think of people by race, so I dismissed racism as a factor. But the discomfort stuck in my mind.

Like most black and white students in my school, Tyrone and I coexisted, having a parallel education that rarely intersected outside of class or sporting events. I knew Ty because he was one of our leading basketball scorers, but it wasn't until my senior year that I got to know him as a person. We were in a psychology class together and in one unit we were studying racism and prejudice. There were twelve white students, three black students, and two Latino students in the class. The conversation was awkward and polite at first, but gradually we began to talk honestly and share some of the situations of discrimination that each of us had encountered. I didn't think I had been discriminated against, but recalled situations in school or around town when I had felt frightened or intimidated when confronted by a group of black or Latino people. I was surprised, and ashamed, when I listened to some of the discrimination that Tyrone and the other minority students had encountered right here at school and in our community. There were some arguments, even a few tears, but gradually we came to understand and care for each other in new ways.

Ty and I discovered that we had a lot of things in common and often carried our conversation beyond the classroom. He was good looking and loved to tease me—he seemed to listen and understand me like no one I had ever known before. We talked about life and jazz and parents and how we felt about everything. Before I realized it, I found myself looking forward to class and searching crowds at school for a glimpse of Ty and his friends. His smile made me blush and laugh. When we brushed shoulders in the hall or leaving class, I felt safe and warm just being near him. I was so taken by Tyrone as a person and the closeness we shared that I think I really believed that race would not be an issue. Ty shook his head and told me I was naive, but I just laughed. I felt wonderful; who could possibly object or even care?

We didn't really date—kids at my school didn't date much, but ran around in groups. Of course, the groups were segregated, so that didn't give me much chance to see Tyrone socially. A couple times, kids from my psychology class got together outside of school and it felt reckless and exciting to sit next to Ty at the local pizza place. That may sound strange to you, but it just wasn't done in my town. One of my friends must have noticed because she asked me later if there was something going on between Tyrone and me. When I smiled and started to tell her, she interrupted and told me she didn't think that it was such a good idea and I better watch myself. My brother told me that some of the guys were starting to talk in the locker rooms and it wasn't very nice talk.

Now, this was a wrinkle. I was surprised anyone would notice and confused that me being with Tyrone would bother them. Ty just rolled his eyes and said "Welcome to the world, little girl." We started to spend hours on the telephone—it was a relief to have his soft voice and comforting laugh with no color attached. We were invisible and in our private world. On our own, other people's comments and concerns seemed silly and powerless; we were lost in our personal thoughts and feelings. Our growing intimacy made me bolder and I began to complain that we couldn't be together in public. It felt hypocritical and unfair. We weren't doing anything wrong and it seemed cowardly to be so secretive. I wasn't embarrassed or afraid. I am ashamed to admit that I never really thought about Tyrone's position in all this—that it might be hard on him to have a white girlfriend. I was in love and was tired of worrying about what other people thought or said.

We sometimes met after school and walked part of the way home together as if we had just coincidentally been going the same way. We met secretly a couple times and went out on a date once to a nearby town. I was nervous, but we didn't run into anyone we knew and it felt wonderful to be together in the open. I was less cautious at school and rumors were flying. Conversations stopped when I approached a group and some people avoided me altogether. I was getting more and more paranoid and uneasy. One day, I had to walk though a large group of students hanging out on the school grounds. Luckily, I had my sunglasses on and books in hand, so I took a deep breath, held my head up, and walked through. One popular boy that I used to have a crush on said, loud enough for everyone to hear, "Why are you wearing shades? You want everyone to look black?" I don't know how I kept walking. These were my friends. What was happening?

From then on, the attacks became more daring and painful. Ty and I watched silently, brought together by our common predicament, but frightened by the disparity between our simple, loving relationship and the anger it seemed to evoke. Ty never told me about the trouble that he was given, but students would yell things at me from passing cars and once dumped a trash can full of garbage on my lawn with a sign that said "white trash." My parents were distraught and worried. Most of my closest friends didn't actually join in, but they didn't defend me either. By now, it was too late to erase anything. I was a scandal before I even realized what was happening. I didn't feel brave; I felt scared. But I knew that our relationship was blameless, that the way we were being treated was wrong, and I wasn't backing down. It wasn't heroic or even a choice—it felt like the only thing I could do.

It was about time for the junior-senior prom, which is a pretty big deal at my school. There was no way that Tyrone and I could go together—that would really be asking for trouble. The black students usually went together as a group and I figured, with all the rumors and harassment, no one would ask me to go. I was resigned to this. Then one week before the prom, in class, in front of a bunch of other students, Roger, the vice president of the senior class, asked if I was free to go to the prom with him. Roger had always been nice to me, he was on the basketball team with Ty, and he was surely aware of what was going on. The vice president of our class was sticking his neck out to ask *me* to the prom. I could feel the tension in the air as I accepted. I have no idea why Roger asked me; we were friends, but he could have gone to the prom with just about any girl in the class. I was grateful—and impressed. I felt that I had naively backed into my peer's wrath, but Roger had stepped in with his eyes wide open, daring anyone to question him . . . or me.

It was the best prom I ever attended. Roger was gallant and friendly—we laughed and enjoyed each other's company, unencumbered by the typical romantic complications. Emboldened by Roger's audacity, I spoke openly with several of my black friends and, on Roger's arm, chatted confidently with some of my white friends who had been shunning me for weeks. My eyes still searched the dance floor to keep track of Ty, but I was content to be at the same dance, with a brave and good friend, my head held high. I had lost track of Ty and his partner when suddenly I heard Roger say "Hey, you two want to switch partners for a dance?" I turned and there were Tyrone and his partner, Renee. Ty and Roger looked directly at each other. Ty smiled slightly and nodded. I could hardly catch my breath, but floated in Tyrone's arms, feeling the astonished gaze of everyone around me at not one, but two, mixed race couples dancing at the junior-senior prom.

It has been years since all this happened. I know it changed me and how I think about what is important and how to live my life. Tyrone was wiser to start with, but I think we both touched and shaped each other in important ways. And Roger. . . . I still admire him. I wonder about why he asked me to the prom and what role Ty and I have played in his life.

PRIVILEGE AND ENTITLEMENT

Hunger

Hunger continues to plague an estimated 800 million people around the world, including 31 million in the U.S.

Hunger kills. Every day, 24,000 people die from hunger and other preventable causes. Nearly 160 million children are malnourished worldwide.

Poverty

1.3 billion people—that's one in six—live on less than $1 per day.

32.3 million people in the U.S. live below the poverty line

70 percent of the world's poor are female

1 billion people do not have adequate shelter, and 2.4 billion people do not have access to proper sanitation. More than 1 billion people do not have access to clean water.

Global Resources

If food were distributed equally, every man, woman, and child would receive 2,700 calories a day, more than the minimum needed for basic survival.

The wealthiest countries, which contain 15 percent of the world's population, account for 78 percent of global consumption.

$40 billion—only .1 percent of the world income—would provide universal access to basic education, reproductive health, family planning, and safe water and sanitation for all.

Education

125 million children in the world do not attend primary school, and another 150 million primary school-age children drop out before they can read or write.

27.6 percent of adults in the developing world—1.2 billion people—are illiterate

Funding universal education in sub-Saharan Africa would require an additional $3.6 billion a year. The region currently spends over $13.5 billion on foreign-debt payments.

Health Care

880 million people lack access to basic healthcare, and 1.5 billion lack access to safe drinking water.

Curable diseases, including diarrhea, malaria, and tuberculosis, kill 17.4 million people each year. Of these, 5 million of these people die due to water contamination.[2]

Luke

When the World Trade Center and Pentagon were attacked on 9/11, I was a junior in high school. I didn't know anyone directly who was hurt, but, like most Americans, I felt a dizzying combination of shock, anger, fear, and confusion. The world of terrorism and desperate ethnic conflict jumped out of my TV and invaded my sense of immunity. Amidst the outpouring of sympathy from around the world, I heard an underlying refrain of "So, now you Americans know the fear and violence much of the rest of the world lives with every day." My mind reeled as I watched people on the streets in an impoverished, Mideast country jump in celebration as they learned of the successful assault on their American Goliath. How could anyone be happy about the violent murder of hundreds of innocent civilians simply going to work to earn a living for their families? How could a people or government so far away despise the United States so much that it would painstakingly plan and execute this symbolic and violent gesture of hatred and vengeance? I resonated with the anger and retaliation spoken by our government, but I was also left with the empty, disturbing question—*"Why do they hate us so much?"*

I watched the news over and over, searching for clues that would make sense of such anger. *"Americans are arrogant—they take what they want, invading less developed countries with their bombs and their businesses." "Americans are greedy—they have so much while others around the world are starving and barely managing to stay alive." "Americans are selfish and shallow—they waste and whine about minor inconveniences while much of the world is struggling with poverty, disease, war, pollution, and despair."* I don't feel arrogant, greedy, or selfish. I consider my warm home, full closet, regular meals, and single bedroom full of gadgets and possessions, and, to be honest, I can't imagine living any other way. I'm not rich, but I have everything I need—and more, I guess. I have never worried about having food and my clothes reflect more fashion than function, but it is hard to see these things as privileges. Everyone around me has them—in fact, many have much more than I do and there is always something I don't have and want to buy. I suppose I waste things or food or money, but it is not intentional or even conscious. When I pay $3.50 for a cup of coffee at Starbucks, I can't really imagine that money would feed a child in Honduras for a week like the *Save the Children* ad says. Who could eat on $3.50 a week?

Once a year, I participate in a community service project at my school called *Los Ninos. Los Ninos* is a nonprofit organization that takes groups of students to Tijuana, Mexico, to work with local people to help build schools, improve housing, and play with the children in the *colonias* and orphanages.* I started going in my sophomore year because one of my friends said it was really amazing. We work hard and it is a lot of fun, but the biggest impact has been on how it has helped me come to understand my privilege and how lucky I am. On the drive down, my mind is usually clouded with homework and problems with friends or family; I want to go, but it always seems that my life is so busy and demanding that I am stressed about all the other things I should be doing that weekend. I know we will be eating peanut butter sandwiches and sleeping on uncomfortable bunks in an adobe bunkhouse without many amenities. We have to be careful about the water and the work is physically hard without any modern equipment—we bring a stack of plastic throwaway buckets that detergent is sold in because even buckets are scarce. I am glad that I brought my Walkman.

As we cross the border, my regular world begins to slip away and I am intrigued once again by the stark difference that a barbed-wire fence can make. The green, watered California lawns give way to the desert and parched landscape of northern Mexico. I watch the border patrol and try to imagine the quiet groups of migrants slipping through the night past river and desert to come to work in the California orchards. We travel through Tijuana, past the tourist section and the Universidad, and into a middle-class neighborhood where neat adobe homes sit next door to more run-down houses, and skinny stray dogs roam the streets. Broken bottles cemented onto the tops of the walls around the courtyards are the only divisions between street and home. Yards are occasional and small with only dirt and a barking dog. The *Los Ninos* house is spare, but comfortable with

---

* Check out www.losninosinternational.org

donated couches and mismatched chairs dotting the sparse, adobe rooms. We all pitch in to cook and clean, and quickly adjust to the lack of luxury. The big pot of spaghetti and warm tortillas taste delicious. We are asked to put the used toilet paper in a can next to the toilet, since the pipes cannot handle any paper. The house has electricity, but only a couple of small lamps, so we huddle together for a game of *Uno* and retire early to our REI sleeping bags on top of thin, creaky bunk mattresses.

In the morning, we are going to a *colonia*, or squatter's camp, to help the residents construct a playground for the new kindergarten they have built for their community. In Tijuana, the government will only provide teachers and funds for a school after the community has built it. The *colonias* are constantly changing and growing as migrants from southern and central Mexico come to the border towns in hopes of crossing into the United States to get work and send money back to their struggling families. Some make it across, some return to their rural homes, but many stay and settle in the border towns, taking jobs in the United States-owned *factorias* and gradually establishing communities and schools. All around, you can see *colonias* in various stages of this evolution. In the beginning, people are living in makeshift shelters, sometimes a large cardboard box from a refrigerator or stove, with no electricity or running water. They scavenge through the large garbage heaps with the seagulls, looking for food and throwaways to furnish their improvised homes. A tortilla shop or small convenience store may set up as the *colonia* grows and gradually the houses become more substantial. The dirt roads become more worn and eventually electricity may be added. Water is still scarce in this desert area and you see canals of iridescent green water and trucks with large bottles of water for drinking and cooking. Children and dogs run happily through these evolving villages and men on beat-up, one-speed bicycles avoid the ruts in the road on their way to work at the local brickyard—hot, heavy work where they will earn fifty cents a day.

The *colonia* that we are working with is well established. They have built a small one-room kindergarten for the younger children who are sitting attentively at a large table inside as we work with fathers, mothers, grandparents, and some of the older children to dig out a section for a playground and mix and pour the cement. One of the men is an experienced contractor and he directs this willing but unskilled group of neighbors and United States students. We are assigned digging, planting, and setting up the lines to prepare the area. The ground is hard and dry; digging is slow, difficult, and unsatisfying. The small trench around the circumference of what will be a playground seems to take forever with our picks and shovels. I wish for water to spare to loosen the soil or a backhoe to relieve my aching shoulders. We take turns and get an occasional break by going in to the kindergarten and helping the two volunteer teachers with the twenty-five children sitting attentively around the tables, gluing beans in the shape of the letters of their names. I sit with a group of children as they bring out their paper bags with a piece of fruit and tortilla or cookie for their lunch. The children carefully section off their small lunches and one little girl notices that I am sitting there with nothing. Shyly, she comes over to give me the orange from her lunch so that I will have something to eat. This leaves her with a tortilla and a small pack of crackers. I don't know what to do. I don't want to refuse her generosity, but I also don't want to take her lunch. Then the others, observing her hospitality, are reminded of their own manners, and begin to offer me things from their lunches as well. I am shamed by their kindness—how can children who have so little be so generous? Emulating them, I finally peel the orange and share a piece with each of the children—a solution which seems to please everyone.

Back outside, we are ready to mix and pour the cement for the playground. Heavy wheelbarrows of sand are dumped into a pile with a bag of cement. Slowly water is added and five or six of us mix the pile with our shovels—scooping it up and dumping it back on top. It is hard, heavy work as the sun reaches its noonday heat. As the mixture starts to set, we shovel it into the waiting wheelbarrows that are wheeled over and dumped on the foundation that we had helped to dig. Nine- and ten-year-old children help move these heavy loads as grandmothers hold the babies and watch the procession. Women pitch in with the men as they all work together to build a school for their children. I try to imagine going to a school that my parents and neighbors had built. I try to imagine mixing cement for the miles and miles of highway and sidewalks and parking lots that I hardly even noticed at home. I try to imagine children being so excited and proud to be able to go to school and share their lunch with a rich American who didn't have one. The workers laugh and help each other; the children inside ignore the activity outside and seriously attend to their studies—even when we have to take a long board off the inside wall to temporarily use as a level for the poured cement. As primitive and simple as our tools and efforts are, there is a sense of community and pride that I have never seen in my own school or neighborhood. Our lunch, pots of homemade food and fresh tortillas made by some of the neighborhood women, tastes exquisite. I feel physically exhausted and pleased with myself as I sit on a rough stool and sip some sort of blue sugar fruit juice with my lunch. The children are admiring our morning's work and happily chattering in Spanish. My world of carpets and cars and dishwashers and Starbucks suddenly seems imaginary and absurd compared to this simple, human world.

We work at a different *colonia* the next day, providing a tie-dye craft project for the local children while their mothers meet with the agricultural consultant to plan how they might grow a community garden in this parched earth. The children love the beautiful new shirts that are hanging out on a rope to dry—rainbows of colors over our school logo on leftover shirts from some fund-raiser back at school. They marvel at our shoes and buckles and take turns trying on the headphones of my Walkman—their eyes wide with amazement as they hear the music streaming out of this tiny box. That night we have a speaker from the *Universidad* talking about the economics of the border towns and the American factories that utilize the cheap workforce to manufacture goods to ship back to the United States. She cites statistics about the border patrol arrests—how they always decrease at the beginning of the growing season and increase when the pickers are no longer needed. Some of the neighborhood teenagers come over to play cards and visit. We play the guitar and practice our Spanish and English skills as we get to know each other. At one point, I am talking about how something is in America and one of the teens gets angry with me and explains that Mexico is in America too—the United States seems to think *it* is America. I am embarrassed and a little offended. I hadn't meant disrespect; I just had never thought about it that way.

The next day, we all work to clean the *Los Ninos* house and wash the vans as our contribution to the program. As we wash the vans, I notice neighborhood people stopping to watch, coming out of their houses to stare at us. I am proud to demonstrate how hardworking young people from the United States can be until one of the *Los Ninos* people tells me the neighbors are actually watching in amazement at how much water we are wasting as we spray down the van and leave the hose running into the streets. Water is so precious and these Americans must have so much they can let it run down the streets. How must it seem to them to be so carefree and wasteful?

On the ride back home, I always think that I will never take so many things for granted again. The problems I had been worried about on the way down seemed silly and pretentious. I think about my warm bed, clean sheets, ten-speed bike, books, refrigerator full of food, and endless supply of T-shirts and vow to simplify my life, share what I have, and be grateful for all the advantages that I take for granted every day. I haven't forgotten these lessons, but I often slip back into taking my affluence for granted and complaining about what I don't have. I pay $100 for shoes put together for pennies by children younger than I am in countries I can't place on the map. I waste food and pay $3.50 for a cup of coffee. I browse in the mall and spend money on things I don't really need, throw away things I might easily fix, expect my day to be easy and full of everything I want. I do community service and try to share things that I don't need, but I don't really make many sacrifices. I expect the world to take care of me and no one would expect me to share my orange if I am hungry. It is so automatic. How must I look to teenagers who wander the wartorn streets in Iraq or Haiti or Palestine? What must I represent to countries that are struggling to provide schools for their children, food for their families? As I let the water run down the street and my country consumes the majority of the world's resources, what anger and jealousy do I evoke? Am I entitled to what I have? What is the responsibility of my advantage and prosperity? What is my obligation to others who are less fortunate? Can we all coexist on one planet with such disparity of wealth and opportunity? How can I counteract the image of Americans—oops, people in the United States——being arrogant, greedy, and selfish?

And what is the price I have paid for my privilege?

PHOTO *by Unknown*

Affluenza

More than ever, we have big houses and broken homes, high incomes and low morale, secured rights and diminished civility. We excel at making a living but often fail at making a life. We celebrate our prosperity but yearn for purpose. We cherish our freedoms but long for connection.—Psychologist David Meyer

Many people in the United States suffer from a condition which social scientists are calling affluenza*—"An unhappy condition of overload, debt, anxiety, and waste resulting from the dogged pursuit of more." Polls show that even U.S. people think that we are too materialistic, too greedy, selfish, and self-absorbed. We are filling our lives with things, but feeling empty and unsatisfied. While the average American now makes more than twice as much, has twice as much stuff, and lives in a house in which the garage is almost as big as the average home in 1957, we report being less happy, more anxious, more rushed, and less contented. Seventy percent of us go to the mall at least once a week (more than go to church or synagogue). The average American spends six hours a week shopping and forty minutes playing with his or her children. Advertising sells happiness—by the age of twenty, you will have seen over one million commercials; approximately one year of your life will be spent watching TV commercials. Two-thirds of the newspaper and 40 percent of our mail is advertising. Laurie Mazur, in her book* Marketing Madness, *states that advertising "encourages us to meet nonmaterial needs through material products." Advertising tells us to "buy these products because we will be loved and accepted. It also tells us that we are not loveable or acceptable without buying their product."*

Advertisers target children. Research has shown that if a product does not establish brand loyalty by the time a child is eighteen, it probably won't, so in 1995, advertisers spent one billion dollars on ads aimed at children. Even schools are being given free materials, flashy sports equipment, and cash incentives that advertise

The obsession to consume has tripled credit card debt since the 1980s, reduced average savings to 4 percent, and in 1996, one million Americans declared bankruptcy. This pursuit of more material goods has had serious social and environmental costs as well. Parents work longer to earn enough money to buy all the luxuries that seem like necessities. People have less time for family, community, and community service. Lower income people see the consumption and feel a heightened sense of deprivation and inequity.

At the same time, large companies are attempting to expand their markets internationally—creating new consumers, new materialism, and new waste. Since 1950, Americans have consumed more resources than everyone who ever lived before them. Americans throw away seven million cars per year and two million plastic bottles per hour. The average American consumes five times more than the average Mexican, ten times more than the average Chinese person, and thirty times more than the average East Indian. If the rest of the world began to consume at the same rate that we do, the world's ecosystem could not withstand the impact.

Advocates for "voluntary simplicity" encourage consumers to buy less, make do, and recycle. Adbusters.com sponsors an annual "buy nothing" day and has attempted to fight advertising by airing "uncommercials" that challenge the consumer lifestyle. They insist that people will be happier and the earth can sustain a comfortable lifestyle for everyone if we:

1. *Explore nonpolluting and energy efficient technologies.*

2. *Produce goods that last longer and require fewer resources.*

3. *Reuse and recycle.*

4. *Reward frugality and penalize waste.*

5. *Narrow the gap between rich and poor.*

6. *Commit our economy to stability, not expansion.*

—From *Affluenza: The All-Consuming Epidemic* by John D. Graaf, David Wann, Thomas H. Naylor[3]

Some Questions from the Affluenza Self-Diagnosis Test[4]

1.   Do you get bored unless you have something to consume (goods, food, media)?

2.   Do you try to impress your friends with what you own or where you vacation?

3.   Do you ever use shopping as "therapy"?

4.   Do you sometimes go to the mall just to look around with nothing specific to buy?

5.   In general, do you think about things more than you think about people?

6.   Do you personally fill more than one large trash bag in a single week?

7.   Have you ever lied to a family member about the amount you spent for a product?

8.   Do you spend more time shopping every week than you do with your family?

9.   Do your conversations gravitate toward things that you want to buy?

10.   Do you feel like you're always in a hurry?

11.   Do you often throw away recyclable materials rather than take the time to recycle them?

12.   Do you spend less than an hour a day outside?

13.   Do you replace sports equipment before it's worn out to have the latest style?

14.   Does each member of your family have his/her own TV?

15.   Do you receive more than five mail-order catalogs a week?

16.   Do you ignore the miles per gallon of gasoline your car gets?

17.   Do you drink more soft drink, by volume, than tap water?

18.   Do you watch TV more than 2 hours a day?[5]

After the bombing of the World Trade Center in September of 2001, a Navajo grandfather was talking to his grandson about how he felt about terrorism and people who are mean and aggressive. He said, "I feel as if I have two wolves fighting in my heart. One wolf is the vengeful, angry, violent one who wants to strike back. The other wolf is the loving, compassionate one who wants to understand and heal."

The grandson asked him, "Which wolf will win the fight in your heart?"

The grandfather answered, "The one I feed."

—Wilden Louis

VIOLENCE

Violence has always been a part of human interaction and the late 1990s and early twenty-first century have seen a dramatic rise in random violence and shootings in schools, workplaces, and communities across the country. In addition to the more notable events, in 1999 the teenage homicide rate was up 300 percent, firearm deaths were up 43 percent, and the suicide rate for 15–19 year olds had tripled since 1970. Eighty percent of all teenage deaths in 1999 resulted from homicide, suicide, or violent accident. An estimated 100,000 students carry a gun to school on a regular basis. Parents have become increasingly concerned—55 percent say that they fear every day for their child's safety at school. Schoolyard bullying and harassment have led to violence on the part of both the bully and retaliation by the victim. Seventy-five percent of school shooters had previously be seriously harassed and bullied.

In the larger world in which children are being raised, frightening and unpredictable acts of violence and terrorism have become increasingly commonplace. Many people in countries throughout the world live a daily life that includes random violence and intimidation. The loss of over 5,000 people in the terrorist attacks on September 11, 2001, brought that reality and fear home to the United States. Suicide bombings, hostage kidnappings, and pointless sniper killings have made the world seem unsafe, incomprehensible, and out of control.

It is difficult to grow up in a wartorn country and not be damaged by feelings of anger and retribution. Grief, fear, aggression, anxiety, and vengeance are all painful by-products of violence. Students and families in many previously sheltered places around the world have lost a fragile sense of security and invulnerability. It is difficult to feel safe or trusting when our structure and moral compass has been so repeatedly violated. Alienated individuals and terrorists have exerted violent power over political, social, or random targets. Chemical warfare and the proliferation of weapons of mass destruction have shifted the balance of power from authority and strength to anyone who is alienated and angry enough to strike out without regard for the consequences. Whether it is an alienated student or a Mideast nation, we are challenged to become more inclusive and understanding of people, religions, and cultures that frighten, alienate, or threaten us. It is increasingly impossible to control the violence of estranged individuals. We must look to the causes of alienation and restructure our world and relationships in such a way that all individuals have a stake in our common survival and well-being.

"BRYAN" by Robyn Strumpf

Fred

In 1999, there were more than 4,000 reported hate crimes based on race, more than 1,400 hate crimes based on religion, 1,300 hate crimes based on sexual orientation, 830 hate crimes based on ethnicity, and 19 hate crimes based on disability, according to the most recent FBI statistics. Colorado is one of eighteen states that do not include sexual orientation in their hate crimes law. It is also one of forty-six states that do not include gender identity. Five states have no hate crimes law.

June 28, 2001

Detectives are questioning three suspects in the slaying of a Navajo boy from Cortez and are looking at his homosexuality as a possible motive for the crime, Montezuma County Sheriff Joey Chavez said Wednesday. Names of the suspects had not been released and no arrests had been made as of press time. Although there had been reports the three had been cleared, Sheriff's Detective Lt. Kalvin Boggs said late Wednesday afternoon that was not the case.

One week ago Thursday, the badly decomposed body of 16-year-old Fred Martinez Jr. was found near the sewer ponds south of Cortez by two young boys who were playing in the area. According to Chavez, Martinez's body had been there nearly a week.

The sheriff's office declined to release any information about what had been the murder weapon, but preliminary autopsy results suggest Martinez had been bludgeoned. "It appeared to be some sort of blunt trauma to the head that contributed to the cause of death," Chavez said. Exposure was also likely a factor, he added.

Martinez, who had just finished his freshman year at Montezuma-Cortez High School, was the son of Pauline Adakai of Elmwood Trailer Park in Cortez. Local students reported that Martinez was a homosexual, and said, in hindsight, they thought he might have been targeted for a hate crime.

Montezuma-Cortez High School sophomore Jessica Wilson said Martinez often curled his hair, plucked his eyebrows, wore make-up and toted a purse at school. "People talked behind his back, but I'm sure he knew," Wilson said.

MCHS sophomore Mandy Rollman also said Martinez was openly gay. She described him as outgoing and happy, with a good sense of humor. "He was really nice," Rollman said. "I can't believe someone would do that to him."

Chavez said detectives are looking at the boy's sexuality, as well as the fact that he was Native American, as possible motives in the crime.

"It could be a possibility that this is a hate crime," Chavez said. "We're not ruling that out, but we're not saying that for sure." Chavez said the three suspects are young adults but not fellow students. "One of them we feel is local and the other two were maybe just passing through," he said. "We're in the stage of ruling them out, and at that time we'll decide through interviews if there will be any arrests."

Martinez was last seen at his home on June 16 and reportedly had said he was going to the carnival at the Ute Mountain Roundup Rodeo. He never returned home. Only after the body was discovered did his family report him missing, according to the sheriff's department. "Evidently, they (the family) didn't report him right away because he frequently left and wouldn't come back for days. They just thought that's exactly what he was doing," Chavez said.

Initially detectives had a difficult time identifying the body because of its state of decomposition and the lack of a missing-persons report. However, a mirror bearing the name "Fred Martinez" was found near the body, according to Chavez. Also found at the scene was a blue handkerchief, but detectives have yet to determine whether it belonged to Martinez or someone else. "At this time it's still part of the investigation," Chavez said. "We don't know that the handkerchief was specifically his."

According to a police report, Martinez was wearing black work boots, tan pants and a gray sweatshirt with his hair pulled up on top of his head in a ponytail when his body was found.

Officials do not know whether anyone saw Martinez at the carnival or if he was with anyone.

"We're still in the interview stages and we haven't determined exactly who he was with," Chavez said.

Because Martinez was a juvenile, the Journal was not able to obtain any information as to whether he had a criminal history. "The sheriff's office has never had any dealings with him, but we think he was familiar with the city police department," Chavez said.

The final autopsy results will not be available for at least another week, he said. It is unknown whether Martinez was under the influence of drugs or alcohol at the time of his death.

MCHS counselor LouAnn Burkett said Martinez did not stand out as a problem child at the school and seemed to be well-adjusted socially in terms of his sexuality. "He was really happy with himself—he didn't seem to have any guilt or any complex about it," Burkett said. "He enjoyed himself and the way he was and kids accepted him."

Burkett said she did not believe Martinez had been a victim of bullying. "I never saw or heard anything—secondhand or from him—that there was anything said at school to him," she said. "Generally, if those kids are having a problem, they'll come in. It was never pointed out to us that he was a problem. I'm just going to really miss the guy."

Anyone who has information regarding the case is asked to call the Montezuma County Sheriff's Office at 565-8452 and ask for the detectives' division.[6]

Media Statement by Pauline Mitchell, Mother of Fred Martinez, Jr.[7]

NOTE: The following statement can be attributed to Pauline Mitchell. Ms. Mitchell is the mother of Fred C. Martinez, Jr., whose body was discovered near Cortez, Colo., on June 21, 2001. Martinez identified as gay, Two-Spirit, and transgender. Ms. Mitchell is releasing this statement in lieu of interviews.

I feel it is time to talk about the death of my son, Fred C. Martinez, Jr.

I am his mother and now I want to make sure the truth is told about Fred by people who loved him. With more and more talk about his death, the police looking into his murder, and the details of my son's personal life in the media, it is time to speak the truth about Fred's life.

The most important thing I can say is that I loved Fred. I loved my son exactly for who he was, for his courage in being honest and gentle and friendly. It is sad that he had to face pain in his daily life and in school.

I am speaking out now because I am angry. I am angry that other people are lying about who my son was, including Shaun Murphy and his family. I want to make sure that Fred has people speaking the truth about his life. I am angry that the police have not taken the time to explain what is happening and help me deal with this. I don't want to read about new things in the newspaper.

I reported that Fred was missing on June 18. Two days later I called the police again, and on June 23 I read about a body being found near our home. I phoned the police again, but they told me the body had not been identified. Since June 25, when the police told me at work that Fred had been murdered, I wondered if it was because of who he was and how he expressed himself. Violence was a common part of his life, and as I learn more, I know that this was a crime based on anger and hate. His friends, other students at school, and family friends have told me things that make me know that Shaun Murphy picked Fred out to chase and beat him.

One of the places that Fred faced a lot of trouble was in school. I blame the people in charge at the school for not making sure he was safe. I am angry that they thought Fred was the problem. Fred tried very hard to fit in. People in charge shouldn't treat children differently just because they aren't like them. I hope that they will listen to me and other people who care about what happened to Fred.

Fred was a member of the Native American Church. A lot of Native American Church members prayed for Fred and his family.

What I wanted for my son was for him to be accepted and loved, just like I accepted and loved him. Fred was always proud to be Navajo. Fred did not struggle with who he was, but he was hurt because of the people who had problems with my son expressing himself honestly. I hope that the police and the District Attorney will talk about this and bring justice for the death of my son. I am grateful to Fred's friends for accepting him the way he was and remembering him for who he was. Fred's family loved and cared deeply for all of who he was. We firmly believe that Fred's murder was a hate crime.

Because he was different his life was taken from him, and we will never know the person Fred would have become.

Kindness

Before you know what kindness really is you must lose things,
Feel the future dissolve in a moment, like salt in a weakened broth.
What you held in your hand, what you counted and carefully saved,
All this must go so you know how desolate the landscape can be
Between the regions of kindness.
How you ride and ride thinking the bus will never stop,
The passengers eating maize and chicken will stare out the window
forever.

Before you learn the tender gravity of kindness,
You must travel where the Indian in a white poncho lies dead by the side
of the road.
You must see how this could be you,
How he too was someone who journeyed through the night
With plans and with the breath of life.

Before you know kindness as the deepest thing inside,
You must know sorrow as the other deepest thing.
You must wake up with sorrow.
You must speak it till your voice catches the thread of all sorrows
And you see the size of the cloth.

Then it is only kindness that makes sense anymore,
Only kindness that ties your shoes and sends you out into the day

To mail letters and purchase bread,
Only kindness that raises its head from the crowd of the world to say

It is I you have been looking for,
And then it goes with you everywhere
Like a shadow or a friend.

—Written by Naomi Shihab Nye [who is Palestinian/American] after the
September 11, 2001 terrorist attacks

Culture Shock

As vast and diverse as the United States is, there is a common culture that is
known and recognized by foreigners as distinctly "American." Visitors from
Asia, Europe, Africa, or even South America can quickly point out ethnocentric
beliefs and behaviors that we tend to assume are universal. Just as we have stereo-
types about other cultures, the American stereotype is easily recognized by visi-
tors and citizens of other countries and forms the basis of many of our
nonconscious attitudes and actions. As much of an individual as we may feel our-
selves to be, each of us has been influenced by this invisible culture and it is a part
of our cultural identity.

Here are some of the "strange" customs and conduct that outsiders have noted
about American behavior.[8]

1. *Americans are typically informal in both social and business situations. They*
    often use first names, avoid titles, and may nod or just say "Hi" instead of
    shaking hands or acknowledging people formally. Americans often speak to
    strangers and value a comfortable equality in their social and business rela-
    tionships. Americans are often blunt and direct, valuing authenticity over
    politeness. Americans don't stand on a lot of protocol or formalities, but they
    are generally polite and respectful of others, including service people.

2. *Americans don't mind showing their feelings and often exaggerate them*
    rather than hide them. (I was furious! You look fabulous!) They talk openly
    about difficult emotions and comfortably express affection and pleasure. Lim-
    ited expressions of anger are acceptable, but Americans are less comfortable
    with feelings of sadness and disappointment.

3. *American life is often fast-paced and mobile. Americans love gadgets and*
    timesaving devices and always seem to be in a hurry. From fast food to chang-
    ing jobs or moving to a different community, Americans can seem rootless

and disconnected. Time represents opportunity; Americans don't like to wait and like things to be quick and efficient. The pace of work and life in general can be exhausting and many Americans have a difficult time relaxing.

4.   *Americans operate according to schedules and value being on time. They dislike human interruptions and focus more on the completed project than the process. They often see only practical and profitable activity as truly valuable.*

5.   *Americans are friendly and may ask personal questions that seem to pry or invade your privacy. Where do you work? Are you married? What are your hobbies? Friendliness, however, is not the same as friendship. Americans are careful not to bother others or become indebted. Friends try not to demand too much of each other and reciprocate whenever possible. In cities and suburbs, neighbors rarely drop in unannounced and sometimes do not communicate or know each other at all.*

6.   *Americans are do-it-yourself people and even wealthy professionals often do their own laundry, shop, cook, garden, and do repairs and projects around the house. There are even large warehouses that cater to do-it-yourself projects. Americans take pride in making things and would rather spend their money on travel or entertainment or appliances.*

7.   *Americans are often uncomfortable with silence and fill it with small talk and background music or TV.*

8.   *Americans believe in planning and self-improvement. They work hard at improving their minds, making money, losing weight, exercising, fixing relationships, building their self-esteem, and creating a more fulfilling life. While seen as already somewhat self-centered, Americans flock to self-help books that promise techniques to help individuals get what they want without feeling guilty or obligated.*

9.   *America is a youth culture. Youth is valued over age and experience. Older people dye their hair and dress in youthful styles. Leaders and cultural heroes are usually young—it is a popular American warning not to trust anyone over thirty.*

10.   *Americans tend to be comfortable about twenty-one inches apart when in conversation—closer than Asians, but more distant than Arabs or South Americans. In crowded situations such as elevators or subways, they try not to let their bodies touch. In conversation, Americans often use their hands and may briefly touch the person they are talking to in a gesture of emphasis or agreement. Extended touch, however, is usually unacceptable.*

11. *Americans love to question authority. Schools encourage students to ask questions and think critically. People will often argue and challenge the status quo or their superiors in an effort to explore an idea. This is not considered rude or disrespectful.*

12. *Americans attempt to control nature rather than live within its limits. American think in terms of harnessing rivers, controlling weather, taming the wilderness, and conquering space.*

13. *Americans value equal opportunity and hard work. Status and privilege should not ensure an advantage or prohibit anyone from getting ahead if they work hard and are talented. Americans are profoundly future-oriented and optimistic. On the other hand, this sense of equal opportunity and possibilities can create a sense of discontent and fear of failure—Americans often feel pressure to get ahead, win, make a lot of money, and prove themselves.*

14. *The American ideal is self-reliant, tough, risk-taking, and independent. Individuals don't like to be tied down and American children are expected to leave home and become independent as early as age eighteen. Young adults are expected to make it on their own and aged parents often are expected to take care of themselves.*

15. *Americans have fewer family ties and obligations than most cultures. Families are important, but they often live far apart and individual members usually carry on separate social lives. Parents and children make up the nuclear family and few people feel much sense of duty to members of the extended family. Older people tend to spend their time with other older people, not their families.*

16. *Most non-Americans are shocked by the informality and disrespect that American children show their parents and other adults. Autonomy and independence is valued over obedience, and American children are often allowed more freedom, choices, and control than children from other cultures. Parents try to respect children's thoughts and feelings and children are encouraged to be individuals.*

17. *Parents may help support their children in college and early adulthood, but few teens or young adults contribute to their family's income. Some have part- or full-time jobs, but use their earnings for personal spending.*

18. *The stereotypical "Ugly American" is loud, arrogant, and insensitive to cultural differences in others. American travelers frequently speak only one language and are not always respectful or aware of foreign customs and expectations.*

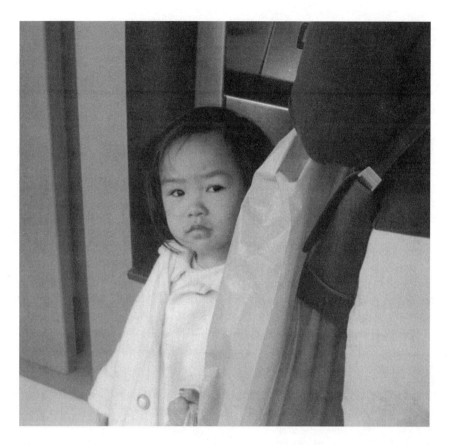

UNTITLED *by Joannie Chui*

Meiko

I first came to school in the United States when I was twelve years old. My father wanted me to learn English for a year before I started high school in the United States, so I went to a pre-prep school in Connecticut—on the opposite side of the earth from my home in Seoul, Korea. When my parents first told me that I would travel to the United States for school, I was very excited. I knew it was an honor and I knew of two girls who had been in the United States for school and they liked it a lot. My school in Korea was not a happy one for me. It had become rough and as a younger student, I was sometimes frightened. My parents did not want me to be worried. I was in the higher track at my school, but it was very strict and I could only take one course of studies. The schools in the United States expected you to think about your work and develop an opinion. I applied to a very good school and was accepted, so my parents decided this would be the best way for me.

When it was time for me to go, however, I was not so happy. My friends were sad to have me go away and my little sister cried and begged my parents not to make me go. My father was to take me to school for the first time and I could see that my mother had tears in her heart. She tried not to show them to me because she knew America would be good for my education. I tried not to show her my tears as well because I knew that she and my father were giving me this wonderful opportunity and I should be grateful to them. But I still did not want to go and would cry quietly in my room before we left. I had taken English in my school for four years, but I did not feel competent enough to manage all my studies in English.

It has been four years now and my English is good and I have come to love my United States school and friends, but when I first arrived, I was sick with worry and sadness. The trip had taken us over twenty-four hours and I was tired and scared. I think my father was nervous for me too and it must have been hard for him to leave me so far from home, but he only told me that I must be brave and learn all that I could in this United States school. I needed to always work hard and make him and my family proud of me. Not many girls have this opportunity and I must be proud and grateful. I must only bring honor to my family and to myself. All this he said to me in Korean and at the end he spoke in English. "You must come to understand the American language and customs so that you can be successful at the American university and bring your knowledge back to Korea. But you must never forget your family and your culture. It is your heritage and strength. Honor your American teachers and American school, but never forget that you are Korean and always honor your Korean ways." That seemed like a big order at the time, but only later did I realize how truly difficult it would be.

Everyone was nice at my new school, but my first comfort came when I saw that I was not the only Korean student. There were four other Korean girls in my dormitory and I could not wait to be alone with them and speak my own language and talk with others who knew how I was feeling. So much information and instruction was coming at me—and all of it in English. I smiled and nodded to everyone, but my head was full of words and confusion that I could not fit together. By the end of the first day, I was exhausted and could not remember anything I had been told. When I heard my language breaking through the haze of disjointed English, I wanted to cry. It was Kim, a Korean girl in my dorm who had been at the school for two years. She reassured me and translated all the instructions and rules I had been given so they would stay in my mind. She told me not to worry;

my English would improve quickly and I would learn a lot at this school. She told me to always smile, because someone will smile back at me. She told me that it was also OK to cry—crying is just a feeling, the same as laughing. The other international students would help me and I would make American friends too. She was so nice and I thanked her for her comforting, but I didn't believe her. I did not think my English would ever catch up with the quick way the Americans spoke and how could I make an American friend if we could not understand each other. While I was relieved to see other Korean students who could help me, I knew that my father did not want me to speak Korean—he wanted me to learn English and learn the American ways. My smile was tired and I knew I could never let anyone see me cry. My father would be ashamed at my lack of courage and ungratefulness.

My roommate, Jennifer, was a very nice and very bouncy girl from New Jersey. She came running up to me during the school tour and gave me a hug, announcing that we were roommates. I was very surprised at her friendliness since she did not even know me. She spoke quickly and I could not understand most of what she said, only her enthusiasm and openness. She seemed nice, but I did not know how to respond to the way she acted as if we were good friends since I had only just met her. One thing she said really frightened me. I did not understand the whole sentence, but she said that she had some "goldfish" that we could eat during study hall. When I asked Kim what a "goldfish" was, she told me it was a little fish like a minnow that Americans kept in bowls. I was afraid to go back to my room that evening and wondered what kind of strange girl I was to room with. I was very relieved to find out that the "goldfish" were just a small cracker, not a fish at all.

The first few weeks at my American school are still a cloud to me; I was so busy trying to understand the English. If I listened very hard, I could begin to understand the main ideas that were spoken to me, though often not the details. Understanding came much more quickly than my ability to answer back, to find the English words to express my answer. Most people were patient and helpful, though occasionally someone would think that I could understand her better if she spoke louder. This could be disturbing since I already thought that Americans spoke very loud. Reading in English was the hardest because I was both translating and learning the subject at the same time. I had to study everything with my Korean/English dictionary at my side and it took me so long. I would study every free minute of the day and study hall and still need to stay up late to finish my work. Jennifer told me that I worked too hard and should relax and learn to have fun. But where it might take her twenty minutes to read an English assignment, it could easily take me an hour just to translate it. I was not really as unsociable as she thought I was, but it took so much time just to keep up.

I was also surprised, however, at how relaxed the American students were about their work. Study hall was sometimes noisy and the students did not always listen when the teachers or student prefects told them to be quiet and work. In Korea, a student would not think of disobeying a teacher and we always knew that we must work very hard to stay in the top track and get into a good university. A student who was not applying herself or obeying her teachers would bring shame on her family and easily lose her rank as a student. American students spoke up—often without even being called on—and thought nothing of disagreeing with the teacher or anyone else in the class. This confident and independent thinking intrigued me, but much of the arguing and outspokenness seemed disrespectful and immodest. Students often interrupted and spoke before they had thought something through. Teachers seemed to accept this kind of behavior and even encouraged me to speak up more and state my own opinion. At first, this was very difficult. I was used to giving "correct" answers, not personal answers; my opinion was just unformed thinking in the face of scholars who had thought long about the subject at hand. As I grew more comfortable with this American way of disagreeing, it sometimes got me into trouble when I was back in Korea. I would never disagree or speak back to my parents, of course, but I had learned to question other adults and authority in ways that were not acceptable at home.

The whole culture in America seemed more informal than Korea. Young people were much more independent and outspoken—I even would overhear students speaking disrespectfully to their parents. In America, someone may say, "Hi. How are you?" and not wait for an answer. Americans are very friendly and good-natured and seem to take everything in a relaxed way. They don't have many strict manners or rituals. Every night, I would finish my homework, take care of my toiletries, fold my clothes and put them away, placing my shoes neatly at the end of my bed, say my prayers, and make sure that my room and desk were in order before going to sleep. Some of the American girls threw their clothes on the floor, left food in their room, and could never find anything on their desk. Even when they would clean for room inspection, their room would be a mess soon after. I was surprised that they were not punished for this type of behavior and that they had not learned how to take care of themselves in a better way.

My pre-prep school and the one I am at now both had lots of rules, but you could never know if they would actually enforce a rule or not. We had a rule that no one was to wear a hat in the dining hall, but people wore hats in the dining hall all the time and the adults said nothing. It seemed like some people would get in serious trouble for violating a certain rule while others might be lightly reprimanded. At some times, the teachers were very strict about having your light on after hours, and at other times, they did not seem to care. In Korea, we did not have so many rules, but every rule was enforced and nonnegotiable. In America, it was hard for me to know which rules were very serious and which rules would usually be ignored. And there were rules that some people enforced and others did not. This seemed unpredictable and disrespectful to me. The Americans thought this showed flexibility, but to me, it just said that they do not honor the traditions and rules they have set up for themselves. If you are not raised in this culture, it is very difficult to know what Americans mean by their rules.

Americans are very friendly and I have many good American friends now. One of them, Ashley, has been my roommate for two and a half years. I stay with her family during some school vacations and she has visited me in Korea. We can talk about anything and she has learned a lot about my culture. Most Americans only speak one language and don't know very much about other countries. I am taking a very big course on American history this year, but many Americans don't know the difference between North and South Korea. Some confuse me with Japanese or Chinese students. Almost no one knows the history or culture of my country. America is big and many Americans never travel to other parts of the world so they do not need to know another language or different cultures. When I first got here, I had stereotypes of Americans that I had gotten from television and movies—they are all rich and violent and disrespectful. I have met many people and most of them are not like that at all. Americans who have never been to Korea probably have stereotypes about my people as well. I hope when they know me they will see that we are not like those stereotypes either.

What I miss most about my home is food. American food is very greasy and it is difficult for me to get good Korean food here. I have come to like pizza, but none of the food really feels like home. There is a Korean market in Boston. I love to go there and just smell the familiar smells and touch the familiar foods. I bring Korean candy and staples back to my room and complement my American diet with familiar tastes and smells. Sometimes my dormmaster will let me cook in her kitchen and many of the students will stop in because of the strange and unusual smells coming from her apartment. I wish I could tell them that is what my world smells like; I wish they could know that their food smells just as odd to me. When I get homesick or miss my family, I just wish I could smell my mother's cooking.

Probably the hardest time for me has been when I have been sick. When I feel sick, it is hard for me to keep up with all of my classes and I miss my mother and the way she would take care of me. In Korea, we use many herbal preparations that help cleanse the body so that the body can fight the illness. We recognize that your mental wellness affects your health and that you must get sleep, good diet, and meditation to stay healthy. My work schedule is so busy that I often don't get the sleep that I need and usually do not have the time to take care of my body. When I get sick, I prefer to use the medications that I have brought from home if I can. The American nurses seem to think that my medicines are superstitious and that their prescriptions are superior and correct. They don't really listen to how I am feeling or value the way I have always taken care of my health at home. Sometimes I am just tired from the stress of trying to keep up with the day and I miss my family and home. I know this can make me feel sick, but the American nurses only look at my temperature and tell me to take Tylenol. I don't want to miss any classes and I want the comfort and familiarity of my own medicines, so I usually stay away from the health center. This is hard when I am feeling very sick. Usually my herbal teas and remedies help in a little while, but it is a lonely time. I don't want to let my family down or risk my attendance at the American school, but I wish there was someone who understood how to take care of me in the Korean way.

Most of all, it is difficult to keep up. My English is very good now, but the work is still often culturally foreign to me. Most of the books we read in English are set in American cities and homes with American relationships and themes. American history rests on the foundation of a hundred stories about George Washington or the civil war or American politics that my classmates have grown up with, but are all new and frequently peculiar to me. I am happy to learn about the American history, but it does not have the same personal importance to me. The schedule at our school is always busy. I am used to studying very hard at home, but Americans insist on many other obligations and activities as well—sports, clubs, parties, student government, being outdoors, and doing community service. At home I would not do these things because of my studies; here in America, I am expected to do them all AND study. American students sometimes complain about how late the international students stay up. Even with my improved English, I do not know how Americans manage to do excellent work at all these things without staying up late.

It is true also, that frequently the only ones awake late at night are me and my international friends. For just a short while, the dorm is ours, the school is ours, and we do not feel like foreigners. Korean is spoken freely;

we imagine what is happening at home which is then in daylight; we can laugh at Korean jokes and commiserate over American misunderstandings or slights. We love our American school and learn much from our studies and the American ways, but it is difficult always to feel in part like an outsider. During the day, this does not bother me; I am used to it and understand that it is a choice I have made for the privilege of attending an American school. But late at night, it is sometimes a relief to put aside this understanding and step away from my cultural differences and just be myself in a familiar world in which I am normal and unexceptional.

The most perplexing realization is that I no longer feel completely normal and unexceptional at home either. The clothes that I wear at school stand out among my friends back in Korea. I often speak up independently in ways that embarrass my family and friends. My friends at home laugh at my American slang and boys are intimidated by my more outspoken ways. I find my mother's submission to my father and other men very difficult to accept. My parents sent me to the States to get a good education and become a doctor when I return to Korea. I have fallen in love with art and now wish to become a fashion designer. My parents cannot imagine that I might go up against their wishes—and I cannot imagine that I might not. I have an American boyfriend—my parents dismiss him as a phase; his parents are intrigued, but ignorant of Korean ways. I want him to come meet my friends and show him around Korea. He wants me to come to the American university and stay in the United States with him.

"Honor your American teachers and American school, but never forget that you are Korean and always honor your Korean ways." I do honor my American education and I cannot forget that I am Korean, but now I am both and I am neither. I understand both Korean and American cultures, but I am not purely either. I miss my Korean food, but love pizza too. I can speak up clearly as a strong young woman, but I am not comfortable disagreeing with my teachers and elders. I have a dream of being a fashion designer in New York City and I want to honor my parents' wishes that I return to Korea as a doctor. I have a foot in both worlds, but neither accepts or knows me completely. You might wonder if I regret coming to America and all these adjustments, but I do not. There are some conflicts in my heart that are difficult to reconcile, but I know more about this world than either my parents or my American friends do. I am not defined or completely known by either culture, but that only makes me more myself. I can live in either world. I know which parts of me are cultural and I can choose to assimilate or be independent of most of them. I am not entirely Korean or American, I am Meiko.

SOCIAL RESPONSIBILITY

From a speech given in 1959 by Phil Graham, publisher of the Washington Post:

. . . When I get in difficulty—at times almost unbearable difficulty—is when I try to examine the meaning of what I am engaged in.

When these difficulties get too great we in the newspaper business . . . retreat to the ritual of reciting old rules that we know are meaningless.

We say that we just print the objective news in our news columns and confine our opinions to the editorial page. Yet we know that while this has some merit as an over-simplified slogan of good intentions, it also has a strong smell of pure baloney.

If we keep wages too low in some few areas where unions will let us do it or if we neglect decent working amenities as long as we can avoid the cost, we defend ourselves by muttering about our concern for stockholders. As though by announcing compassion for a relatively anonymous and absent group we can justify a lack of compassion for people we spend our working days with.

If we are brutally careless about printing something that maligns the character of some concrete individual, we are apt to wave the abstract flag of freedom of speech in order to avoid the embarrassment of a concrete apology.

If we are pressed even harder, we may salve our consciences by saying that after all there are libel laws. And as soon as we say that we redouble our efforts to make those laws as toothless as we possibly can.

And if we are pressed really quite hard, we can finally shrug our shoulders and say, 'Well, after all, we have to live.' Then we can only hope no one will ask the ultimate question: 'Why?'

I certainly have been guilty of all those stupid actions—and a great many more stupid. And I suppose that more than a few of you have done as poorly.

What I prefer to recall are those rare occasions when I have had some better sense of the meaning of what I am engaged in. In those moments I have realized that our problems are relatively simple and that simple, ancient, moral precepts are often reliable business tools. In those moments I have been able to keep in mind that it really doesn't matter whether I am kept in my job. In those moments I have been able to look straight at the frailty of my judgment. And finally I have been honest enough to recognize that a few—a very few—great issues about the meaning of life are the only issues which deserve to be considered truly complex.

. . . by paying attention to the broader meaning of what we are engaged in, we may be able to join our passion to our intelligence. And such a juncture, even on the part of but one individual, can represent a significant step forward on the long road toward civilization.[9]

Steven

Steven Toney is a private fellow, but I heard through a mutual friend that he was having some financial troubles. Mainly, he was late with his rent. So I stopped by to see him, and he said that yes, he was having some financial troubles, but he didn't want any details in the newspaper.

No details then. But in general terms, Toney's problems have nothing to do with his lifestyle. He lives simply in a small apartment. It's a nice place, though. His apartment is in the back of the building, and when you open the door, you don't see the street. Instead, you see trees. He appreciates that very much.

He has a job with a rental car company at the airport. He works about 25 hours a week. The airport-rental car business has never really recovered from 9-11, and there's not much chance that Toney's job will go full time any time soon. It's a nice job, though. Sometimes the company sends him places to pick up cars. He likes that. He does not want to be cooped up in an office.

He was cooped up for a long time. In 1982, he was given a life sentence for a rape conviction. He had been picked up on a bad check charge—he was quickly cleared of that—but he was put in a lineup on a rape case. The victim identified him as her attacker. He professed his innocence from the very beginning. "How much time would you be willing to accept?" his public defender asked him. "Not a single day," he said. He went to trial, and the rape victim—a woman Toney had never seen—testified that he was the rapist. Thirteen years and 10 months later, he was released after DNA testing excluded him as the rapist. Was not him. Could not have been him.

First thing he did when he got out was to get a strawberry milkshake. Later, he met with reporters and said he did not intend to dwell on the negative.

He has been out of prison for five years. He's 55 years old.

In March, he went to Jefferson City to testify on behalf of a bill that would establish some kind of remuneration for people who have been wrongly convicted and imprisoned. It went nowhere.

"One of the legislators asked me where they were supposed to get the money," Toney told me. "Like I should know?"

Actually this is an issue that the Legislature has to address. Fairness demands it. New technology is making it possible for some wrongly convicted people to prove their innocence. On the national level, more than 100 people have been freed in the past decade, thanks to DNA testing. Here in St. Louis, Larry Johnson was recently freed after spending 18 years in prison for a rape he did not commit. The good news—good on several levels—is that there is not going to be an endless stream of these cases. After all, we're talking about people who were convicted before DNA testing was readily available.

In the meantime, though, what do we owe somebody like Steven Toney?

He's a high school graduate. He served in the Army and did a hitch in Vietnam. He received an honorable discharge. He later got in trouble, which is not unusual in these cases. Most people who get caught up in the system have been in it before. In Toney's case, he did two and a half years on a robbery charge.

Of course, that was years and years ago. Now he lives quietly. He doesn't even own a car. He takes the bus to work. He has an occasional beer, and now and then, he'll go out to dinner, but nothing fancy.

We talked for quite a while when I visited this week. He's a contemplative man, thoughtful and intelligent. He seems largely at peace with himself, and I suspect a lot of that has to do with what he said five years ago about not dwelling on the negative.

Still, it is hard to be positive when you're having trouble with the rent. Toney said he wasn't sure what he was going to do. He said he could move in with somebody, but he was hoping it wouldn't come to that. I like the solitary life, he said.

He deserves some solitude. It's something you can't get in prison.

—Bill McClellan, reprinted with permission by the
St. Louis Post-Dispatch, October 2, 2002

"TWO MIRRORS" *by Jiyoung Kim*

THE SEARCH FOR MEANING

Saroya

I just graduated a month ago and after the ceremony and all the parties, a friend came up to me and said "If I never see you again, have a good life."

The friend and I are not that close, but she is one of the people that I have seen almost every day of my life since kindergarten and her words came as a jolt. Yes, we are all heading off into different directions and different colleges and my plans don't include hanging around my hometown much—I want to get out and see the world. But when my friend said that, I realized for the first time that I really am heading off on my own. I have spent the last eight months complaining about how ready I am to be out of my home and school, with all their rules and expectations. I'm excited to make my own choices and stop having everyone else run my life for me, but finally standing here with my life in my own hands, I have more questions than answers.

". . . have a good life." I was so sure I knew what that meant only a year ago, back when I was fighting against everyone else's version of "my" good life. My dad was sure that my good life included going into business—a career that had made him a lot of money . . . and not much time for anything else, including me, as far as I could tell. My mom just kept saying, "Don't limit your options—girls today can do anything. You should become a lawyer or doctor. Don't get tied down with a man and family until you are ready." My best friend was sure "our" best life was going to the state college together and joining the same sorority and just having some fun. My art teacher told me it would be a crime if I didn't pursue my art talent. My grampa was so excited for me to apply to his alma mater, "the school that has educated four generations of Lansons."

My boyfriend isn't going to college for a year and he encouraged me to get off the treadmill with him and discover what life is really about. Everyone was so sure they knew what I should do with my life and I was so sure that I knew better than all of them. I wanted a college, but not one where my best friend or four generations of my family had gone. I wanted a college that was about me and the things I care about. I wanted to get off on my own, away from all these people who had been defining me all of my life. I love my art, but I don't want to turn it into drudgery by making it a career, and a business or law office is the last place I want to spend a quarter of the rest of my life. Independent and sure of myself, I politely told everyone to bug off. I can take it from here, thank you very much.

Now, it is *here. Here* I am. This is it. Off to my good life even if I never see you again. It is exciting, but it's big, too. Knowing what *I* really want, what *my life* is really about, is a lot more daunting than knowing what I don't want. If not art or business, what? If not my hometown, where? If I get off the treadmill, where will I be? What will hold me up? What will be important? If not the same person I have been gridlocked into being for the last four years, who will I be?

And some of the things that I have been pushing away, suddenly seem precious and fleeting—friends I have taken for granted; the security of my hometown where people know me; my family who has shared so much of my life up to this point; even the nagging and restrictions that gave me predictable and safe boundaries. My bedroom suddenly seems safe and comforting, full of the pictures and artifacts that have made up my life for the last eighteen years. What is me and what are all the things around me?

What will I take with me and what will I leave behind? The real possibility of regret is new to me. Before, nothing was really so unpredictable or irretrievable. I was protected from big mistakes and the little ones were easily fixed.

Now all the *"paths less traveled"* are spread out in front of me like a game show—behind door number one, is it the *"good life"* or a year's supply of peanut butter? Choices seem more critical; if I charge off in one direction, will all of the other potential paths of my life disappear—and will that make *all the difference?*

What is the meaning of my small but personal little life? What do I want? What will make me truly happy? Is there something more important than happiness? What do I want to accomplish? Should I work hard and do good—or should I just make a lot of money and have a good time? What am I willing to sacrifice to get ahead—free time? family? friendships? pastimes I enjoy? my health? my honesty? What will give my life meaning and significance? Is there a plan or purpose to all the things that happen to me or to anyone? Or is my life just a random speck of idiot DNA signifying nothing? What happens when I die—heaven or hell, reincarnation, or just decomposition? Is there a God who is masterminding this whole world of life or is it all some grand, indifferent coincidence? If there is a God, is he compassionate or vengeful—or just slightly curious? If I am a part of some larger plan, how will I know my part? The dumbest ant seems to know just where to go and what to do, and I am clueless.

Along with the deliciousness of my new freedom, I find these questions running through my head, no longer tied to the simple answers of my childhood. My family has never gone to church much, but over the last few months, I found myself talking with the school chaplain. He answered most of my questions with more questions, but he listened and smiled at my attempts at humor and sympathized without condescension with the depth of my questioning. He said that to ask these questions was the core of my own spirituality. It was not a church thing or a shared thing, he said, but "my deeply personal engagement with the mystery of human experience." He is Episcopal, but he gave me books on Buddhism and philosophy and Native American beliefs in addition to suggesting readings from the Bible and prayer book. He said that it was the search itself that would reveal my spiritual faith as I read and talked and measured each idea against my own inner knowing.

We talked about the existence of God. I don't how I define God or even if I believe in some omnipotent power. The world is beautiful and functions reasonably well when mankind is not screwing it up, but then, if God is the creator of everything, he made mankind too. Science explains the physical world reasonably well, but lacks the sense of magic and majesty I cannot help feeling standing next to the ocean, watching a sunset, or observing the perfect colors of the feathers of the smallest hummingbird. There is art to it and a beauty that is unnecessary, but spectacular. I can't help believing there is something more to existence than the sum of cells and molecules. In its splendor, nature makes me believe in a God, but nature's impersonal wrath and devastation also makes me wonder what sort of God that might be, one that creates the tenderest flower or new life and destroys thousands as they sleep in the wake of an earthquake or volcano eruption. Is it a kind and compassionate God who comforts and forgives? Or is it a grave, unforgiving God that demands strict observance of its commandments and feels no anguish or concern for human suffering? Or is it merely an indifferent God who simply provides the objective circumstances and patterns of our lives leaving it to us to make the best of things—creating our character out of the remnants of our experience?

Whether my life is cunningly planned, fated, or capriciously evolving, I am always faced with the choices of how to react to my experience. I can act in my own self-interest regardless of how it might affect others. I can act in the interest of those that I love, disregarding my own personal gain or pain. I can choose to be a part of some group—friends, a community, a nation, a club—and surrender my own personal wishes for the best interests of the group. Or I can choose to act based on a larger principle, like Mother Teresa, basing her decisions on compassion for the poor—or in my smaller way, recycling or telling the truth or standing up to a bully or discrimination. I once heard a speaker say that whenever you have a difficult decision, always come up with five options. Inevitably, at least one of those options will be ethical.

Ethics seems like such an old-fashioned, moralistic word—certainly one that most people in my school find archaic and impractical. I doubt if there is anyone in my school that hasn't cheated on some test or project and some people cheat whenever they can get away with it. It is only wrong if you get caught. Nobody really thinks about cheating as an ethical problem; it is just a pragmatic choice to get a better grade or get into a better college. If you don't cheat, you are at a disadvantage—or simply naïve. Parents cheat on their taxes and on their spouses; companies rip off their stockholders and employees; sports celebrities cheat to win and make more money; elected officials lie and make deals in back rooms. There is certainly no scarcity of examples to justify a little cheating on a math test.

Is there any good reason to behave ethically even if nobody else is—even if there is no chance of getting caught? Someone said that your character is defined in those moments when no one is looking. Should I behave in ways that I believe are right and good just to be right and good? Is it better to be right and good than to win? Or am I just being naïve? People get away with being dishonest all the time and it is usually to their advantage. What price do they pay? What do I gain by resisting?

On the other hand, if the world has gone ethically mad, does that justify my own corruption? What kind of world is our mass dishonesty creating? On a school level, it makes learning cheap. You don't have to work for it, you probably won't learn much, and there is little personal satisfaction in the achievement—unless you build your reputation on getting away with things. You can't really trust anyone if everything is open game. If you work hard on a project or test, it can provide an easy A for someone else who didn't do anything. I have seen friends steal from friends, students take papers from the Internet, and AP biology fruit fly lab experiments sabotaged in order to beat the curve. It might make you mad if they were your fruit flies, but it is no outrage. We all somehow excuse each other for doing whatever we need to do to get ahead. This has created a paranoid world—do unto others before they do unto you.

Nice guys finish last—and nice girls don't even make the lineup. Do I buy into that? I make these kinds of choices every day. Do I make them out of principle or convenience or self-interest? Does it matter? Is God keeping score? Is the world worse or better off because of my choices? Am I worse or better off because of my choices? If I screw over my friend, lie to my coach, cheat on a sports event, win, take home the trophy, and a $2000 prize and never get caught, am I better or worse for my choices? And should I care?

A lot of people get to the top by not playing straight—some people call it *the real world*. Enron cheated on its books, making a lot of money for some people and stealing the life savings of others. President Clinton lied about his relationship with a female intern—what else was he lying about? Advertising is a series of well-choreographed exaggerations and fabrications. Sammy Sosa used an illegal bat—was it just this once, as he claimed, or was cheating responsible for his 500 homeruns? He seems like a nice guy, but when the world is based on dishonesty and personal gain, it is hard to believe anybody. I guess I take everything with a handful of salt and my whole generation is pretty cynical and disbelieving.

I don't like it. I don't like watching my back and I don't like not being able to trust people to tell me the truth, whether it is my best friend or my president. I don't like being ripped off whether it is on the French test by the kid who sits next to me or by the advertiser who makes false promises to get my money. I don't like wondering if Congress is acting in my best interests or at the bidding of the lobby group that has the most money or offers the best kickbacks.

I'm just eighteen. I should be out there saving the world and it is hard to muster up a good reason. What can one person do? And, as the attractive, slimy, soon-to-be-senator character in *The Emperor's Club* said, "Who the hell gives a shit?" The Buddhists say I can only impact the world by being pure myself—adding my one drop of integrity into the mix. Social activists say I must speak up and fight injustice and oppression. Religion says I must live rightly and have compassion for others. Machiavelli says take care of yourself and let others get out of the way. My parents say I can't take on the whole world and my boyfriend says I have to take on the whole world; if I am not a part of the solution, I am a part of the problem. Existentialists say none of it matters except what you decide matters. And that will get you right back to door number one.

Death plays an interesting role in the way I think about all these things. If life is just a biochemical coincidence in an indifferent universe and I will just decompose when I die, what's the point? Having a good time while I am alive? Making it a little nicer for someone else? Contributing something to a meaningless swirling planet of life that will eventually disintegrate into the universe regardless of my efforts? If you go to heaven or hell after you die, the options are obvious. The big question there is, how tight are the entrance requirements and how forgiving is God? If I continue after death in some form—a spirit or a frog or an evolved state of light—that suggests that there may be some evolutionary purpose to my life. Lessons to learn, karma to pay for, or experiences to add to my evolving spiritual self. That makes life pretty serious and I need to pay attention. Suffering and mistakes become my teachers, opportunities to grasp something larger than my immediate human experience.

My gramma died about two years ago and that scared me. She was pretty peaceful and reassuring about the whole thing, but suddenly she didn't exist anymore. She didn't help with Thanksgiving dinner or send me birthday presents or listen to my stories or sit in her favorite chair in our living room. I try to imagine her watching over me, but the fact is, she wasn't at my graduation and won't be there to see how my "good life" turns out. She was always my champion and defender; she believed in me and kept my secrets. Where is she now? I miss her and want some sign that she still exists in some form.

One afternoon while I was sitting on my bed, thinking about her and trying to make sense of death, the sunlight came through a prism that was hanging in my window. Distracted by the tiny rainbows that were danc-ing around my room, I imagined that the prism was death and the color-ful shards of light were individual lives, distinct expressions of life. After death, on the other side of the prism, they rejoined the sun or source of light. On one hand, that created a scary and hollow feeling in me—to be absorbed and indistinct. Gramma would no longer exist as a distinct en-tity and I would never rejoin her after my life and I would someday melt into that same nameless globule of light.

On the other hand, as I felt the warmth of the sun fall on my hand, it felt powerful and warm and unbroken. It filled all space and its energy gave life to everything in the world. Its force was good and comforting, metaphorically getting rid of the darkness. It created life as surely as my grandmother's dance of color on this side of the prism had created me, and I was here, now, creating my *good life.* It was a moment that didn't an-swer all of my questions, but gave me some reassurance for living out those questions. I can try to live my life true to that lightness. If I am a speck of that light, I need to reflect it plainly. In my short life, I already know that is not always easy. I know when a choice makes me feel good and light, and when it makes me feel small and disconnected, but it is still not always easy to make. Doing the right thing often requires wisdom, courage, or uncommon effort and may not be rewarded or appreciated by others. But I need a connection to something larger than myself in order to make sense of my life. I see so many people around me gathering things, winning races, collecting accomplishments and yet gaining no satisfaction or connection. And instead of questioning their methods, they frantically work to gather, win, and collect more, feeling more lost and empty in the effort.

I don't know if I will have a *good life* or if I will ever see that friend again. I do know that I alone am responsible for my choices and I can either di-minish or amplify the light that I give out and take back through the prism. No one else can do that for me or stop me from it. That is the only thing I understand, and for now, it is my measure, my guide, the light that I can see by.

Artwork:

Jessica Webb
Viewpoint School

Artist
Unknown

Robyn Strumpf
Viewpoint School

Joannie Chui
San Domenico School

Jiyoung Kim
San Domenico School

Notes

[1] Gloria Steinem. *Revolution From Within: A Book of Self-Esteem.* Little, Brown and Company, 1992.

[2] www.Oxfamamerica.org

[3] John DeGrace, David Wann, Thomas Naylor. *Affluenza: The All-Consuming Epidemic.* San Francisco: Berrett-Koehler Publishers, Inc., pp. 168–70.

[4] Ibid.

[5] Ibid.

[6] From the Cortez Journal, www.cortezjournal.com, by Aspen C. Emmett, June 28, 2001.

[7] http://www.temenos.net/remember/martinez/article_3.htm

[8] Esther Wanning. *Culture Shock! USA.* Printed in Singapore by Chong Moh Offset Printing Pte Ltd, 1991.

[9] Katharine Graham. *Personal History.* Random House, First Vintage Books Edition, March 1998.

As I see it every day you do one of two things: build health or produce disease in yourself.

—Adelle Davis

Chapter 2.

Living in Your Body

The adolescent growth spurt is a rush of hormones and physical changes that affect every part of your life for several years. The slow and steady growth of childhood is abruptly replaced by great spurts of height and weight as well as internal and external changes in the way your body looks, feels, smells, and moves. Your soft baby skin may be covered with pimples and patches of strange new hair. The shape of your body changes, not necessary in a coordinated way, starting with gangly feet and hands that may seem out of sync and clumsy. Muscles, breasts, hormones, curves, height, weight, and proportion change in their own good time, rarely on demand or at the same rate or time as your friends.

And it doesn't help that girls tend to enter this growth spurt a couple years earlier than boys. Or that your body may look eighteen while you are still fourteen— or look fourteen when you are eighteen. You can't judge a book (even your own) by its cover, but people often do. Making friends, dating, getting a job, being taken seriously, and feeling good about yourself can all be influenced by the way you look. This can create a lot of pressure around something over which you have little control. Focus on what you can control—staying healthy, eating well, getting enough sleep. Don't lose track of who you are. Appearances may fool others and even make you question yourself, but true friends and self-confidence come from who you really are. That may be little solace if you not sure what you really think and feel much of the time, but remember, you are not finished and never will be. It helps to be patient, curious, and forgiving. All these changes are temporary and important. Don't lose your sense of humor—especially your ability to laugh at yourself. Physical and emotional maturity come when you have learned how to take care of and accept yourself, warts and all.

THE CHANGING BODY

Sam

Let me start by saying that I used to be quite cool. Not bad looking, a good athlete, plenty of friends—I played lead guitar in a band and was high scorer on our soccer team. We were pretty good. Girls liked me and I was elected president of my seventh-grade class. Really, check my junior high yearbook—I was definitely cool. I am still pretty much the same, so what happened?

Actually, that's the problem—nothing much has happened. While all my friends started growing and shaping muscles, even a few facial hairs, I am sitting here with not so much as a pimple. I look like a seventh-grade version of Tom Sawyer. Thinking she is cheering me up, my older sister tells me I am "cute." Senior girls think I am "adorable" as they pat me on the head and walk off with their boyfriends. Charley has been my best friend since we were in elementary school and we still hang out, but these days that just highlights our differences. Charley is now a lanky 5'11" with the body of a growing man. He is the only freshman on the varsity soccer team and even older girls think he's hot. Just a couple years ago, we were playing soccer together and *he* was passing to *me*. Now all 5'1" of me can still dribble circles around half the varsity team, but one good check and I'm flat—I just don't have the bulk. Coach says in a couple years I should be seeing some good playing time. A couple years, heck. I will practically be a senior. What am I supposed to do in the mean time? Play kickball on the playground?

It is really unfair and misleading because I am definitely older than I look—in fact, for as different as Charley and I look, we still feel and act pretty much the same way. We still like to screw around and play video games and watch *Saturday Night Live* and steal his older brother's girly magazines. But people treat Charley like he is older (I am actually older by two months) just because he looks older, and they treat me like a kid. They expect me to say dumb things and act immaturely, but when Charley does the exact same things, they don't think he is dumb or immature. In class, I swear teachers don't take me as seriously. I don't even think it is intentional, but they give more credit to the guys that look older. They have never once asked me to monitor the room while they step out for a minute and they have asked Charley three times. What a joke. Charley is the biggest cutup in class, but the teacher thinks he is *mature* because he has to shave now and then. She needs a monitor for her monitor.

And girls. That's a whole other sad story. First off, they all grew back in junior high, so even the genetically short girls are taller than me. I come about eye level with their boobs when I try to dance—needless to say, I don't dance much. Even the girls who had crushes on me a couple years ago back when I was cool have passed me by. A couple girls like me "as a friend" and even ask my advice about how to get "a boyfriend"—like I'm some sort of third gender or reject. Even when they discover how cool I am inside, I just don't fit the boyfriend look. One girl I really liked actually told me that if I were just a little taller, she might even like to go out with me. Thanks a lot. You can imagine what all this does for my emerging sex life. When I try to drop a line or give girls a sexy look, they just start giggling and say, "Oh Sammy, you're so cute." *Cute* is not the look I am after.

The locker room is another of my favorite places—if you want me to look even younger, just take off my clothes. All the guys are parading around with hair growing in all the manly places, flexing their muscles, and flaunting their—uh—"equipment." I will go for the next three years without a shower if the only one available contains a group of my well-developed peers. I have already been humiliated in PE class, joked about when we have to do lay ups, and ignored when either strength or height are required. One afternoon, a couple of seniors actually lifted me and put me in the trashcan. Now try looking mature and sophisticated climbing out of a trashcan. I try to get shin splints or sprain my ankle whenever possible so I am excused from sports—me, the future soccer champion of the world.

And my parents treat me like I am still in elementary school—my mom even calls me "Sammy." Sam is a decent manly man name, but Sammy sounds like I should be put down for a nap. It is hard enough for my parents to accept the fact that I am not their little baby anymore without me looking like one. When I ask if I can go out to a party, they practically ask if we will be playing pin the tail on the donkey. If they even knew what really goes on at those parties, they would ground me for ten years. As I mentioned, I don't get much action in the girl department, but I can still show people I am not a kid by smoking and handling my share of the beer and buzz. Actually, my body can't hold as much alcohol, so I tend to stick with the pot and minor drugs that show up at our parties. I can toke up with the best of them, but eventually they all tumble off in pairs and I am left with the clean-up patrol. Hardly cool.

My dad says that he matured late too and not to worry; by the time I get to college I will be strong and studly. Is that supposed to make me feel better? I should just sit out the next three years of my life in hopes of getting some playing time in the fourth quarter? Here I am in high school which is supposed to be the best time of my life and I'm not big enough to make the team, manly enough to get the girl, or tall enough to see over the girls in front of me at the football game. I'm a joke. If I had always been a joke, it would be one thing, but I was once cool and am meant for better things. I mean, what if I never grow? What if I look fifteen when I am trying to run some important board of directors meeting? Or if I have to look to elementary school to get a date for the senior prom? I have tried working out or making a name for myself in debate club or being a party animal, but it still looks like *cute* little me pretending to be a stud. It is all well and good to say you don't judge a book by its cover, but it's the cover that makes the team and gets the girl and my cover looks like one of the Hardy Boys.

Call me in a couple years and I will let you know if I'm cool again yet.

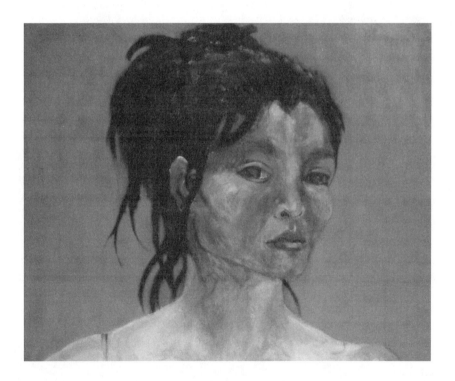

SELF-PORTRAIT *by Suki Boynton*

EATING DISORDERS

Research suggests that about 1 percent of female adolescents are anorexic and 4 percent of college-aged women have bulimia. Fifty percent of recovering anorexics develop bulimia during their recovery. About 10% of people diagnosed with eating disorders are male. Eating disorders can affect children and older adults, but most anorexics and bulimics are in their teens and twenties. About 72 percent of alcoholic women younger than thirty also have eating disorders. Without treatment, up to 20 percent of people with serious eating disorders die. With treatment, that number falls to 2–3 percent.

With treatment, about 60 percent of people with eating disorders recover. They maintain healthy weight. They eat a varied diet of normal foods and do not choose exclusively low-cal and nonfat items. They participate in friendships and romantic relationships. They create families and careers.

In spite of treatment, about 20 percent of people with eating disorders make only partial recoveries. They remain focused on food and weight. They participate only peripherally in friendships and romantic relationships. They may hold jobs but seldom have meaningful careers. Much of each paycheck goes to diet books, laxatives, exercise classes, and binge food.

The remaining 20 percent do not improve, even with treatment. They are seen repeatedly in emergency rooms, eating disorders programs, and mental health clinics. Their quietly desperate lives revolve around food and weight concerns, spiraling down into depression, loneliness, and feelings of helplessness and hopelessness.

Please note: The study of eating disorders is a relatively new field. We have no good information on the long-term recovery process. We do know that recovery usually takes a long time, perhaps on average three to five years of slow progress that includes starts, stops, backward slides, and ultimately, movement in the direction of mental and physical health.[1]

Clara

I came to Groton from a small town in Pennsylvania, entering the third form in the fall of 1984. I arrived anxious about everything: my clothes, my athletic ability, my roommate. I worried that I would not be able to do the work, or that no boys would speak to me. I probably felt no differently than the others girls who were standing awkwardly around me as our parents unloaded the cars on the first day, but I never found out. I have never shared my feelings well and so assumed that my anxiety was mine alone. Here, perhaps, was the first sign of trouble, if hunting for reasons is important to you.

My first year went well. I made many friends, loved playing sports and did well in my classes, though I worked desperately hard to achieve the highest marks possible. I struggled in math, and needed extra tutoring to catch up with my class. This was an embarrassment to me, and, I assumed, to my parents. I had control, but barely.

I had never encountered eating disorders before my arrival at Groton. I do not think that I even knew the terms until it became obvious that a girl in my dorm was bulimic. I was horrified that someone could do something like that to herself, but also intrigued. Why was she so desperate to be thin? Was there something I was missing? I thought a great deal about her, and wondered if I, too, needed to worry about my body. I brought a scale back with me after Thanksgiving break and began to weigh myself every day. It would take me eight years to break myself of that habit.

I lost weight slowly, but steadily, during the fourth and fifth form. No one noticed, or at least no one mentioned it. My strategy was simple: skip breakfast, eat crackers or salad for lunch, and salad only for dinner. I did not stick to the regimen at first, as I still enjoyed pizza with friends, dorm feeds, and meals with my parents who visited regularly. At some point though, my goal to lose weight overrode all other interests. I began to devise elaborate routines and strategies in order to avoid situations where I would be forced to eat. I knew exactly what I would eat before I ever climbed the winding stairs to the dining hall and had no trouble avoiding temptations once I was there.

There is an incredible power anorexics find in their ability to refuse food. I discovered my ability to not eat was my greatest strength. Here, I was in complete control. While I could not guarantee my grades or win every tennis match or be sure that I would be asked to dance on Saturday night, I was confident that what I ate or did not eat would be entirely under my control.

Despite the habits I was developing, I do not believe that I became truly "anorexic" until sixth form. Some signs were obvious, some more subtle. I continued to skip meals, as much as I could, and significantly increased my exercise. While I played field hockey and ice hockey, I kept my exercise at a reasonable level. Breaking my collarbone in one of our first ice hockey games was a significant blow. However, I now know that the break was most likely due to the brittleness of my bones than to the force of my impact with the boards. Since that accident eight years ago, I have had five stress fractures due to overtraining and bones weakened from the impact of malnutrition. A recent bone scan revealed that I now have the bone density similar to a woman in her sixties, an effect of six years of anorexia that I will never be able to entirely reverse. With my arm in a sling and unable to practice with the team, I was suddenly left alone to find a way to sweat off the minimal calories I was still consuming each day. I discovered the weight-room bicycle, which I pedaled until I was so lightheaded I could barely stand up. I have few distinct memories of that winter, but a day in December does stand out. It was my seventeenth birthday, my early acceptance to Dartmouth had arrived that morning, and I had stepped on the scale to discover that I had lost two pounds. I did not find it at all unusual that I considered my weight loss the best part of my day.

My collarbone took a long time to heal, but by the spring, I was playing tennis and pleased that my skirt from fifth form no longer fit, but had to be pinned. Not convinced that tennis burned enough calories, I began a running routine that would become compulsive by the time I got to Dartmouth. I ran every day. I ran because I enjoyed the time away from the dorm and my classes. I loved the surrounding countryside and the emerging signs of spring. I loved the sweat and the pounding of my straining heart.

I talked to no one about my weight and eating habits, and few people ever said anything to me. Friends asked me to come along to meals at first, but eventually gave up. My adviser was the first adult to confront me. I was a prefect in his dorm. His was the first voice to question what I was doing to myself. I denied everything, of course. I brushed aside his every approach. He never let me forget that he was aware of my struggle, however. Though I pretended to be aloof to his concerns, I felt less alone than I had in months. Someone had finally entered the world that was slowly beginning to consume me.

My best friend and I drove up and down the East Coast during senior week, visiting classmates' houses. I returned for graduation tanned and at my lowest weight in five years. My adviser told my parents of his concerns after the ceremony, a simple act which helped to save my life. Completely unaware of my struggles until that day, my parents began to accept that their "perfect" daughter had a problem and started educating themselves about the disorder. I spent only a few days at home after graduation before I drove off to Maine to work as a summer camp counselor. I avoided most of my responsibilities at the camp, eager only to run around the lake every morning and to Rollerblade every afternoon. I ate nothing at meals, as my ten-year-old campers watched me in puzzlement. I was dismissed from that camp halfway through the summer. The camp leaders recognized my illness and pleaded with me to get help. My parents picked me up and brought me home. I visited my pediatrician, was weighed, and was put on a food plan. I was significantly below the normal weight for my height, but eagerly agreed to gain a few pounds and made quick excuses for the loss. I told no one of what had been going on over the last few years, and no one asked. I managed to gain a few pounds before I headed off to Dartmouth.

My first month at Dartmouth was wonderful. However, as the workload increased, I slowly began to return to my running and stopped going to meals with friends. These runs increased in intensity over the fall term, until I was running two and half hours every morning before my first class. One day during hockey practice, we had to weigh ourselves and have a treadmill stress test. I lied to the therapist about my weight as he strapped on a heart-rate monitor. We were supposed to run until exhaustion, but the trainer stopped the treadmill after only ten minutes. My coach cornered me as I entered the rink later that afternoon. Irregularities in my heartbeat had been recorded and my weight, even though I had secretly added ten pounds to the true figure, was dangerously low. I would not be allowed to practice and was told to report to the hospital for more tests.

I had been found out, once again. This time, I would not be able to escape, though I continued to spiral downward that winter. My heartbeat was, in fact, irregular. Because I gave myself so little fuel, and had no fat reserves, my body was feeding upon itself, slowly consuming its own muscles, including the lining around my heart. Other physical signs of deterioration were painfully obvious. I could not sit for long in class as my bones lay sharply on the hard surface of the chair. Walking hurt, as I no longer had any padding on the bottoms of my feet, though, of course, I continued to run. Doctors monitored my heart, nutritionists advised me on my diet, and I met with a counselor three times a week. Despite the attention I was receiving, my weight dropped drastically that winter, until my five-foot-nine-inch body was well below 100 pounds. I, like other anorexics, always had a certain goal weight in mind; a magic number that, when reached, would instantly solve all of my problems. I was working so hard because I was convinced that when my digital scale finally read that certain number, I would finally be the attractive and popular person I had always wanted to be. Whenever I got near a supposed goal weight, one look in the mirror convinced me that the number had to be altered. Five more pounds and I would be perfect. Even at ninety pounds, I had already shifted my goal to eighty-five.

I went through eight counselors that winter. Finally, hands in the air, my doctors told me that I would not be allowed to enroll for the spring term unless I gained five pounds. Such a goal was impossible for me to reach, and I did not, in fact, return to Dartmouth again for a full year. That year away from Dartmouth was an exasperating one for my parents and for me. Since the day that my adviser had told them of my problems, my mother and father had supported me and tried to find help, but were completely unprepared for the state I was in when I returned from Dartmouth. I spent the next year visiting doctors and counselors daily. I was miserable, but slowly began to relax my tenacious hold on my old habits. My weight gain was slow, but I recovered enough physically and mentally to return to Dartmouth the next winter. I returned to a support system waiting for me. I continued to be weighed weekly by a doctor and was required to join group and individual counseling, which I continued for three more years. Though I experienced a few relapses, I never fell as far as I had my freshman year.

Anorexia is not a disorder I will ever entirely recover from. I do not have a story that ends with a miraculous recovery, and I would be suspicious of anyone who claimed that they had completely gotten over an eating disorder. I continue to struggle with worries about food and my body. I exercise every day without fail. I am prone to stress fractures and will mostly likely encounter early osteoporosis due to the irreversible effects of starvation on my bones. I am lucky that I should be able to have children someday, though many long-term anorexics are never able to.

Despite these lingering effects of the disorder, they pale in comparison to what I consider to be the most detrimental of all. When I look back on those six or so years, it sickens me to realize how much of my life I missed. I allowed my obsession with my weight to take over my life, so that every waking moment was spent worrying about fat, avoiding fat, and exercising. I was one of a lucky few to attend schools such as Groton and Dartmouth, yet I had isolated myself so drastically that I never took advantage of all of the opportunities I had at either place. So lost in my solo quest for a thinner body, I spent most of my days alone, studying for perfect grades and running for a perfect body. It was an entirely selfish quest and one that I executed without emotion. It was not until I began the recovery process that I ever expressed any grief or anger. It took me years to recognize how lonely I had been.[2]

—Written by Clara A. Zurn, 1997

What Can a Friend Do?

If anything that I have said strikes a chord in your own mind, please find someone to talk to. Once anorexia envelops you completely, you will never seek help yourself, but hopefully someone will step in on your behalf. There is no magic solution to eating disorders, but there are ways to support and to help a friend whom you suspect may have a problem.

- First, educate yourself about eating disorders. Learn about the symptoms, habits, and danger signs. Read articles and ask questions.

- Trust your intuition. If you suspect there is a problem, there probably is.

- Get support and advice from people you trust. Talk to a dorm head, a teacher, a coach, a friend, or someone who has experienced an eating disorder personally.

- Write down specific instances of the person's problematic behavior.

- Communicate directly to the person the seriousness of your concern and your conviction that treatment is necessary.

- Do not play food police. Do not argue about how much should be eaten or attempt to threaten or bribe a problem eater. Avoid giving simplistic advice about nutrition.

- Try to remain calm and nonjudgmental.

- Try to establish and maintain a healthy atmosphere in the dorm and to include the problem eater in group activities. Encourage him/her to pursue interests and to see friends.

- Be patient, but do not let yourself become completely wrapped up in your friend's problems. You need time away to maintain your own mental and emotional health.[3]

DISABILITIES AND DIFFERENCES

Anne

I have heard people say that they would rather die than end up in a wheelchair for their whole life. I guess before my accident, I might have said that too. I couldn't imagine not being able to move anywhere I wanted or play sports or take a walk or be able to take care of myself. I was full of life and, while I took it for granted, I thought being physically independent was an essential part of who I was. I have come to understand that my physical self is only a part of who I am; that my life has been different than I thought it would be, but I am just as alive and capable regardless of my physical circumstances. When you look at me, you may see a wheelchair and limitations. When I look in the mirror, I have come to see myself—strong, happy, and powerful.

I was an active child, coordinated and strong. I was the fastest runner in my class and could climb anything I put my mind to. I swam and dove and played field hockey, basketball, and lacrosse—loving both the physical activity as well as the fun of playing on a team. I was the middle child of five and enjoyed the protection of my older brother and sister and the admiration of my younger brother and sister. We had a close and loving family—I felt lucky and sheltered, enjoying an easy life with lots of good friends and nothing much to worry about.

Every summer my family went away for a summer vacation. The summer between seventh and eighth grade we spent a month at my grandmother's house in Maine. I enjoyed the independence I had when I was there. My brothers and sisters and I could ride our bikes to the pool and tennis courts or walk to town to buy penny candy or watch the windjammers come into the harbor. It was a wonderful month of family time and new friends. I had several friends I had met summers before and we looked forward to reuniting so we could swim, sail, and hang around the lifeguards who we idealized. It was a safe and friendly community. We could run around together without worry or supervision.

I had invited my close friend from home to visit for a week. Pam and I had known one another a little less than a year but we were two of a kind. We would wake up early in the morning and as we were eating our breakfast we would make our plans for the day. Our day consisted of swimming, playing tennis, or hiking up a nearby mountain and returning to the pool for an afternoon swim before returning home to a family evening.

At the pool, we would play endless games of Marco Polo and race each other back and forth in the pool, laughing and creating water ballet or handstands. The lifeguards knew us well and, aside from an occasional "no running" whistle, they let us play and hang out without much hassle. Our daily ritual was to ride our bikes to the pool and race to see who would be the first to brave the cold Maine water. It was the same every day, the laughing dash to the pool and quick dive into the deep end. Only this morning, the sand-bottomed pool that was adjacent to the regular pool had been drained for cleaning and was not back to its normal depth.

I told Pam I would get the inflatable raft that was floating at the far end of the sand-bottomed pool. I stood at the edge of the pool and took my normal dive, but the missing foot of water threw off my depth perception. In less than twenty seconds, my life was to change. I remember the dive and vaguely remember hitting my head and then just floating there in the water, my head bobbing as I gasped for air. My head had hit the bottom of the pool without any warning or protection. Pam came over to see where I was, but stopped short when she saw me floating there, realizing that something terrible had happened. She ran for the lifeguard who managed to pull me to the surface and up on the small patch of beach. There was a bleeding gash on my head and all I remember was trying to move any part of my body that I could. As my mother knelt beside me she kept telling me everything would be all right. The doctor and the ambulance were called and the lifeguards were instructed not to move me until they arrived with a brace for my neck. The more movement there was meant an increased risk of damaging more nerves.

The lifeguards were tested in all the training they had hoped never to need, and everyone gathered to help or comfort or hold their own children tightly. It was all quite a shock for this quiet, charmed beachside, but I am told that everyone worked together in the way that people do when they are frightened and needed. A neighbor whisked off my younger sister and Pam. My father, who had taken my younger brother off fishing for the day, was notified. He raced to the hospital to be with my mother. My parents don't talk much about that time, but did what parents do—somehow working through their disbelief and shock to answer questions, arrange for my brothers and sisters, and begin to make medical decisions that had been totally unfamiliar to our lives. My mother accompanied me in the ambulance, continuing to assure me everything would be all right. The local hospital was unprepared for an emergency of this measure and we set off on an hour ride to Bangor.

I was met in the emergency room by a neurosurgeon who tested me from head to toe with a safety pin asking if I could feel anything and, if so, was it sharp or dull. The only real feeling I had was on my upper torso, neck, and head. I was transferred to intensive care. I only remember a disembodied fog. I couldn't locate the pain; it filled my whole body and the space around me. I floated in and out of my body. My vision was blurred and my mind couldn't focus on anything for more than a few seconds. As soon as I saw or thought of something, it drifted away, out of my grasp. I couldn't place the sequence of things and nothing around me made any sense. I have vague memories of my parents, but I couldn't touch them or form the words to call to them.

I had broken my neck at the sixth cervical and my parents knew immediately that I was seriously injured. I didn't know any of that, but I was increasingly aware of a distance between myself and what was happening around me. I watched my father sit silently by the side of my bed for hours with uncharacteristic tears forming in his eyes. My mother checked with the nurses, tended the nursery of flowers that filled my room, and spoke firmly with visitors, family, and doctors—her stepfather had been a doctor and she had learned to oversee medical proceedings with a careful eye. Even as it became clear that the pain I felt was blocked at the nerve endings in my neck and I could not move 90 percent of my body, there was never a question that I wanted to live. *How* I would live and what all this would mean to my life was secondary. Faced with the very real possibility of dying, I got my first awareness that my life was not seated in my body; that no matter how restricted and disconnected my body was, I was still full of life and will.

This was the beginning of the fight that has seen me through many physical breakdowns and countless personal challenges. There were many times I could have given up or sunk in self-pity, but I never had the time or inclination. My parents insisted that I would be strong, and my friends and family would hear of nothing less. I guess we all prayed for a miracle, but we were also determined to look this situation straight in the face and beat it—even if beating it meant I would live fully without ever walking again.

My dependence cultivated a patience that had never been a particular strength of mine as an impetuous, active thirteen-year-old. I learned how to accept help with grace and to ask for help without apology. I learned how to help my friends and family with their awkwardness. I welcomed their attention and taught them how to talk openly about the physical realities I was facing. The hospital gave me plenty of time to think before I had to actually confront this new world of arms and legs that had lost their connection to my will. It felt so wonderful to actually get out of my hospital bed that a wheelchair seemed like a Masseratti. I was anxious to get home and figure out what parts of my life were still intact and what parts needed to be redefined.

My parents had added a small bedroom and bath to the first floor of our house—a concrete ramp barged through my mother's tulip garden, giving me access to the house. Many family friends had helped finish and decorate my new quarters and it was full of sunlight, flowers, and cards of congratulations and well wishes. I did feel that I deserved to be congratulated—I still had to begin rehab, but I was home, I was alive, and I was determined. My older sister became my nurse extraordinaire. She lifted, dressed, carried, and anticipated almost everything I was thinking or feeling. We occasionally talked with tears in our eyes, but never allowed self-pity or limitations to shadow our efforts. There was much laughter and even more determination during those first months at home while we tried to let my body heal enough to begin physical therapy. My bedroom became the family gathering place, my medical rituals set the family schedule, friends added daily visits to their school routine, and finally, we were able to set up a TV monitor system so that I could see and respond to my classes from my bed. For over a year, I was to be a television presence in my school classroom. Friends came in to class early to chat through the speaker system and my overview of the classroom often caught antics that the teacher missed. They couldn't actually see me propped up in my home hospital bed, but I could talk through the speaker system and join in the discussion. My teachers regularly came by the house to bring materials and answer my questions.

While I think that some people felt sorry for me or didn't know what to say, most people close to me learned to accept the reality of my situation and began to relate to the person I was, independent of my body. My family and friends became my confidantes, inspiration, and companions. They thought I was the most amazing, courageous, strong, and stubborn person they had ever known and they never let me forget it. This came in handy as I began rehab with the daily struggle to hold a spoon, brush my hair, prop myself up so someone could help me dress, and gradually regain small measures of coordination and strength so I could transfer to the wheelchair or bed and eventually even a car. It was physically exhausting and frustrating to struggle so hard to do such a simple thing as hold a telephone. At times I thought that I could keep up my mental attitude, but the physical challenges were so discouraging. The changes came slowly and sometimes I surprised myself with how mobile and strong I had become. Once I got some coordination back in my hands, my spirits revived and I went back to the cumbersome tasks that someone else could do for me so easily, but which kept my body strong and my sense of independence alive. Gradually I could transfer, brush my teeth, feed myself, answer the phone, whip anyone at Scrabble, navigate my wheelchair—and go to school.

My school had added ramps and switched rooms so that all my classes were on the first floor. Friends had signed up to help me get from class to class and my friends gave me a very stylish backpack to attach to the back of my wheelchair. We had bought an old van with a wheelchair lift and my sister smiled and rolled her eyes with me as my father muttered about all the buttons and getting the "damn thing" to work right. He eventually became pretty much of a pro and insisted on being my chauffeur since he was the only one "who really knew how to work the damn thing." My mother had everything organized and stood at the door with proud tears in her eyes as she watched me venture out to take on the world. I had become confidant and competent in my own room and home and now it was time to negotiate with the larger world. The principal was out at the dropoff to greet me. My father got the wheelchair out of the back and I tried to transfer out of the van as gracefully as possible in order to make a grand entrance. Of course, the lift got stuck, my father started swearing under his breath, my books fell out of my lap, the principal bumped into my wheelchair as she stooped down to get my books, and my friends burst out laughing. I sat there stranded halfway down on the lift unable to do anything. I could either cry or join my friends in their amusement at my foiled entrance, so I laughed and soon we were all laughing—except my father who was still trying to get the "damn thing" to work. He was finally successful and I regathered my books and dignity, and I entered the side entrance where the ramp had been erected. The door had been opened for me and I determinedly gave the wheels a couple of pushes to get me through. I made it to my first classroom and watched a little nervously as Pam and Betsy, my best friends, left to go to their classes. I caused quite a stir in the beginning, but soon the teacher had us settled back to Algebra II. A couple minutes before the bell rang, a friend I didn't know very well arrived and said he was my second-period chauffeur. He chatted comfortably as we wheeled quickly through the empty halls, hoping to get to our destination before the bell rang and the traffic became more considerable. I made it to three more classes before lunch and was pretty exhausted. This was a lot more activity than I had had in a long time. I thought perhaps I would slip into the infirmary and just rest during the lunch break, but Pam and Betsy showed up and begged that we go to lunch first—they were starving. Lunch was the last thing I wanted, but there was no arguing with my loyal managers.

As we pushed through the dining room doors, there was a hush and I saw a giant banner edged by helium balloons and covered with hundreds of signatures. It read "WELCOME BACK, ANNE" and before I could realize what was happening, the whole room burst into applause and cheers. Pam and Betsy just stood there as smug as cats and I was moved and embarrassed to be the cause of such uproar. Pam and Betsy leaned over and gave me a hug and whispered, "You're incredible." I did feel pretty incredible, but more important, I felt like myself—unforeseen and different, but still the same me inside. Life hands out adversities that shape us in ways we never expected. We are all set to go one way and suddenly that door is closed. But if we are careful, it is neither the trials nor the closed doors that define us. It is the muscle that we gain in the struggle; the courage we muster in our fear; the patience and grace we gain in the unfolding; the friends who insist that we are incredible. If we dare to persevere, a wheelchair can be a vehicle for many things.

—Written by Anne Hotchkiss, 2003

DEALING WITH STRESS

For many reasons, students today experience a different kind of stress and anxiety than teenagers have in the past. Affluence, options, and perfectionism have created pressures to perform and constantly improve. We have somehow convinced ourselves that you can have it all—and if you can have it all, there are few acceptable excuses for not having or achieving everything. With all the right lessons, opportunities, equipment, and expectations, why shouldn't you be able to accomplish anything? Perfection seems like a real possibility if you work hard enough. Who you are becomes based on what you do. It is hard to accept failure or imperfection if everything is positioned for your success and your identity lies in the balance. Failure is a natural part of life—never planned or enjoyable, but inevitable and educational. If you are never allowed to fail, the possibility looms larger and scarier as time passes. Failure allows you to fall on your face and realize it is not the end of the world. It teaches you humility, humor, and perseverance. Perfection creates an illusion of invincibility—and the stress of having to maintain that illusion as well as the worry of what will happen if you don't.

SELF-PORTRAIT *by Teresa Wan*

Rosalie

If I work hard enough, worry long enough, and prepare carefully enough, I can be perfect. People say that nobody's perfect, but maybe nobody has really tried hard enough. If a little is good, a lot is great. If a two-page essay is good enough, a six-page paper is excellent. If others study three hours for a big test, I study five. If a research project requires six references, I provide twenty. I take pride in staying up the latest, working the hardest, and not wasting my time with foolishness. If I never let down my guard, I am convinced that someday I can be perfect. When others fall to the wayside, I compete with myself. I keep up my own pressure to be better, smarter, faster, and more successful. Mistakes or inadequacies are unacceptable. The early bird catches the worm; grasshoppers will starve while ants bask in their accomplishments; all work and no play may be dull, but it will also get me into Harvard. An "A–" could bring down my average which could lower my GPA which could keep me from getting into the best college which could keep me from making the contacts I need to get into the best company in my field which could keep me from making a significant contribution to the field of my choice and making lots of money which could spoil any chances I might have for being happy and successful. Viewed in this light, you can see why even the smallest assignment requires vigilance and sweat.

Now you may wonder why I set such demanding standards for myself. My parents are very proud of my academic success, but insist that grades aren't everything—as long as I do my best, they will be happy. My best, of course, means working to the best of my ability, which means no time for slackers. I mean, if my "best" is not THE best, what does that say about me? My teachers are pleased with my work, but sometimes suggest that less work and fewer words might produce better results. Imagine. A teacher asking a student not to work so hard. My fellow students are hardly motivation for my perfectionism—they make fun of my scholarly answers in class and hop around like party-grasshoppers while I toil away at my homework. They are wasting their time and potential, but few seem to care. Actually, there are others who work and worry, but I excel at that too. Worry is my defense against mediocrity. I attend a competitive school, take all honors and AP classes, and offer to do extra-credit work whenever possible. I have always been good in school and have ribbons and trophies to prove it. It came easily to me in elementary school and I was a model student with time to spare for the jungle gym and silly socializing. But now I have put away childish things in my pursuit of perfection.

Why is it such a big deal, you ask?

I think it may come down to cursive writing. It was second grade and I was in the advanced writing group. My printing was beautiful. The teacher displayed my handwriting samples prominently on the bulletin board and if anything needed labeling, I was asked. My "G's" and "Z's" had just the right slant, I never got my "S's" backwards, and my capital "Q" had a lovely understated curl on its tail. The teacher suggested that the other students study my capital and small "K" to understand how they were done properly. I had mastered the paper with three lines to keep your printing straight and could even write without any lines at all. In fact, you might say that my printing was "perfect." I was modest and helpful in spite of my obvious superiority, even writing out words for some of the students who couldn't seem to keep their letters straight. My parents proudly put my beautiful perfect papers on the refrigerator and bragged to their friends about the honors and accolades that came from my perfect handwriting. Life was good and I never worried about my place in the scheme of things.

Then one day during free-writing period, my teacher approached the advanced group and announced that she thought that we were ready to learn cursive writing—a strange, grownup handwriting that connected the letters of each word together. This sounded very exciting and the teacher had prepared a special worksheet for us to begin tracing over the familiar but slightly slanted and disguised letters. I grabbed my pencil and the worksheet, eager to add this new skill to my handwriting expertise. The other students shyly looked to me to lead the way.

I couldn't do it.

No matter how hard I tried to make my perfect handwriting slant and connect, my pencil wobbled and created ugly, uncontrolled lines on my paper. Some letters like "R's" and "S's" didn't even look like real "R's" and "S's." My hand strained to adjust to the new way of writing, but with no luck. To make matters worse, several other students in the group seemed to switch to cursive writing quite naturally, exclaiming that it was "easy." I wish I could say that they treated my temporary incompetence with grace and encouragement, but that was not the case. One student even offered to write my cursive letters for me since I "wasn't very good at it." I burst into tears, quietly crumbling my paper and putting it in my desk. The teacher came over to see what was wrong, but I was too embarrassed and crying too hard to explain. One of the other students said quite loudly, "She's no good at cursive writing." I was mortified and only cried harder. The teacher tried to comfort me, but to no avail. When the others went out to recess, I stayed in and the teacher helped me practice. The letters still looked horrible, but the teacher assured me that if I worked really hard and kept practicing, I would get it.

I worked for hours at home and even stayed in during recess, working on my letters. It took almost two weeks before the letters started to come together and over a month before they came anywhere near my old printing standards. Eventually, my cursive writing was quite good, but I never regained my position as the handwriting expert. Some students with terrible printing actually excelled at cursive writing and had their papers put on the bulletin board. My parents kept my old printed papers on the refrigerator and told me that many successful scholars preferred printing to cursive writing. But I knew they were ashamed of my fall from grace. I was determined to never let this happen to me again.

Clearly, no matter how good you are at something, there might be something new and difficult around the corner to knock you flat. You need to build up some reserve credit to prepare for such an eventuality. The harder you work, the safer you may be, but you always need to be prepared for the curve ball—then work all the harder. Luckily, I can count on other students to goof off and not spend as much time working as I do, so even if I stumble, I have some room to regain my balance without losing the lead. The students that I hate are the ones that do almost as well as I do with half the effort. I can still manage to stay ahead out of sheer persistence, but it is exasperating to watch them work less and still do well. They don't take all this seriously at all. As hard as I work, I worry that it isn't enough or that there will be a pitch I can't hit. Any mistake or setback could ruin everything.

But I try not to obsess on those things. So far, I have managed to handle everything that has come my way—well, after second grade anyway. I know that my efforts will pay off in the long run if I never let my guard down. Perfection is just an assignment away—and there is always room for improvement.

by Anna Petry

LOSS

Greg

I had never faced death before. Sure, as a young American teenager immersed in American pop culture, I was no stranger to it. I could read the news, watch television—see the bodies of people in faraway lands sprawled out in the dust only to be forgotten during the next commercial break. But that's not death—that's like going to a zoo to look at a lion instead of seeing it in the wild. And let me tell you, for anyone who has *watched* someone die, the real thing is far more terrifying.

My brother was seven years older than me, and I always looked up to him. Where I considered myself a nerd, he was cool. He had the taste in music, the artistic talent, the build of my father, the older, wiser friends. He would invite me into his room to listen to the newest Digital Underground tape (CDs weren't the norm back then), and he would rewind the best lines over and over and sort of laugh his deep, even chuckle when I would frown in confusion at the meaning of the lyrics.

We shared a love of video games. He would watch me play Nintendo, and I always encouraged him to play as it was the one thing I could beat him in. When his girlfriends would come over I would shy away to my room, but he always tried to get me to spend time around them, even though older women petrified me.

"Man, if you don't practice talking to them you'll have problems later on." That would prove to be very sagacious advice, although that is another story, I think. Due to our age difference we never argued. There was nothing to argue about. If he needed to use the car, I was too young to drive. The shows we watched came on at different times, and in the house he'd either be working on his music or drawing.

The point is, he was my brother, and I loved him. To think that I was to lose him was as real to me as my own self one day sprouting wings or winning the lotto. Like most young people, I thought that I was immortal, and other young people, by association, were immortal as well.

Cancer changed all that. Looking back, I'd say it all started with a fall. When moving out of his apartment the year he graduated from college, my brother fell on his knee. It bruised up, but the swelling went down. He went to the doctor to have it X-rayed, and they found nothing wrong.

Looking back, I wish I had a time machine to go back and slap that X-ray doctor around a few times.

The bump went down, but then, weeks later, something strange happened—it came back. So he went to the doctor again and they stuck this needle in the leg and I'll never forget how *long* that needle was. And this old Indian doctor, who seemed in my opinion to be way too calm for the news he bore, tells us he believes the bump to be malignant, and just to be on the safe side they'd do an operation and remove it.

The week before the operation was difficult because I didn't really know how to talk to my brother. What comfort could I give him? I was petrified of the needle; I was *terrified* of the thought of the knife. I remember thinking how brave he was, how I would've busted down crying or praying or something.

For anyone who has dealt with cancer, you know what I mean about the "false hopes." The doctors would lay everything out, and would make it seem so simple. One little operation, remove some tissue, and it's *done*. You want to believe it's simple. So I got all my hopes up that this would be over with one operation. That would make the weeks to come all the more difficult.

They performed the operation, and afterward the doctor told us that we'd have to wait awhile to see how my brother's body responded. Again, I found myself furious at the man's demeanor. This wasn't some random person he was working on—it was *my brother*. The least he could do was *feign* concern.

Later, they tell us that the first operation wasn't successful, and that they didn't get it all. I thought I was angry before, but this time, it took everything I had to keep from doing physical harm to the doctor. I didn't understand why they just didn't play it on the safe side and take *more* of the bad stuff out—even a little of the good tissue if it improved my brother's chances. My parents felt the same way.

And it got harder at home because now I saw real traces of fear in my brother. The doctors wanted to put him on chemotherapy, but he refused, saying that he didn't wish to poison his body. He wanted to try alternative treatments, and my parents and he had big arguments over this. (Especially my father, who had lost many brothers to the streets, and wasn't about to lose one of his sons.) I wanted him to take the chemo too, but after what I perceived as the bumbling of western medicine thus far, I thought the alternative treatments couldn't hurt.

My father won out in the end, and he was placed on chemo. Chemo is hell on earth. I swear, from what I have seen, if I were ever given the choice between chemo and death, I'd choose death. If you think this is too harsh a judgment, then you don't know what chemo is. It really is poison. They hook you up to an IV and it drips into you. It is effective at killing cancer cells, but the damned thing's an equal opportunity killer, killing the good cells—your hair follicle cells, your immune cells—right along with the bad. It's not a precision weapon. It's like using a tactical nuke to kill a couple of flies.

I don't like talking about the effects. To see someone who is healthy slowly deteriorate is indescribable—like a Clark Kent Superman transformation in the reverse. Bit by bit they lose their strength, their appetite, and thus their weight. Then, they're sick—not flu sick, or cold sick, but *virus*like sick; vomiting, chills, and random infections that occur from having a weakened immune system.

That's the worst thing about cancer. I would rather have a family member murdered, or hit by a car, than have them die of cancer. Cancer is tricky. How can I put it into words? It's as if someone took *pieces* of a loved one from you one part at a time (which cancer can literally do, but I'll come to that soon enough). With my brother, it went into remission a few times, and each time, I had that false hope that he'd beat it, and all would be as it was, and for a while, it was.

He was accepted into Cornell architecture program, and he went and began study. I longed for the day when I would have him design my house and we would sit and talk about women, and cars, and music, and life, and hard times past. But that was shattered when the cancer came back, and spread. My brother refused to go back on chemo, and I couldn't blame him. Like I said, if you've seen it, you know.

But he didn't give up. He tried other remedies, like East Asian stuff, and herbs, and other things. But none of it worked. Without the chemo, the cancer spread violently, and at this time, the doctors said they would have to amputate his leg from the knee down to make sure it didn't spread. All I could think of was the doctor who first took the X ray when it was a little bump. I wanted to amputate *his* leg. And an arm or two. Maybe his eyes as well, seeing how I thought he was already blind as to not catch this all those months ago.

But my brother, never one to give up, opted for the operation, and again, we were given false hope that this was surely the *worst* that could happen. But the cancer had already spread into the lymph nodes, and it was carried throughout his body by then. Then he went blind, and then he died. And I was left with nothing but anger. Anger that I lost a brother for no reason, and anger that those stupid doctors, with all their technology, could do nothing but cut and poison, and they couldn't even get that right.

So in order to cope, I just didn't think about it. I just buried it deep down. Even here, I didn't go into all the details, because I don't like to think about them. I sometimes slip when people ask me if I have any siblings and say I have an older brother and a younger sister. And then they ask me about them, and what they do, and I inevitably have to tell them that my brother passed, and the really stupid people ask me how, and I have to tell them, and I don't bother hiding my frustration when I do.

There is no happy ending here. I wish there was. I have no advice to give you about facing death except that I hope you have as little experience with it as possible. I, personally, don't think it's an experience that makes you stronger. It only made me angry. It drains you. Leaves you weaker inside. When faced with death, I saw just how powerless I was to stop it, and that in itself changed me.

I began to realize how short life was. I had wanted to be a doctor, but I switched my major to history. I wasn't about to spend all those years studying to be a doctor only to face the possibility of dying at any time. I was going to *live* my life, not waste it studying away. Yet most of the decision stemmed from the fact that I also was thoroughly disgusted with the medical profession. They think they're making a difference, but I think doctors suffer from delusions of grandeur—they can't stop death any more than driving the speed limit will keep you out of an accident.

So I'm pursuing my passions—my writing, women, travel—all the things that I would be thankful for doing if I found myself in front of some unsmiling, cool toned oncologist. I hope that you do the same.

—Written by Gregory Lemmons, 2003

SELF PORTRAIT *by Claire Min*

AGING AND DEATH

Big Mama

The old rusting chair sighs in protest as Big Mama leans back on it. She crosses her legs at the ankle and, being the Southern lady that she is, pulls the thin material of her housedress over her knees. Her skin holds the color of dark dirt just after a rainstorm. Even after eighty years of use, it shows almost no signs of aging. Her face is not wrinkled, but lined; these lines add wisdom to her countenance. She has no hair on top of her head, and the hair around the sides is thick and curly. She keeps it braided close to her skull. Her eyes, distanced from the world by a pair of thick spectacles, are a watery blue. She is a mystical creature, and as she rocks in her chair, humming forgotten hymns and spitting juice from a mouthful of snuff, I watch her.

To the mind unversed in the rigors of rural Southern life, she is just another relic, dying slowly as her body succumbs to a slow betrayal. But to me, she is a collage of experiences—every part of her body is significant. Her legs, which by rights should be flabby and varicose veined, are muscular and toned. Those legs are the result of a lifetime of working in the fields, first as the virtual slave of a rich landowner, then as a sharecropper, and finally on her own land. Her stomach is pouchy and her waist almost nonexistent, but this fact causes her no grief. She knows that from her womb emerged fifteen children, twelve of whom are still alive. Her blue eyes and curly hair are a tribute to her mother, who was a full-blooded Cherokee woman, and to her father, a Black man. This woman's body is a shrine—she could tell you her life's story without uttering a word.

Myriad of feelings build inside me as I watch her rocking in her chair. I am proud that I have her blood in my veins. I am awed by the fact she is almost one hundred years of walking history. But mostly, I am afraid. I am afraid because I know that in less than ten years the chair she sits in will be empty. She has suffered two heart attacks, a stroke, and even temporary blindness. She is a diabetic and has been hospitalized several times. Three children, four sisters, and her husband have preceded her in death. Each time she buries a loved one, another brick is added to the load she carries on her back. Although she is the strongest person I have ever met, I know that not even she can defy the law of nature forever. I've always thought that I would be near her when death came to claim her; now I know that won't be the case. When she dies, I won't be there to hold her hand, pray with her, or kiss her good-bye. I might not even make it to the funeral. I am afraid because I know that when she goes to her eternal peace, I will be left behind.

—Written by Tamara Bynum, 1994

Artwork:

Suki Boynton
Purnell School

Teresa Wan
Mercersburg Academy

Anna Petry
Mercersburg Academy

Claire Min
Newark Academy

Notes

[1] From ANRED, Anorexia Nervosa and Related Eating Disorders, http://anred.com/welcome.html

[2] Excerpted with permission from *My Private Disorder* by Clara A. Zurn, *Groton School Quarterly*, May 1997.

[3] Ibid.

"Many highly intelligent people are poor thinkers. Many people of average intelligence are skilled thinkers. The power of a car is separate from the way the car is driven."

—Edward de Bono

Chapter 3.

Your Brain and Your Mind

EACH BRAIN IS DIFFERENT

Our brain is the tool through which we receive, interpret, and respond to all of our experience. Far from being an exact, undeviating machine, the brain is incredibly complex, containing over 100,000,000,000 neurons with at least 100,000,000,000,000 potential points of connection. No two brains are wired exactly the same, and this wiring affects our perception and processing of experience. Strengths in different parts of the brain may give you talent in art, music, memory, problem solving, carpentry, or conversation. Weaknesses in other parts of the brain may give you trouble with directions, reading, expressing your thoughts, learning a second language, or drawing a picture. Weaknesses in one area are almost always balanced by strengths in another, but understanding how your brain works and how to use your gifts is an essential component of learning and understanding who you are.

Let's imagine that you are blind. Now, this can be a disability for certain activities, like, say, crossing a street. There are several ways that you can respond to this problem.

1. *You can say "I am blind; I cannot cross the street." This keeps you on one side of the street and can get boring.*

2. *You can say "I am blind, therefore, you have to walk me across the street." This solves the immediate problem, but leaves you at the mercy of others about when and how you will cross the street.*

3. *Of course, you can just say "I am not blind" and get run over by a truck or stand frozen at the curbside wondering how everyone else gets across without being run over by a truck.*

4. *An alternate response is to say "I am blind and I can't cross the street in the same way you do. I have to learn how to cross in my own way. In fact, I have noticed that I hear much better than you do and I may be able to use that to get me across safely."*

Now you still probably won't pass a driver's test. Is that fair? Heck, no. Should you get a driver's license anyway? Heck, no. You're blind. There are some things that you must do differently, there are some things that you can do better than other people, and there are some things that you just can't do. And none of that has anything to do with your inherent worth or value or intelligence. It is just the shape of one piece of your life and the road in front of you. You inevitably have strengths and power to compensate for your weaknesses in delightful and inventive ways. The back side of a disability is often a gift—a way of seeing the world and approaching a situation that creates new insights and possibilities.

Cher

The second week of eleventh grade, Cher Bono left class and said "I'm not coming back." School was frustrating and difficult. Cher learned almost everything by *listening* and later admitted that she was eighteen or nineteen before she read her first book. Her teachers insisted that she was smart, but her grades were erratic—an A on one assignment and a D on the next. Her report card always said that she was not living up to her potential, but Cher found it difficult to keep up with her daily work, much less her potential. Reading and writing took exasperating hours to complete and never looked like she had put in any time at all. Her papers were difficult to read and didn't reflect what she knew or the depth of her ideas. Her mother couldn't understand why she could do well in a class one semester and fail the next. Cher couldn't understand that either.

It wasn't until Cher was thirty and her daughter, Chastity, was experiencing similar problems in school that both were diagnosed with dyslexia. Dyslexia is a learning disability with a strong genetic component that hinders a person's ability to process written letters and numbers, making reading, writing, spelling, or math difficult. Fifteen to twenty percent of the population have language-based learning disabilities, including very bright, talented, and successful people like Pablo Picasso, Winston Churchill, Walt Disney, Nelson Rockefeller, Nolan Ryan, Danny Glover,

Magic Johnson, Agatha Christi, Whoopi Goldberg, Robin Williams, Ted Turner, Steven Hawkings, and Tom Cruise.[1] (*And many others—see below.*)

But dyslexia can make school very difficult and undermine a student's confidence, particularly when it is not diagnosed or understood. Cher now understands her problems with reading and has learned how to compensate. She never reads cold for an audition and her brain has compensated by enabling her to memorize scripts after only one or two readings. She still has trouble mixing numbers in dialing the phone or misreading words when she has to read quickly, but as a successful and multitalented singer and actress, she has learned to take these things in her stride. "I couldn't care less today if people know I have dyslexia; I'm handling it. I just wish it hadn't made me so insecure. I'm insecure about everything from my talent as an actress to my skill as a mother to how I look. It doesn't take much to completely shake my confidence to the bone. That insecurity stifles everything. But then I keep coming back—I'm a survivor."

Dyslexia is one of several distinct learning disabilities. It is a language-based disorder of constitutional origin characterized by difficulties in single word decoding, usually reflecting insufficient phonological processing abilities. These difficulties in single word decoding are often unexpected in relation to age and other cognitive and academic abilities; they are not the result of generalized developmental disability or sensory impairment. Dyslexia is manifest by variable difficulty with different forms of language, often including, in addition to problems reading, a conspicuous problem with acquiring proficiency in writing and spelling. (The International Dyslexia Website, http://www.interdys.org/index.jsp)

Do you know the following famous people with learning disabilities?[2]

1. *This brilliant Italian artist, scientist, and scholar left all of his notes in perfect backward mirror writing, a common writing characteristic of some dyslexics.*

2. *Played by Julia Roberts in a movie about her accomplishments, this young woman struggled in school, but later was able to help win a $333-million-dollar settlement for the townspeople of Hinkley, California, the largest U.S. direct-action lawsuit.*

3. *This famous dyslexic writer said he had the lowest SAT scores in the history of Philip Exeter Academy where he attended and his stepfather taught. He learned perseverance through high school wrestling and applied it to his writing. As an adult, he noted, "It was not easy to be slow as a student when you are judged by how quickly you can absorb and retain a wide range of infor-*

mation. I could never be a good student. I don't have any difficulty being a good writer."[3]

4. *This creative inventor who was the forerunner of all modern technology dropped out of school in Michigan where he was failing dismally and his mother slowly taught him a basic academic curriculum at home.*

5. *This popular TV and movie star was held back three times in school and read his first book* (Soul On Ice) *as a senior in high school after his drama coach told him that he had talent, but would never make it in theatre if he didn't learn how to read.*

6. *This president did not learn to read until he was eleven and struggled with everything in school unless it relied on speech, where he excelled.*

7. *Severely dyslexic in school, this man went on to become the founder and chairman of a holding company that engages in securities and related financial services with assets exceeding $800 billion.*

8. *Considered "backward" at his first school, this brilliant scientist did not talk until he was four or read until he was nine. He failed math under traditional instruction and did not begin to show any intellectual promise at all until late in high school.*

"WONDER" *by Balinder Tarta Singh*

WHAT DID I DO???

How Attention Deficit Disorder feels—Quotes from ADD students

How does A.D.D. make problems for you at school?
- *Thoughts just pop into my head and when I get back to the conversation, I am on the wrong subject.*
- *I don't just interrupt other people; I interrupt myself.*
- *I can't filter out sounds, textures, touch, movement—everything distracts me.*
- *I miss meetings and get into trouble.*
- *When someone talks slowly, I cannot stay focused. I want to yell at them to talk faster and get to the point.*
- *When I space out, I try to just smile and look like I am paying attention.*
- *I get so scared of taking a test that I can't remember anything I used to know.*
- *Sometimes I know that I know something, but I can't find it in my brain.*
- *When I get bored or frustrated, I just give up.*
- *I can't stand to double-check my work, so I make stupid mistakes.*
- *I hate it when people tease me or ask if I forgot my medication when I do something dumb. It makes me feel like they don't like me unless I am on my meds.*
- *I can never tell what I am going to remember. I can give you the last detail on some trivial thing that caught my attention and not remember anything about something else that was important.*
- *Procrastination is my worst enemy—it takes so long to get started and by then I have lost my interest.*

What makes your teachers mad?
- *Tapping my pencil.*
- *Not raising my hand, but just blurting things out.*
- *When I can't sit still or stop bothering other people.*
- *Interrupting—I usually blurt things out so I don't forget what I have to say.*
- *When I stare out the window or at the clock—they think I am not paying attention even when I am.*
- *When I forget my homework or book or pencil.*
- *I ask too many questions.*
- *I am afraid to ask questions when I don't understand; then I get lost; then I space out.*
- *I argue about everything or ask questions the teacher thinks are not important. Sometimes I just ask questions even when I already know the answer—I don't know why.*

What makes your friends mad?
- *When I change my mind and switch plans for no reason.*
- *I always exaggerate things to make them more interesting.*
- *I am indecisive—I keep going back and forth when I am making a decision. Drives my friends crazy . . . me too.*
- *My moods can change dramatically without warning or reason.*
- *I tend to tell everyone everything about myself—but not many people really know me.*
- *When I interrupt them when they are talking or studying or doing something.*
- *Sometimes I interfere in my friends business and get bossy.*
- *When I start things, but then lose interest.*
- *I am always losing things.*
- *I am pretty dependably late all the time.*

What do you worry about?
- *EVERYTHING.*
- *School, parents, friends.*
- *Failing or screwing up.*
- *What people think of me.*
- *I put a lot of pressure on myself. I want to be perfect and do well, but I keep screwing up.*

What helps?
- *Writing things down on a list—if I don't lose the list. . . .*
- *Cleaning or organizing something.*
- *Sometimes I work better when I am stressed out and under pressure.*
- *Not having a roommate—it is so hard to focus when someone else is in the room.*
- *Working or reviewing with someone else—actually saying my work out loud helps me focus and re-member.*
- *Smaller classes really help. I don't get as distracted and I have a chance to talk without waiting or ask questions without feeling dumb.*
- *Knowing that my teacher really likes me and understands. Teachers who are a little ADD themselves seem to understand.*

What would you like teachers to understand about A.D.D.?
- *I really don't mean to fidget.*
- *I really am trying.*
- *I can tell when a teacher gives up on me.*
- *Sometimes I just need a little extra time and I can do it.*
- *Please just give me some slack—I really do want to learn and do well.*
- *I really am listening when I am staring or doing something else at the same time—sometimes.*

- *I make a lot of excuses or get mad because I am embarrassed.*
- *I don't think most teachers understand how hard I work just to do as well as I do. I would love some appreciation for my effort and work even when it doesn't turn out as well as I would like.*
- *I can always tell when a teacher believes in me, and that makes it easier to keep trying.*
- *Please understand when I forget and cut me some slack—help me figure out how to remember better.*
- *Some days my brain just clicks and I can do anything. Other days it is like wading through quicksand. Just because I could do it yesterday doesn't mean I can do it today. I know that sounds crazy, but I am not making it up.*
- *It is so frustrating when a teacher thinks that I am just making excuses or that everyone has the same problems paying attention and I should just try harder.*
- *Some teachers don't believe A.D.D. is real—they think I am just lazy or dumb.*
- *Some teachers think I just don't care—that's not true, even when I give up.*
- *I like learning; I just hate repetition and I hate failing.*

People with ADD are often noted for their inconsistencies. One day they can "do it" and the next they can't. They can have difficulty remembering simple things yet have "steel trap" memories for complex issues. To avoid disappointment, frustration, and discouragement, don't expect your highest level of competence to be the standard. It's an unrealistic expectation of a person with ADD. What's normal is that they will be inconsistent.

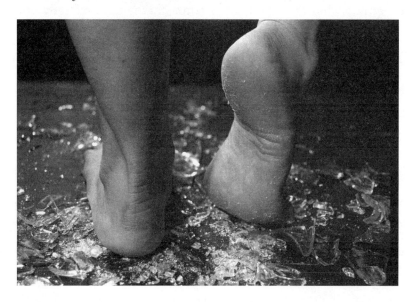

UNTITLED *by Landi Guidetti*

CHOOSING NOT TO USE

Brandon

"Just say no." Technically, I suppose that would work, but it's a little more complicated than that in my school—at least for me it is. In the first place, people don't usually "ask" you to do drugs. It's there, it's part of the party, and it may even be assumed that if you're there, you want in. It's not really pressure; but if you're not a user it's like wearing clothes in a nudist colony or listening to Beethoven at a rock concert. You stand out. Now that is not an inherently bad thing, but, in most high schools, it is not the way you want to stand out either. Being popular makes high school more fun—or at least it seems that way. And the popular kids at my school party. I don't know if they party because they are popular or if they are popular because they party—either way, if you "just say no," you stand out.

I don't use drugs or drink. It is a personal decision that I have made for reasons I won't go into. I don't try to make a big deal out of it; I just don't use. I am a good athlete and make good grades and I have a lot of friends, but my social life is pretty much a bust. Most people at my school say they respect me for my decision—but they usually don't invite me to their parties. They assume that if I don't want to get high or trashed that I wouldn't want to be included in the party. I admit that it can get pretty boring watching a bunch of people get wasted, but it is also pretty boring spending my weekends in the library or with people that the only thing we have in common is that we don't use. I don't pick my friends by their party habits, but on the weekend, it often filters down to that. I know some people who use just in order to have a social life, but that is lame.

People who are partying often aren't comfortable having nonpartiers around—we are "no fun." If you think about it, some of the "fun" that goes on at parties is pretty stupid—even to the participants after they sober up. Drinking games are really only fun because you get stupid. I guess nonpartiers are like stupid-ometers. It is no fun to have someone around who actually witnesses how stupid everyone is being. Drunk jokes are not usually that funny. Running naked through your parents' cocktail party is only momentarily amusing. Watching a couple have everything but intercourse on the couch next to you is awkward. And watching people throw up in the sink is no fun at all.

And when stupid gets dangerous, I start to feel like a parent or a cop. *You can't drive home; you're drunk. No, I don't think it is such a good idea to go find those guys and start a fight. No, stealing more beer from the 7-11 is illegal and stupid—they have cameras all over the store.* I have probably saved a few of my friends' butts over the years, but it is never a very popular position at the time. There have been times when I have watched friends make some pretty scary decisions and felt helpless to stop them.

There are also some pretty negative stereotypes of nonusers. We are naive, geeks, party-poopers, babies, chicken, nerdy, goody-goodys, losers, or just plain uptight. Some people think we act holier-than-thou just because we aren't using, but I think that is just their conscience giving them a hard time. I guess some nonusers might get moralistic, but I'm not judging anyone else—I am just trying to make my own choices without being treated like a social pariah.

If you do get invited to the party, nonusers often become the baby-sitters. I don't mind being the designated driver, but I don't like having my car puked in—especially when the puker is too messed up to help clean up or even remember to apologize later. I try not to worry about furniture getting wrecked or a drunk girl stumbling into the bedroom with some guy she just met, but when you are sober, it is hard not to notice. If somebody passes out or starts tripping, what if they are not OK? I've had friends beg me to sneak them into their house or lie to their parents that they are with me because I can make the phone call. I know that my friends know they can depend on me to stop them from getting too crazy, but that is not exactly what I am looking for on a Saturday night out.

So why do I want to go to these parties if they are so stupid? Good question, I guess, but there is a lot more to a party than getting wasted. I like to relax and have a good time. I like being with my friends. I like music and beaches and girls. I don't like feeling left out and I don't like feeling like the odd man out. I just don't want to use drugs. If you think I am just making all this up, check out the next party you go to. How many nonusers got invited? How much of the "fun" revolves around using? Most nonusers would never say the things I have just said—I don't say them to my friends either. But they are true. Try not using at a party yourself and see if my story doesn't make more sense. Nobody at my school would ever make fun of me for not using or force me to have a drink, but peer pressure comes in different ways. To me, it is anything that makes it hard to respect your own choices and not have them dictate your whole social life.

NICOTINE—A "MINOR" ADDICTION

More U.S. youths have been taking up the smoking habit in the 1990s, according to statistics released by the Centers for Disease Control and Prevention.

More than 6,000 youths under the age of eighteen try a cigarette each day, and half of those become daily smokers, according to a CDC report assessing adolescent smoking trends from 1988 to 1996. About 1.3 million people under the age of eighteen became daily smokers in 1996 compared with 708,000 in 1988, the report said.

In the 1960s and 1970s most smokers took up the habit on a daily basis between the ages of eighteen and twenty-five; by the late 1980s, as many people under the age of eighteen began daily smoking as did the older age group. The CDC also found "young people vastly underestimate the addictiveness of nicotine." Among those who thought they wouldn't still be smoking in five years, 75 percent of them continued to smoke five to six years later.

At least 4.5 million adolescents between the ages of twelve and seventeen smoke cigarettes, the CDC said.[4]

Leslie

I started smoking when I was thirteen. It was just a social thing. Several of my friends were trying it and I wanted to see what it was like. I don't think I ever intended to smoke much and I certainly didn't ever imagine being addicted to cigarettes. How pathetic would that be? To tell you the truth, I didn't even like smoking at first. I didn't inhale until one of my friends noticed and asked why I wasn't inhaling. I made up some lame excuse about a cold or something, but then figured I better learn how to smoke right if I was going to smoke.

The first time I inhaled, it made me sick. I coughed violently and got dizzy and felt nauseous. Luckily I had decided to try inhaling on my own so I didn't make a complete fool of myself in front of others. I had to sit down and wait for the bad feelings to pass. Yuck. When I started feeling better, I took another drag. Pretty smart, huh? I figure a rock wouldn't need to try something twice that made it feel sick. But I was determined. When I look back on it, it was the first time I had purposely put a mind-altering drug into my body. I didn't think of it that way. I wasn't really thinking about the chemical effects of tobacco on my body at all. At that point, I wasn't smoking to calm down or feel differently or get a buzz. I am embarrassed to admit it, but I was really just going for the look—you know, the careless, worldly,   blowing-smoke-over-your-shoulder-while-you-flirt-with-the-older-guy look? I didn't really think about smoking as a drug, more like an accessory—a prop for parties, something to make me look a little older, a little more reckless, an independent woman making my own choices. When I think about the millions of advertising dollars that had been spent to make me feel exactly that way, I feel like an idiot, but at the time, I just felt liberated and pleased with myself. My parents didn't know and would be furious. That added a touch of excitement and secrecy to the mix and I liked that. I was usually such a "good girl" and it felt good to challenge my parents and my acquiescence in such a discrete, but undisputable way. Just walking around with a pack of cigarettes hidden deep in my purse seemed like my own little secret life that my parents didn't know anything about. When a friend asked for a smoke or I was with a group lighting up, I could nonchalantly rummage around in my purse and pull out my own personal pack—the obvious sign of an experienced, sophisticated smoker. If I sound ridiculous, wait; it gets worse.

Once I got used to the buzz, I could inhale smoothly and blend smoking around my conversations and actions like I had been smoking all my life. I even got pretty good at blowing smoke rings and French inhaling. No longer a newcomer, I could master the art of smoking—tapping down the cigarette for reasons known only to me and other experienced smokers; looking up sexily over the tip of a cigarette as I lit it; carelessly blowing a perfect smoke ring while I peered deeply into a guy's eyes; throwing out a careless *"Boy, do I need a cigarette"* as a punctuation mark for anger, relief, happiness, frustration, a big test, or a boring spot at a party. For a long time, it was all social and image. It wasn't even really for other people, though they were definitely a part of my audience, but it was about me trying on different personas and looks. I could go days or weeks without a single cigarette and not notice any cravings or need to smoke. Of course, I never did that—why would I? I was just smoking because I wanted to, not because I needed to. And I usually wanted to many times a day.

I can't really pinpoint when *"Boy, do I need a cigarette"* became a reality. It was subtle at first. When I got mad or hurt, I didn't really *need* a smoke, but it sure made me feel better. I then found myself looking forward to a smoke after dinner long before the meal was over. Pretty soon, I woke up looking forward to my first smoke of the day. Before, I had never smoked in the morning, often not much until the evening in social situations. After I had been socially smoking for less than six months, I started smoking earlier in the day and more and more often when I was just by myself. If I went more than one or two hours, I found myself tuning out of what I was doing and thinking about a cigarette and when and where I could get one. Running out of cigarettes was no longer funny—if I couldn't get another pack, I would find myself rummaging through an ashtray or trashcan. Strangely enough, none of these things seemed odd or compulsive. All my smoking friends acted the same way and we would laugh about it and compare notes. I think there was almost a sense of honor that meant you were a *real* smoker.

It wasn't until after a year or so that smoking began to seriously inconvenience me and make demands on my life. There were parts of my life that were necessarily "smoke free." My parents still didn't know I smoked, so I couldn't smoke in the house and had to be careful about my breath and hiding my smokes. I started to really like—need?—a smoke before I went to bed—it helped me relax and fall to sleep more easily—but that was difficult since I live with my parents. I would sometimes sneak out to the garage or climb out onto the little roof outside my bedroom, if I was really desperate.

And yes, I have to admit it, I was occasionally getting desperate. Long family trips, holiday meals at my grandparents, school, sports trips—all started to last longer than my no-tobacco comfort zone. I started sneaking around at school—yes, I even had a smoke in the bathroom once during a really hard test—and was occasionally late to class or meetings because I snuck off school grounds to have a cigarette. I have a couple of friends who were really antismoking and I found myself avoiding them for activities that would outlast my nicotine cravings. I would cut off really good conversations with people I liked a lot because it was time for a cigarette. And more and more of the good friends that I really liked had either quit or never started and I downplayed my smoking. I subconsciously found myself choosing activities based on how well they fit with my smoking schedule. I didn't even notice these things at first—I always had other excuses. The class trip would be boring. I have outgrown soccer. Family gatherings are for kids; I hate being cooped up with my grandparents. My parents don't have any right to tell me if I can or cannot smoke. It's my body. Is there any law against going out for a walk at night? I can finish this conversation another time. Why are those nonsmoking friends so militant? I sure never want to be uptight like them—I don't tell *them* whether or not they should smoke.

Now if you went back and substituted alcohol for all the places where I said cigarettes or smoking in the last two paragraphs, we would both say, "You're an alcoholic." Can't go for more than two hours, medicating feelings, looking forward to the next hit, panic if I can't get it, starting earlier and earlier in the morning, avoiding nonusing friends and activities, focusing my time around my use, sneaking around, breaking rules and trust to get it. But I still didn't think of it as an addiction—that was just the way everyone smoked. Well, almost everyone. I know a few people who can have a cigarette now and then at a party and never think twice about wanting another one, and I am envious. Usually nicotine doesn't discriminate—it is an equal opportunity addiction. (If you were just thinking that you would probably be one of the occasional smokers, I am all over that. I was *positive* I would be.) The simple truth is, if you smoke long enough, you will need to smoke. It is a physical fact of addiction. I am not sure when I crossed the line from trying to wanting to needing, but it became increasingly clear that I was no longer calling the shots. As ridiculous as it may seem, I would go to great lengths, take great risks, cut off great conversations, lie, sneak, and hide just to have a smoke.

And if I needed any further proof that nicotine was addictive, I got it in spades when I tried to quit. I was in denial for a long time—I could quit anytime I wanted to; I just didn't want to. I had all the basic denial systems working: I don't smoke that much, I smoke only filters or low-tar cigarettes, I am quitting right after exams, I will switch to a "safer" brand, or if you were under as much pressure as I am, you would smoke too. These dodges all worked for a while, but my cough was getting worse, my parents were getting suspicious, it was harder to find a place to smoke freely, cigarettes had gone up to $3.50 a pack, and my friends were on my case about it. Three of them had quit and were born-again nonsmokers. My boyfriend was a nonsmoker and said that kissing me sometimes tasted like licking an ashtray—how sexy. Then my favorite uncle died of emphysema and it wasn't pretty. He knew I was smoking and begged me to quit—said dying and going through what he was going through wasn't worth one drag of a cigarette.

Okay, I thought, no big deal. I don't need to smoke. I will just quit. After this pack. Well, perhaps one more pack, to really get my mind-set right. Okay, okay. This pack and that's it. Cold turkey, none of this tapering off silliness. I counted the smokes left in the pack and drilled myself whenever I wanted one—*Do I really want this cigarette? There will only be ten left. . . . Ten is plenty.* I got a little more selective when I got down to the last four, but it wasn't much more than two days and they were all gone. Final. No more smoking. I felt fine and proud of myself for the first couple hours and then I started coming up with very good reasons why quitting wasn't such a good idea. *I really don't smoke that much. Cold turkey is not a good way to quit. Whose business is it anyway if I smoke? I'll quit long before it really hurts my body. Smoking helps me relax; I study better when I smoke; what's so bad about smoking? There are lots worse things I could do.*

And I was feeling *very* irritable. It was as if I was looking for a fight or excuse to go have a cigarette. At one point, I even caught myself thinking "Who wants to live anyway if you can't smoke?" See, I told you it would get more pathetic. I began to bargain with myself—well, actually, lie and haggle with myself. *If I just have one cigarette now, I won't have any more. How about if I don't have any cigarettes all day, I can have one at night after dinner? What if I just smoke half of each cigarette this week, a quarter next week, and gradually just a puff or two, then nothing.* Yeh, like that would work. . . .

Then I stopped actually buying cigarettes. All my smoking friends would see me coming and hide their packs. *Hey, I have really quit, but could I just bum one off you?* I even found a liquor store in town that sold singles—how desperate is that?

I must have quit eight times in the next two years. I tried the patch. I hid my cigarettes where it was hard to get them. I flushed them down the toilet. I rewarded myself for not using. I took deep breaths and made myself wait twenty minutes before lighting up. I prayed for help. I tried just to keep busy and stay away from places where people were smoking. Just watching someone light up in a movie or on the street would send me into nicotine fits. Eventually I could talk myself out of quitting by simply asking myself, *Why go through all this suffering when you know you will start again?* And every time I started smoking again, I was right back where I left off—moderation was no longer a possibility. If I slipped and had one, I was back to a pack a day. I began to understand why an alcoholic could not just drink in moderation. It was like all your resistance and resolve was washed away once the floodgates were opened.

Clearly I wasn't getting the upper hand. Everything seemed to remind me of having a smoke—a cup of coffee, a certain location, after a certain activity, after a certain class, when I got mad, when I was scared, when I wanted to celebrate, when I wanted to comfort myself. Any time was a great time for a smoke. Not my cough or my dead uncle could compete with my clever smokescreens. I even started using my addiction as an excuse to keep smoking—*Yeh, I know, it's terrible, but I'm addicted.* . . .

I have heard people say that nicotine is just as addictive as heroin and while I haven't tried heroin, I wouldn't be at all surprised. Withdrawal makes you want a cigarette so badly that all the good reasons for quitting seem distorted and silly. And it is so easy. This cute little pack of smokes fits anywhere—just one hit, how bad could that be? Lots of people smoke and they don't die. If you ever run out of excuses, give me a call and I can probably give you a couple that you haven't thought of.

I have been off cigarettes for two years now. I feel terrific and I am proud that I finally did it, but I don't take my smokelessness for granted for a minute. I don't crave them like I used to, but I know for sure that if I just had one, I would be back on the treadmill. I am a *recovering* nicotine addict and always will be. There are times when I miss smoking or am tempted by a situation or place or person. But for the moment I know quitting was just too damn hard to get started again. I always thought I was different; I could control smoking. Wrong. Nicotine is not about willpower or intelligence or bravado. It is just a drug—a very addictive drug.

by Mo Higby

ADDICTION

David

Ross General Hospital 11-22-83

REVIEW OF SYSTEMS: *Patient describes chills and sweats five to six times a day beginning 24 hours after the admission and says he "feels bad all over." . . . Describes ringing in the ears and a dull headache in the frontal and occipital areas. He has stomach ache with nausea but no vomiting. . . . There is a past history of seizure on one occasion when he was in an apartment with friends. This was apparently a witnessed grand mal tonic colonic seizure and may have been related to drug intake, but is not known. . . . The nasal septum is perforated with some purulent material . . . multiple pigmentation in the lower legs from dependent edema and hemorrhage of small capillary vessels. . . . On the upper extremities, his skin is characterized by healing staphylococcus lesions which are pink, macular and slightly depigmented. There are these lesions as well as multiple burns on the fingertips of his right hand, more than left hand, where he has apparently suffered some flash fires handling the freebase unit need to produce his cocaine for inhalation. . . . There are several open draining wounds on the neck with stph purulent exudates not apparent since he has been on Dicloxacillin.*

BEHAVIOR DURING TEST PROCEDURE: *This large framed, moderately obese 42 year old male patient was at initial contact only minimally cooperative and obviously very tense and apprehensive. . . . The presence of a chronic and recurrent agitated depression that has kept on varying in intensity in a characterologically poorly integrated, emotionally tempestuous, intrinsically restless, and impulsive man. The indications are that this patient has used drugs over the years to contain his agitations and his depressions. Restlessness is very pervasive and there are strong suggestions that even as a youngster he has not coped well with external strictures imposed upon him or with rules and regulations in general. . . .*

These test results describe him as a basically intelligent, sensitive, affection- and attention-seeking person who has, however, always been afraid of establishing closer relationships with others or of making a commitment that would be a prerequisite for such relationships. In recent years, he has felt increasingly lonely, alienated, and embittered...

In spite of the absence of positive organic findings, it will be imperative to persuade him to terminate resolutely all further drug abuse since there are strong suggestions that—contrary to his intentions—such is likely only to exacerbate his agitations and his restlessness. . . . Suicidal attempts cannot be ruled out should he be forced to spend a significant time in jail.

David Crosby went to jail twice in the next two years, eventually spending a total of more than a year in prison. He was paroled from the Texas Department of Corrections Prison in Huntsville, Texas, in August of 1986. During the intervening period he had not only done jail time, but had managed to tour both as a solo artist with his own band and as a member of Crosby, Stills, and Nash for two national tours. When David surrendered to the FBI in Florida in December of 1985, he was heavier, dirtier, sicker, and more addicted than when he was examined at Ross General Hospital in 1983. He and his girlfriend, Jan Dance, were consuming approximately seven grams (a quarter of an ounce) of cocaine a day, as well as half a gram of heroin, mostly by smoking the vapors in a glass pipe. They had no money, his home was being seized for payment of back taxes, and he had sold all his possessions or pledged them to dealers for more drugs. The money to get David and Jan from Marin County in Northern California to Florida came from the sale of his last remaining possession of any substance, a grand piano.

At the time of his surrender, he had shaved his mustache and bought some cheap wigs in a pitiful attempt to disguise his distinctive appearance. Jan weighed less than ninety pounds, hadn't washed her hair in more than a month, and was increasingly catatonic and withdrawn. Both of them smelled bad, looked worse, and were without true friends. Their families had written them off. They were sleeping on the floors of only slightly "safe" houses owned by nervous dealers in the Miami area.[5]

Two years later, clear-eyed and engaging, David spoke to students at Beverly Hills High School about his drug experience.

I told them I had all the advantages, like most of them. I came from a nice family. I had a happy childhood, a reasonable situation with good schools, neither of my parents was an alcoholic, and they didn't beat me with baseball bats. Still, I wound up in a cell in a Texas prison. We're not talking the drunk tank here. We're talking serious business: barbed wire, machine-gun towers, and a three-hundred-pound guy with no neck and a cowboy hat saying "Hey, rock star, git over here, boy." The only thing that saved my life was being physically, forcibly separated from my stash. It had to be taken out of my control. The way they do that is to sentence you to do time, then detoxify you. This is how they detox you in prison: they lock you in a steel box that's about five feet by nine feet, they feed you through a hole in the door, and they don't let you out at all. You get a little shower and a shitter and that's it. You don't leave. If you get a phone call, the guard hands you a tele-

*phone receiver through the slot. You beg people in the hall to bring
you books and the food is part of the punishment. After I told them all
that, a student asked me "Were you ever onstage stoned?" The answer to that is that never once, until I got out of prison, did I ever
record, perform, or do anything any way except stoned. I did it all
stoned.*[6]

David Crosby was born in Hollywood, California, on August 14, 1941. His
father, a New York boy and graduate of St. Paul's School in New Hamp-
shire, was a photographer for motion pictures. As a child, David was a
loner and a rebel, second fiddle to his older brother, Ethan. He attended
the UCLA Lab School in Los Angeles and then moved to Santa Barbara.
Ethan went off to Verde Valley boarding school in Arizona and David attended Crane School, a small private elementary school outside of Santa
Barbara. In seventh grade, he played the First Lord of the Victorian
British Navy in Gilbert and Sullivan's *H.M.S. Pinafore* and awed the entire audience with his clear tenor voice and stage presence. He attended
Cate School, a nearby boarding school, for two years. He loved the
school and the education it gave him, but remained a short, slightly
overweight, detached and abrasive outsider—bright, but unmotivated,
talented, but undisciplined. David wasn't involved in much except science fiction, rifle practice, mischief, and his music—music was his saving grace and talent. Tired of the bell-run routine, one night David and
his roommate devised a scheme to shut down the automatic bell system
and cut down the school bell that hung over the dining hall. Their plans
were successful, but their glory was short-lived. They were summoned
to the headmaster's office the following day and spent the next week re-
porting in at every bell and providing a vocal singing of "Hell's Bell's"
to wake up the dorms in the morning. At the end of the year, David was
advised that he should not return for his junior year. He enrolled in the
local public school where he cut classes and flunked classes, finally set-
tling for a high school equivalency diploma.

At the same time, David's parents got a divorce and his father remarried,
becoming even more removed from David's life. David was angry and re-
bellious. He started hanging out and drinking rum and Cokes at a local
jazz club where his brother, Ethan, was playing. He ran with a fast, mon-
eyed crowd in Santa Barbara and they started experimenting with cough
syrup and anything else that would give them a high. It was a wild and
crazy time of getting high, petty theft, driving fast, getting laid . . . and
music.

Music was the passion that kept David coming back through this haze. He
learned to play the guitar and started moving around to play coffee

houses and jazz joints. It was in this world that he first tried marijuana—and liked it a lot. He moved from LA to Arizona to Colorado to Greenwich Village. It was the early '60s and drugs started showing up in the clubs and on the streets—marijuana, psychedelics, and methamphetamines. David's lust for girls and music and drugs was insatiable. He followed the party to Miami and Chicago and then back to Los Angeles. Folk and pop music were starting to blend and then the Beatles arrived from England, setting a whole new direction for American music.

David made his first record with the band that would become the Byrds. Giving the Bob Dylan classic "Mr. Tambourine Man" a West coast, British sound, the Byrds cut their first record and became popular in the clubs. That was the beginning of road trips, fan clubs, good money—and more drugs. This time, heroin. Pot, acid, mushrooms, speed, and occasionally cocaine were in fashion, but heroin was assumed to be off limits. But

> *Heroin was always a constant presence and the stereotypical junkie musician nodding on the stand was not the average rock 'n' roll smackhead. . . . There was always a subculture of heroin users in the business and a network of suppliers to feed them. Remember that the average pop music star or recording artist doesn't face the disabling side effects that are a constant problem to the street junkie. . . .*
>
> *Later, in the seventies, when pop stars in their twenties checked out before their thirties, the fatal potential of heroin, opiates, barbiturates, and alcohol would become apparent. In 1968, heroes could die young in a plane crash or a wrecked car, like Buddy Holly or James Dean. Nobody thought we'd begin finding rock 'n' roll's best and brightest all cold, stiff, and blue, chocked by their vomit on the floors of cheap hotels.*[7]

David kept his hard drug use private, extolling the merits of pot in public and shooting up heroin and coke with friends like Cass Elliot in private. He broke up with the Byrds and met Stephen Stills and Neil Young. He joined the Monterey music scene where Blue Cheer, White Lightning, and Purple Haze psychedelics were the drugs of choice. When Crosby, Stills, Nash, and Young started up, the party was in high gear, the sound was smooth, and David Crosby was on a high. Singing the opening anthem at Woodstock put the group on the national music charts.

Soon after, Christine Hinton, David's live-in partner, was tragically killed in a car accident. The whole music group living outside of San Francisco was in shock and David was inconsolable. A friend brought him some heroin, which stopped the pain, but set up a prolonged and protracted spi-

ral of suffering and medicating his pain. Later that year Janis Joplin over-
dosed in Los Angeles and Jim Morrison died on tour in Europe. David
was saddened, but didn't see any relation to his own life or drug use.

Writing music, performing, and sailing, David became more rich and successful—and less dependable. He bailed out of a contract to write the
soundtrack for a movie. He was arrested for drugs in Hawaii and Mexico.
He had a harem of attentive women and fathered a baby by his good friend,
Debbie Donovan, and then took up with one of his eighteen-year-old
groupies. His nasal septum was collapsing after years of snorting cocaine.

In 1976, David met Jan Dance and a month later, he was introduced to
smoking freebase cocaine. The constant use of cocaine had constricted the
blood vessels in his noise, shrinking the capillaries, and killing the blood
supply to the cartilage, creating a perforated septum. Continued use could
begin to eat into the sinuses and eventually the brain. Freebasing provided
a new, nonnasal method of ingesting cocaine.

> *In Florida, I had the opportunity to meet Jan Dance, which turned out*
> *to be one of the smartest things I ever did. She was an incredibly viva-*
> *cious, funny, bright, happy, smiley human being and I fell in love with*
> *her. I fall in love with her probably two, three times a day nowadays. I*
> *also turned her on to base and eventually heroin, which was not a real*
> *nice thing for me to do. She had a strong constitution and lasted a long*
> *time before it got to her, but eventually it did affect her very adversely.*
> *I'm probably guilty of using drugs as a mechanism for controlling. The*
> *only mitigating factor was that we loved each other. We went down the*
> *tubes together, but we did it with our hearts intertwined.[8]*

By 1979, David was seriously addicted and his music contacts were falling
apart, even his close friendship with Graham Nash. He turned more and
more to drugs to keep from the chaos that was closing in around him.

> *There is a human mechanism that says "I want it, I want it, I want it,*
> *I got it!" It's the one that gets built up in humans when we want cig-*
> *arettes or sugar. I am just now being able to beat the one on sugar. I*
> *beat the one on cigarettes many years ago. Beating the one on heroin*
> *was difficult because it involved physical illness. You get very sick*
> *when you kick heroin and your endorphins are nonexistent so you feel*
> *terminally fucking awful, but the psychological dependency on base is*
> *the most obsessive of all. . . .*

> *The nature of base smoking is that once you get started, you do it a lot.*
> *After your first taste, the next day you do it a lot. It's a peculiar drug*

that way. You become obsessive with it immediately. It doesn't take a week and it gets worse. You get obsessive and want to do it until you fall out. A lot of times it happens to people the very first time—base gets you loaded if it's made properly. It's a quick rush then it's gone. So you want to do some more right away and then you want to do some more and then you want to do some more and some more and some more. . . .

I used to smoke some base that wasn't good, feel sick, and want some more. That's totally fucking crazy. The point that is best learned from the whole experience is the craziness, the completely illogical short-circuiting of the normal human mental process that takes place in obsessive addiction. You no longer have control of your mind or your spirit or your choices. You just don't. When you become severely addicted you do stuff that doesn't show any sense at all. There are definitions for addictive behavior: one of them is doing the same thing repeatedly and expecting different results. Another is doing something that you know is self-damaging and doing it anyway. Another is deliberately destroying your social circumstance, knowing that you're blowing your job, you're wiping out your savings, you're smoking yourself out of house and home, you're selling the car, and you're doing it anyway—just so you can do more dope. That's what being an addict is really about.[9]

In 1981, David had his first grand mal seizure while on tour in Europe. It spooked his friends and when he and Jan got back home from the tour, twenty of his best friends, a physician, and a psychiatric social worker were waiting for him. David tried everything to avoid the love and demands that were coming at him as his friends insisted that he get help. After four hours, including a couple trips to the bathroom to get high, he finally agreed to check into a rehab center as long as Jan could come along. Graham Nash agreed to foot the bill and Jackson Browne chartered a plane to take David and Jan to Scripps Hospital outside of La Jolla, California. After forty-eight hours of begging and baby-sitting, Jackson and Carl Gottlieb checked them in to the hospital and took the plane back to Burbank and went to bed. At nine o'clock the next morning, Jackson received a call that David and Jan had checked themselves out of the hospital and taken off. At that point, David's closest friends gave up. They had done everything they could. David and Jan were not ready to confront their drug use and, as hard as they tried, nobody could do anything about it.

David and Jan clung to each other throughout this whole nightmare, and many of their friends and business managers thought they were dragging each other down and tried to separate them. Conventional drug treatment discouraged trying to get clean and sober with a partner who was also addicted and, indeed, David and Jan used each other to excuse their drug use and reinforce their denial in an increasingly critical world. Jan became more withdrawn and dependent on David. She lost weight and her optimistic, outgoing personality. She was always there for David, but he became her supplier as much as her lover. David was protective of her, but also allowed her to take the fall for him in Kansas when his luggage was discovered to contain drugs and his .45 caliber automatic.

On March 28, 1982, David had a seizure driving southbound on Route 405 and crashed into the center median. Police found a glass bottle with two pipes extending from it, a film canister of baking soda, a bag of drug paraphernalia, Quaaludes, cocaine, and a .45 caliber automatic. He was charged with driving under the influence and carrying a concealed weapon. Out on bail, David went to a gig at Cardi's Rock Club in Dallas, Texas, two weeks later and was arrested for drugs and weapon possession there. June 3, 1983, he was found guilty on both charges and in August he was sentenced to five years on the drug charge and three years on the weapons charge, to run concurrently. His lawyers immediately filed an appeal and David was let out on bond awaiting a retrial. During this time, he was in and out of treatment centers and returned to touring with Stills and Nash. In the fall, he got arrested in Marin County for reckless driving on his Harley, possession of drugs and paraphernalia, a concealed weapon, and driving with a revoked license. Texas was not pleased. David promised to enter a locked treatment center instead of jail, but in December, his guilty verdict was overturned in appeal and David thought he was free and clear—and no longer needing to appease the court with promises of treatment. The appeals and retrials went back and forth and finally the judge insisted that David await the final verdict either in locked treatment or in jail. David checked into the Fair Oaks Hospital in New Jersey. He hated it, but spent seven weeks without using drugs. Then he slipped out and went into New York City to get high. In less than twenty-four hours, the police picked him up. He was extradited to Texas where he spent almost four months in the Lew Sterrett County Jail. When his lawyers finally got him out on bail, he went straight to LA and started freebasing again. *Spin* magazine came out with an article titled "The Death of David Crosby."

A disheveled, unshaven figure staggers into the living room. . . . His stomach is bloated, his thinning, frizzy hair leaps wildly into the air. A few of his front teeth are missing, his pants are tattered, and his red plaid shirt has a gaping hole. The most frightening thing is his pale swollen face, riddled with thick white scales, deep and encrusted blotches that aren't healing. Looking at him is painful. A fourteen-

year addiction to heroin and cocaine has caused David to resemble a Bowery bum. The spiritual leader of the Woodstock Nation is now a vision of decay.[10]

It wasn't long before David got busted again—this time for possession and a hit-and-run accident with a fence. Texas scheduled a new hearing and David knew that if he showed up, he would go back to jail. So he and Jan took off for Florida, intending to sail to Costa Rica. This added *interstate flight to avoid prosecution* to his legal troubles. Friends and family in Florida told David and Jan that they loved them—but they wouldn't help. It wasn't long before they were out of money, options, friends, and hope. In a moment of desperation and clarity, David Crosby got a ride to the FBI office in West Palm Beach and turned himself in. By Christmas of 1985, he was back in solitary confinement in the Dallas Government Center. But this time was different—David had hit bottom and was determined to get free of his heroin and freebase cocaine habit.

After David turned himself in, Jan checked herself into a hospital and resolved to break her habit as well. For the first time, the two of them thought that just maybe it was possible. As David's body slowly cleared of drugs, he began to write six to eight letters a day to old friends to try to make amends. He wrote the song Compass and believed for the first time that he could make it. David was transferred to the state prison in Huntsville and assigned to the Wynne Unit, known for the best band in the Texas prison system. There he played in the prison band, worked in the mattress factory, and learned how to live and play music straight, for the first time in twenty-five years. He participated in a drug therapy group of bright, hard-core addicts led by Thomas Colkin, a young counselor for the Texas Department of Corrections. Tom noted:

That group had so much energy in it that David went from sitting by himself to actually being some kind of leader. You could see the energy flowing out of that guy and he worked the group as if it were a concert, except that the members of the group took turns being the performer and getting feedback and strength from the others. The spirit coming out of that group made your hair stand up. It was wonderful. I think David was learning that if you really liked yourself, if you're the whole, functional individual God or whatever meant you to be, there's no need to give your reality away to a chemical, to food, or even to another person, unless they are there to dance with you the rest of your life in a good and healthy marriage. If you really know yourself, then, truly that's what recovery is—going back and getting in touch with who you really are, being able to answer the question "How well do you want to get?"[11]

On August 8, 1986, David left Huntsville State Penitentiary determined for the first time in twenty-five years that he could stay sober. Jan had progressed well in her treatment and was living in a halfway house, helping with the other patients. She had gained over twenty pounds and looked much more like the vibrant, healthy woman she had once been. With generous help from their many relieved friends, David and Jan set up a new home and began to build a new life, career, and relationship. On May 17, 1987, they were married. They both continued to work at their sobriety and help each other stay straight. Both of them were learning how to deal with life without drugs, a new, exciting, and scary prospect.

> *The meetings and fellowship they offer have been tremendously helpful to me and I go to them regularly. The people I respect in the music business and in motion pictures are all coming to the same conclusion or have already come to the realization that if you want to do anything, if you want to be a creative force, if you want to write, if you want to produce, if you want to direct, if you want to write songs, if you want to play well, if you want to make records, you can either do drugs or your art. You can't do both and survive. . . . Everywhere we turned, there were old friends freed of their addictions and dependencies. Paul Kantner (of Jefferson Airplane) says cocaine is an intelligence test. If you're taking it, you fail.[12]*

Staying clean was not easy and David still had to deal with the physical and emotional impact of his years of drug use. He was writing good music again and his voice regained its strong, mellow quality, but he had to restore his reputation with the music industry and many of his fans. He owed the IRS almost a million dollars in back taxes and spent years regaining his financial stability. He had to make amends and confront the many friends he had hurt, lied to, and disappointed. He discovered a son, James Raymond, a musician and composer, the product of a brief relationship in the early sixties who had been placed up for adoption. In 1995, David's liver failed as the result of an undiagnosed case of hepatitis "C" combined with his history of substance abuse. David was given an emergency liver transplant—a serious scare that his second chance would only be short-lived. He survived and in 1996, when David was fifty-five years old, he and Jan finally started a family with the birth of Django, named after the legendary French jazz guitarist, Django Reinhardt. Both parents were older, wiser—and straight.

> *I don't want anybody to think that it's all Pollyanna peaches and cream because it's not. If you're an addict, you have to deal with it for*

an extremely long time while you're recovering, and the early stages are hellishly tough. I don't want to give anybody any misleading ideas that recovery is easy. It's not easy; it's difficult, but it's worth it. That's the key: it's not easy but it's worth it.[13]

Special thanks to David Crosby for permission to use his story and excerpts from his autobiography *Long Time Gone*, 1988.

July 1, 1986

It's Tough to Break the Grip of that Wonderful Stuff that Kills

Let's clear up one misconception right here at the start—cocaine is wonderful. Doctors who heal the lives it fractures will tell you as much. Cocaine is a rocket launch. You're the rocket. It is also a soft June moon or a Bob Dylan concert or a flight in a glider or hot apple strudel or a stolen kiss in the dark, depending. That's the sad truth.

Cocaine is also the stranger's car your momma told you never to get into. But, hell, it's long and low and sleek and the pipes have an Indy car's bubble and it's only a short ride and everyone knows how it's fun to go fast.

I'm convinced the reason Len Bias and Don Rogers are dead, the reason John Lucas isn't playing pro basketball and Steve Howe isn't pitching in the bigs and Mercury Morris went to jail, the reason Alan Wiggins is an Oriole instead of a Padre and Vida Blue never plans his life more than 24 hours ahead anymore is that nobody levels with the youth of America.

We righteously say drugs will take you to hell and make your hair grow in green and drive you crazy and give you pimples . . . but then they try them and find out they're wonderful, and so they think they've been conned, and then they do them some more.

Which can get you dead, we've been reminded in recent weeks.

Cocaine is euphoric. Everything's right. There's a feeling of power. You feel no fatigue. That's the truth of the matter. It's wonderful stuff.

That's the problem. As good as it makes you feel in the beginning, after a while that's how bad it makes you feel. And you know you could feel better if you could just take some more. . . . It's tough to get off this drug.

A Len Bias or two may not make much of a dent. Roger's death is evidence of that. People forget. Sometimes people want to forget. That's another sad truth.

—Written by Joe Hamelin, McClatch News Service

M.I.A.

Match each of the following stars with their untimely end. "We just want to remind all the little stars out there who are growing into the Big Stars of the future that the choices we make today can be terribly important, and little mistakes can cancel out massive gifts and spectacular talents."[14]

John Belushi	*Kurt Cobain*	*Marilyn Monroe*
Len Bias	*Chris Farley*	*Keith Moon*
Notorious B.I.G.	*Jimi Hendrix*	*Elvis Presley*
Humphrey Bogart	*Shannon Hoon*	*Tupac Shakur*
	Janis Joplin	

SMOKING   ALCOHOL/PILLS   BARBITUATES   COCAINE COCAINE/HEROIN   HEROIN   SPEED   SUICIDE   VIOLENCE

Check out the footnotes or www.doitnow.org/pages.mias.html *for the answers.*[15]

GROWING UP IN AN ALCOHOLIC FAMILY

Randy

I go to Alateen. I am not an alcoholic or anything, though I do have to be careful because it definitely runs in my family. Alateen is an organization for teens who have somebody in their family who is an alcoholic or drug user. I knew that my mom's drinking worried me and sometimes scared me, but, before I started going to Alateen, I didn't realize that it had affected my whole life. Alcoholism isn't just about the person who is drinking; it affects everybody who loves them too.

My mom is an alcoholic. I guess she was having problems when I was really young, but I just remember her as the best mom in the world. She was beautiful and always there for me with just the right cookie, words, or hugs. I am the youngest of three boys and she always made time for me when my older brothers didn't want me tagging along. I was seven years younger than my next brother, so they thought I was a pest and Mama's favorite. That worked out OK since Mom was nicer to me than they were anyway.

When I was seven, Dad left. I didn't really understand what was happening, but there was a lot of yelling and a lot of tense silence before he left, so in some ways it seemed better to have him gone. I later learned that Mom had been drinking before, but after he left, things got worse fast. At first, it just seemed like Mom was depressed. She cried a lot and spent a lot of time on the phone with friends. I tried to cheer her up and sometimes it worked. I began to smell alcohol on her breath more and more often and sometimes at night, she would fall asleep on the chair while we were watching TV together. I was too young to understand what was going on, but I began to associate the smell of alcohol with her crazy mood swings. She would be all crying and sad and then get lighthearted and silly, telling me all kinds of things about my dad and how much better she was without him. That would work into anger about how he had left her and didn't understand her and didn't care two bits about his family. Eventually it would return to tears and, if I was lucky, she would fall asleep. I say lucky, because when she was awake, I never knew exactly what she would do and I felt in charge of protecting her. When I think back, that is kind of silly and sad—to think of a little seven-year-old boy trying to protect a full-grown woman—but I thought I could.

I was in second grade that year and my brothers were both at the high school. They were gone a lot and started spending more time at my dad's on the weekends. I would go over to my dad's some of the time, but I was scared to leave my mom alone for long, so I usually made excuses. I wished that my brothers would stay home and help me, but I could never really ask them or admit that I needed help or even that there was a problem. They mostly were fighting with Mom anyway. I would sit in my room listening to them fight, scared they would hurt each other. I never told my dad what was going on—I didn't want him to be mad at Mom. I guess I was still hoping that he would come back and everything would be like before. I thought that my brothers must have said something because once Dad asked me if I was OK and wanted to know how much Mom was drinking. I said I was fine and I didn't think she was hardly drinking at all anymore. I don't think he believed me, but I insisted. We were fine.

Things went on like this for about four years or so—sometimes better, sometimes worse. When I asked Mom if she was OK or if we should get some help, she insisted that everything was just fine; she had no idea what I was talking about. She had just been a little upset or sick or tired, that's all. And some days she was so good and like her old self, that I believed her. What had I been thinking? What kind of son was I to think such things about my mom? There was always an excuse for every incident, and I guess I was eager to believe them. I just wanted my happy mom back and the only time she seemed happy was after a couple drinks—before it turned bad. I sometimes thought perhaps I was just imagining things and everything really was fine. I worried silently, but tried to convince myself that all these things were normal or temporary. If I could just be good enough or helpful enough or understanding enough, all this would go away.

The scariest times were when Mom was driving. She drove fast when she was drunk, and she laughed dismissively when she did things like drive up on the lawn or turn down a one-way street the wrong way. One day when she picked me up from school, the whole car smelled of whiskey and she was laughing loudly and calling out to the teacher on duty. I was embarrassed and wanted to get her out of there as quickly as possible, but I was also nervous about her driving through all the kids and their parents getting into their cars. The line was slow and my mom never liked to wait when she had been drinking. I tried to distract her by showing her the "A" I had gotten on my science project, but she was in high spirits and had no time for science or slow car pools. She gave me a wink and said "Watch this." As she drove across the center island and did a bumpy U-turn, I sank in my seat, afraid to look back at my friends and their parents. She just laughed and waved flippantly at the waiting cars. Empowered by her boldness, she drove faster than usual, weaving past the cars obeying the speed limit. About four blocks from home, she had just started to settle down when we heard the police siren.

I knew we had been speeding, but had only a vague understanding of the laws about drinking and driving—I just assumed that everyone drove whether they had been drinking or not. I could tell my mom was nervous, but she quickly flashed on the charm and started telling the officer how sorry she was for going so fast, she didn't know what had possessed her except that her little boy was chattering on about school and his science project and she just hadn't been paying attention. It sounded pretty good to me, but I guess the smell in the car was a giveaway. The officer asked her to get out of the car and I suppose would have asked her to walk a straight line or something if she hadn't just fallen out of the car. She explained that she hadn't been well and was feeling weak and told me to tell the cop that she had been feeling badly. I backed her story—she *had* been feeling badly as far as I could tell—but the police officer took us both down to the police station.

They took me to a smaller office where a nice-enough man in a suit asked me all kinds of questions about my mom—how much did she drink, had she ever been drinking while she was driving, stuff like that. I played dumb and told him that she didn't drink very much at all and that she hadn't been feeling well lately and that she had just been at a friend's birthday lunch and she wasn't normally like this, etc, etc. I don't know if he believed any of it, but he was nice and told me that he had called my dad to come pick me up. That scared me. Where was Mom and why wasn't she going to take me home? The man said they needed to talk with her longer and he didn't want me to have to hang around the police station. I told him I didn't mind and couldn't I just see my mom—I was sure that I could help her explain everything. He said no. I felt powerless and scared. I guess I was crying when my dad finally got to the station. I was so relieved to see him that all my stories and defenses fell to the side. I ran into his arms and, for just a moment, let him take care of me.

We didn't go straight home, but stopped at a little restaurant, Peggy's, that we used to go to all the time when my dad lived at home. It was quiet and only a couple tables were occupied. We sat in a booth toward the back and Dad ordered me a chocolate marshmallow sundae, my favorite. I didn't think I could eat anything, but when it arrived, I thought I could eat forever. Dad asked me how I was and what had happened. I started to lie, but I was too exhausted and scared. I told him about school and how Mom would drive fast and fall asleep pretty soon after dinner most nights. Suddenly, I thought that maybe if Dad knew how bad things were, he would come home and take care of everything. I told him about the crying and the fits of anger. I told him about how I would put myself to bed and find Mom still asleep on the couch in the morning. I was sure he would see how much Mom needed him and come home.

But it didn't go that way. Dad told me that Mom was an alcoholic. It had mostly been binge drinking before he left, but that had created real problems in their marriage because she would disappear for days and come back remorseful, promising that it would never happen again. Dad would believe her and take her back and everything would be good again for a while. Dad said that he had been doing something called *enabling*—covering up for her, protecting her from the consequences of these episodes, hiding his own feelings, denying that there was a problem, but worrying all the time. That sounded familiar, but I didn't want to believe anything that Dad said. Alcoholics were drunks that fell down in the streets and smelled like cheap wine and ended up in jail. Falling out of a car that smelled like expensive scotch and going to jail for speeding was different.

Dad told me that was called *denial*. Making excuses, questioning your own judgment, believing that each time will be different, thinking that you can make everything better if you just. . . . He said he knew all about it because he had done it for years, hoping Mom would stop drinking or stop disappearing. Vaguely I began to remember times when Mom had suddenly gone off to stay with her sister for a few days or had a business trip from which we weren't exactly sure when she would be back. Could all this be true? Dad said that he had tried everything to get Mom to go into treatment, but she insisted she was fine, that she didn't need any help, except perhaps with the kids and the housework, which was why she sometimes needed to get away from it all in the first place.

Finally Dad went to get help for himself. He was angry and scared and resentful. Nothing he did seemed to make any difference and his health, family, and career were all suffering. The therapist that he saw helped and told him he was trying to control something over which he had no power. He recommended Alanon—a support group for grown-ups living with an alcoholic. Dad finally told my mom that if she didn't stop drinking, he was going to leave until she had gotten some help. He started to believe that was all he had needed to do—everything went really well for almost a year. Then, when I was seven, she went on a ten-day binge and when she came back, Dad left.

Dad told me that Mom loved me very much and had been worried that she might take off on a binge and leave me by myself. That was why she had started drinking more regularly—in a crazy way, to try to be a responsible mom. My older brothers, who were now in college, knew what was going on, but avoided dealing with it by staying away. Great. Dad takes a stand, stops enabling, and leaves. My brothers want their own lives, leaving me alone to take care of Mom. It was easy for them. They all knew that I would be there for her if things got rough or she was in danger. They could leave knowing she wasn't alone. What about me? If I left, no one would be there to put her to bed or hide the bottles or car keys or keep her from falling down the stairs. They were all great at giving advice about not enabling and setting boundaries, but none of them ever had to leave her alone. I was there.

I haven't been able to do that either. It has been five years since we ended up at the police department. I stayed with Dad for a while, and he took me to an Alateen meeting. I wasn't ready. Alateen has lots of slogans and sayings, one of which is that everyone gets to Alateen at exactly the right time—it will work for you when you are ready. I actually liked the people that I met at those first meetings and their stories sounded familiar, but I wasn't ready to admit that *I* had a problem. I was just getting used to the idea that my mom had a problem. She went into treatment for a little while and I went to some family sessions while she was there. They were big on the idea that alcoholism is a family disease. Like every object on a mobile, if one is moved or removed, the whole mobile is set into motion. They explained the enabling and denial that my dad had talked about. As destructive and crazy making as all these behaviors seemed, they were just everybody's way of trying to stay connected with someone that they loved—to keep alcohol from breaking up the family.

They talked about the *family hero*, the child who tries to do everything right and win all the awards in order to cover up for the family's problems. My brother Bill was like that—star athlete, honor student, accepted at Yale. I can remember thinking that since Bill was so great, it must be my fault that I felt so bad since he seemed to be doing all right. My other brother, Hal, was the *family scapegoat*. Since the perfect child position was already taken, he went the other way. He drank a lot, got in trouble at school, stayed out late and was always fighting with my mom about something. If Mom did drink a little, who could blame her, since she had to deal with Hal and all his problems? He was the scapegoat for our family. I was kind of a combination of the lost child and the family pet before Dad left. The *lost child* just hides away and acts as if nothing is happening while all the drinking and yelling goes on. The *family pet* is an amusement and diversion for the whole family to let off steam and lighten the mood. I would be cute and entertaining unless the tensions got too high; then I would go to my room and play with my Legos and talk to my dog, pretending not to hear the fighting or the yelling.

After Dad left and my brothers were not around as much, I alternately took on all the roles, a pretty exhausting assignment. I tried to be perfect, distracting, naive, and amusing all at once, all the while keeping an eye on the liquor cabinet, the car keys, and Mom. I must say that I was actually pretty good at it. It wasn't until the end of junior high school that I began to feel the pressure. The treatment program hadn't worked for Mom, but it had given us all just enough terminology and insight to be able to manipulate each other. Mom knew all the right things to say—and not to say—to keep me off balance, and I knew the threats and tricks that could keep her in line for a time. But as I got ready for high school, I started to resent all the time and energy it took to live in my house. I never knew what mood or shape she would be in when I got home from school and I was afraid to go off with my friends for too long a time, not knowing what she would do. It was even hard to have friends at all because I never wanted to bring them home for fear of what we might find. I would make plans with some friends, only to cancel them at the last minute because of the latest crisis. Most of my friends got tired of the hassle.

I was mad at my dad who thought it was so easy to "detach with love." He had a girlfriend now, which not only distracted him from me, but also sabotaged my hopes of him and Mom getting back together. My brothers were off on their lives and would only call when it was convenient, giving me advise like "don't let her run your life." Right. Mom was up and down, in and out of treatment, hopeful and despondent, always apologizing for her lapses and promising to do better. And no matter how bad things got, she could still make me smile. Sometimes I hated her, but I never stopped loving her either. When she was drinking, she looked a lot happier than I had felt in a long time, and when she was out drinking or in treatment, I was home cleaning and taking care of everything and worrying. Everyone was getting a lot better deal than I was. I felt pretty sorry for myself and took it out on everyone by nagging and complaining. It was no fun being me and I made sure it was even less fun being around me.

Then one day, everything just snapped. I quit. I was tired of taking care of everyone. Nobody appreciated me yet still knew I would clean up their messes and responsibilities. I was just a fifteen-year-old boy and I felt like a hysterical housewife. It was Tuesday and I remembered that an Alateen meeting was that night. I didn't fix dinner, I didn't worry about my Mom's plans for the evening, and I didn't even tell her where I was going—let *her* worry for a change. When I got to the meeting, I only recognized two people from before, as it had been quite a while since I had been. People were laughing and telling each other about their day. It pissed me off and I almost got up and left, but the meeting started. We all repeated the Serenity Prayer: *God, grant me the serenity to accept the things I cannot change, the courage to change the things I can, and the wisdom to know the difference.*

For some reason, all of the sudden, it was like I heard these words for the first time. I wanted serenity—freedom from all my fear and worry—more than anything, but I was trying to find it by controlling all the things I had no power over: my mom's drinking, my dad's decision to leave my mom, my brothers' responsibility to our family, my own fears and feelings. And I couldn't imagine the courage to face the things I really did have some control over: my own choices, boundaries, responses, and well-being. I had been worrying about everybody else for so long, I didn't even know how to begin. For the first time, I honestly did *admit that I was powerless over alcohol and that my life had become unmanageable.* I had never even had one drink, but I was powerless over alcohol. All my efforts, defenses, and excuses just plain didn't work. As I admitted this to myself in resignation and defeat, I felt lighter and listened to the experience, strengths, and hopes of each member in the group with new ears and a new openness. I couldn't control my mom's drinking and that was OK. I was scared and that was OK. I wasn't even sure there was a higher power and that was OK. I had no idea what I would do next and that was OK too. Just for today, I would listen and let go of all the things that were not my business. I would keep it simple and come to meetings. One of the other group members was saying how hard it had been for her to trust a higher power, or anyone else, to take care of her—her hopes had been let down by her alcoholic parents so many times. Her sponsor had told her to "fake it 'til you make it"—just thank your higher power, whatever you think that is, for taking care of you in advance, as if you are absolutely sure it will.

I can almost do that. I have been good at faking a lot of things, and I just might be able to *imagine* serenity until I actually have it. Serenity, courage, and wisdom come slowly and intermittently, but I am not alone with all this any more, and I have stopped expecting myself to fix everything and everybody. I even believe that I can be honest and be myself and at least my Alateen family will understand and be there when I need them. Whether I was the family hero or family pet, these were all my desperate and unsuccessful attempts to control my world and my family. It is scary to let alcoholics take care of themselves and even harder to really begin to take care of myself. *Progress, not perfection.* So I just thank my higher power in advance, reach out for help when I need it, and take it one day at a time. So far, I'm OK.

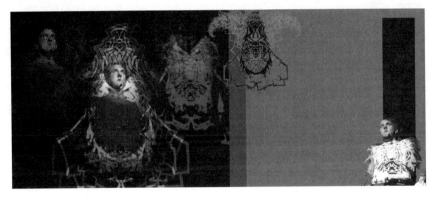

by Mo Higby

MANIA AND DEPRESSION

I have often asked myself whether, given the choice, I would choose to have manic-depressive illness. If lithium was not available to me, or didn't work for me, the answer would be a simple no—and it would be an answer laced with terror. But lithium does work for me, and therefore I suppose I can afford to pose the question. Strangely enough I think I would choose to have it. It's complicated. Depression is awful beyond words or sounds or images; I would not go through an extended one again. It bleeds relationships through suspicion, lack of confidence, and self-respect; the inability to enjoy life; to walk or talk or think normally; the exhaustion, the night terrors, the day terrors. There is nothing good to be said for it except that it gives you the experience of how it must be to be old, to be old and sick, to be dying; to be slow of mind; to be lacking in grace, polish, and coordination; to be ugly; to have no belief in the possibilities of life, the pleasures of sex, the exquisiteness of music, or the ability to make yourself and others laugh.

Others imply that they know what it is like to be depressed because they have gone through a divorce, lost a job, or broken up with someone. But those experiences carry with them feelings. Depression, instead, is flat, hollow, and unendurable. It is also tiresome. People cannot abide being around you when you are depressed. They might think that they ought to, and they might even try, but you know and they know that you are tedious beyond belief: you're irritable and paranoid and humorless and lifeless and critical and demanding and no reassurance is ever enough. You're frightened and you're frightening, and you're "not at all like yourself but will be soon," but you know you won't.

So why would I want anything to do with this illness? Because I honestly believe that as a result of it I have felt more things, more deeply; had more experiences, more intensely; loved more and been more loved; laughed more often for having cried more often; appreciated more the springs for all the winters; worn death "as close as dungarees," appreciated it—and life—more; seen the finest and the most terrible in people, and slowly learned the values of caring, loyalty, and seeing things through. I have seen the breadth and depth and width of my mind and heart and seen how frail they both are, and how ultimately unknowable they both are. Depressed, I have crawled on my hands and knees in order to get across a room and have done it for month after month. But, normal or manic, I have run faster, thought faster, and loved faster than most I know. And I think much of this is related to my illness—the intensity it gives to things and the perspective it forces on me. I think it has made me test the limits of my mind (which, while wanting, is holding) and the limits of my upbringing, family, education, and friends.

The countless hypomanias, and mania itself, all have brought into my life a different level of sensing and feeling and thinking. Even when I have been most psychotic—delusional, hallucinating, frenzied—I have been aware of finding new corners in my mind and heart. Some of those corners were incredible and beautiful and took my breath away and made me feel as though I could die right then and the images would sustain me. Some of them were grotesque and ugly and I never wanted to know they were there or to see them again. But, always, there were those new corners and—when feeling my normal self, beholden for that self to medicine and love—I cannot imagine becoming jaded to life, because I know of those limit-less corners with their limitless views.

—From *An Unquiet Mind: A Memoir of Moods and Madness* by Kay Redfield Jamison[16]

Meitar

Those cycles . . .

. . . of mania and then depression—or depression and then mania—can last as long as years, or as short as minutes. For me, the cycles are generally either hourly or daily. I really enjoy the mania. I can get a lot of work done, and I always enjoy doing the work too. When I'm in a period of mania, I can feel my heart beating rapidly in my chest. I jump around a lot and move really fast, whether I'm walking, running, or doing something else, like typing. I'll often put on some very grand or fast music and listen to it while I work or play. Chances are that I would probably be laughing a lot, and I am sure to be having lots of fun no matter what I'm doing.

And then . . . then the realization that it's all going to end soon. The feelings of happiness and joy will slowly seep back into the recesses of wherever they came from. In their place, the dark and searing pain of depression will ooze out. When it's really bad, I feel my heart being impaled by a huge spear. Sometimes it will physically hurt me. This swing can be triggered by almost anything, but when it's not I go into a neutral sort of mode. Just waiting. . . . Waiting for whatever will set off the spark that will cause me to explode. Depressive episodes are usually coupled with irritability. When my fuse runs out, my hands and toes get numb and I can feel a wave of the pins-and-needles sensation course through my body in a circling outward motion emanating from the middle of my heart. It causes me to tense up and when I finally relax I have no more energy left. It's awful.

At the most basic level, I am constantly confronted with the challenge of making good choices despite the fact that I cannot accurately rely on many of my perceptions of reality. Few people realize how much impact emotions have on our interpretation of the world around us. Mood disorders like bipolar disorder act a lot like false radar-blips on our emotional radar screens, confusing us with misinformation. While the emotion is real and valid, no matter how extreme, it is not necessarily appropriate or in proportion to the situation. It's exceptionally difficult to respond rationally to your mother when she tells you not to forget your coat if, upon hearing the sound of her voice, you suddenly feel attacked and enraged. That has been the source of many fights and lots of confusion in my family.

The very first thing you need to do is begin to educate yourself and your family on your condition. The more they know about it, the more they will understand you. I highly recommend reading *An Unquiet Mind* by Kay Jamison. This is one of the most famous and personal stories of a bipolar woman. It will help you and your family understand so much more about why you feel the way you do. Most important, however, it will show you that you are not alone. Reading personal accounts such as this can also provide you with a vocabulary to communicate your thoughts and feelings. The book *Emotional Intelligence* by Daniel Groleman is also an excellent work (though not a personal account), which explains a lot about the anatomy of emotions. It is a little difficult to read at first because of its focus on biology in the beginning few chapters. However, what follows is the best source of ammunition against "emotional hijackings" I have ever collected.

Another exceptionally helpful thing to do is to keep a written record of how you feel from day to day. You can use a journal, or make a chart. I do a lot of free typing. Free typing is basically just typing whatever's in your head, without thinking or censoring yourself. I usually do it when I'm feeling really depressed or really manic, and the results are always very telling. For example in a depressed state, I write in short, rigid sentences that seem to mimic my stiff body language. In a manic state, my sentences are miles long and contain redundant adjectives or made-up words. Writing like this has always helped me center myself, feel more in control, and I suggest trying it yourself when you're feeling out of control.

I always save what I write, no matter how short it is or how much I may dislike it. The point is to get a better understanding of my own mood patterns, and what triggers the swings in them. It's a lot like keeping accurate financial records if you owned a business. The more accurate and detailed your records, the more precisely you can predict future fluctuations in cash flow (mood) and thus plan for the unexpected (a major mood swing). Anticipating these swings is the first step toward avoiding destructive behavior.

Over the years, I have discovered specific things that trigger both upswings and downswings. If I haven't left the house in four days, then I know from experience and record keeping that my family will likely trigger a downswing. When my brother asks something of me that ticks me off, I have to say to myself, "You're unusually irritable, so don't snap at him just because you're feeling upset." During times like these, I try to give myself some breathing room from my family. Knowing how to avoid the things that trigger you is a great tool in helping to sidestep a possible mood swing. If the trigger is unavoidable (math class in school was a huge one for me), one of your most powerful preventative weapons against a swing is the old "think before you act" exercise. I understand it's easier said than done, but if you simply remember it enough times, even if you don't do it that particular time, you'll find yourself taking that deep breath earlier and earlier.

When talking to people, being completely direct is extremely powerful. A simple line like, "Mom, I'm feeling extremely irritable right now and if I can have twenty minutes alone, I'll feel more able to talk with you," said in a calm, respectful tone, usually halts any unwanted intrusion into your personal space. Being respectful is key, but this should not be a one-way street. You should be getting the respect you deserve too. Mental illness still carries a stigma with it, even if it's not as heavy as it used to be. If you're not being treated fairly, expressing your concern respectfully and clearly on the matter is the only way you will be.

Don't ever let anyone have you believe that you are weak or "just can't cope." In fact, you are stronger for asking for help than trying to handle everything while in the closet. Parents who have been diagnosed often tell me about how they feel guilty for giving themselves mental-health days away from their family. While I empathize with the feeling, it is important that they understand how vital those mental-health days are for *their family* as well as themselves. Ultimately, in order to take care of your responsibilities, you must first take care of yourself. For me, this translated into re-prioritizing many things in my life, most notably homework and medicine.

Nobody likes taking medications, but here's the bottom line in my opinion: If you are prescribed medication by your licensed psychiatrist, *you must take that medication as directed by your doctor because your life does, in fact, depend on it.* The single most common pitfall is taking your prescribed medication for several months, or maybe even a few years, and then feeling "cured." I will admit to falling into this trap, and it almost took my life. I was first prescribed medications (Depakote along with Zyprexa, and then later lithium) when I was at the tender age of twelve. Ever since then, I have hated my medication with a passion rivaling my personal beliefs and convictions. Two years later, and during a particularly stable period, I felt like I didn't need to take the medications anymore. I could handle it, I thought to myself. I stopped taking my medicines, hiding that fact from my parents, for almost two weeks. No sooner was I convinced that I was indeed right, that I could handle it, when I started spiraling into a pit of depression so deep that I attempted suicide one week later. My confidence shattered, my moods cycling out of control, it was the beginning of one of the longest and darkest periods of depression in my life.

Looking back on the experience with twenty-twenty hindsight, I can see that I felt better *because* I was taking the medication. This highlights the fundamental danger of mood disorders: They strip us of our ability to make rational choices. For literally years after that incident, I began training myself to react to situations based on factual information I could gather. No longer, I promised myself, would a cup of spilled milk bring tears to my eyes, or failure to complete an assignment in school cause a temper tantrum. Neither would a manic episode cause me to abandon my responsibilities in favor of a creative all-nighter. Mania, in fact, can be just as dangerous if not more so than depression. The reason for this is that during a depression, you are more in touch with your feelings than you are when you're manic. Medications are an essential tool that helps me manage these extremes and make my life livable. They are not miracle pills that solve all my problems. All they can do is take the edge off most of the extreme emotions racing inside me. Taking control of my own reactions still requires me to think before I act, to stay *aware*.

Medications, by the way, need a lot of fine-tuning to work properly, just like any car engine. Taking the right medications for you, at the right dosage, is critical. The right medicine and dosage for you is whatever medicine at whatever dose allows you to function in your life. It took me a full year to find the correct dosage of lithium that I am on now and, from the many people I have spoken with, my understanding is that one year is an awfully short time. I was lucky; finding the right medicines and fine-tuning them to the right dose can take much longer. Patience is not just a virtue; it's a necessity.

Once you've found a working treatment, it's helpful to understand that these medicines are variables in an equation designed to help you function in your life. If at any point things aren't working, altering your medications may be the best course of action. Any time I am thinking of altering my medications I first discuss it with my therapist and with my doctor. They are always receptive, even if they don't always agree with me. When they don't, it is a sign for me to look over the situation and reevaluate my choices. In the end, my treatment is just that—*mine*—and I've found that it is both more effective and easier to handle emotionally if I'm the one behind the steering wheel. However, I am always aware that both my therapist and my doctor are an important part of my treatment. They provide me with vital information, which influence my choices. I

trust them because of the good working relationship we have created together. I have had several doctors and many therapists before I found ones
which I liked, and I believe that finding the right doctors was just as important as finding the right medicines.

I once heard an estimate that approximately 1 percent of the world's population has bipolar disorder. Just think about that for a moment. Out of
every one hundred people I've seen on the street, at least one of them is
struggling with the same things that I am struggling with right now. In my
experience, many of the people whom I've told that I'm bipolar have already had a previous experience with someone else that has bipolar disorder. Rarely is anyone unfamiliar with it these days. Sometimes, if a
person doesn't know what "bipolar disorder" is they are still well aware
of what "manic-depression" means.

In the few cases where my friends didn't know what I was talking about,
all they wanted was to know that I'm still the same person they be-
friended. I suspect the same will be true of your friends. If you don't feel
comfortable explaining the biology, refer them to a Web site or other resource where they can learn the particulars on their own.

Bipolar disorder is something that affects the very core of who we are. Of-
tentimes, it becomes important to distinguish my feelings as entities separate from my actions and even separate from myself since I can't always
trust them to represent reality accurately. I need to teach myself to stay
aware of my feelings, of the situation around me, and to control my reactions to other people and to triggers that might set me off. Most of all,
though, I need patience from myself and from my friends and family to let
me go through my cycles—to have that sad mood swing or that giddy
night. Sometimes I feel like my moods are a monster within me. I've learned
that awareness and knowledge are the tools with which to defang that monster. I still go through those cycles of mania and depression, except now they
don't bite me as hard as they used to.[17]

AboutOurKids.org   A wonderful resource for parents about all kinds of
parenting and mental health issues listing disorders, symptoms, and help
centers.

Mental Health Matters.com   This site hosts a wealth of detailed information and resources for consumers, professionals, students, and supporters.
Get educated, get involved, and even get help all right here!

DepressionRemedy.com   Information on depression, depression symptoms, types, and research on natural and herbal remedies.

MentalHealth.com   A Web site so vast in its coverage I simply had to include it. This is a great place to start learning about and gathering information about any mental health issue.

Jane's Mental Health Source Page, chinspirations.com/mhsourcepage,   Much more than just a personal page, this Web site delivers content that is both useful and inspiring.

Pendulum Resources, pendulum.org   Information about manic-depression and bipolar disorders. The site contains articles, writings, humor, and links. One of the Web's oldest sites on bipolar disorder.

The Winds of Change, thewindsofchange.org   Frank and personal look at living with bipolar disorder. Lots of links. Clear and very informative—a must visit site!

Because Depression is an Illness, geocities.com/hotsprings/villa/5712/links.html Both informative, and inspiring, this page has many links to sites devoted to mental disorders as well as to support groups nationwide.

The Mercurial Mind, home.att.net/~mercurial-mind/dysphoria.html   This is an extraordinary page which both discusses the personal side of bipolar disorder, and gives many, many links to more useful resources on the net. It is brutally honest, and extremely revealing. I very highly recommend this site to anyone who seeks an insider's look at the bipolar experience!

Depression Central, www.geocities.com/pood_72581/   The depression information site. It has way more information on about every kind of imaginable depression I'd ever like to try and think of.

About.com-bipolar disorder   A comprehensive collection of net resources under the umbrella of a commercial site. Very well organized and easy to search.

The Bipolar Planet, www.bipolarplanet.com   A page dedicated to the self-exploration of the bipolar disorder.

Bipolar NOT Bonkers, www.kiva.net/~sjb/   A site dedicated to those living with bipolar illness. This is a wonderfully compassionate Web site, which shares the author's personal struggles. A great reminder that there *is* light at the end of the tunnel!

*HealthyPlace.com *Bipolar Section*   HealthyPlace.com is a collection of online communities. Organized by topic (ranging from addictions, to eating disorders, to sex and sexuality), this is a well presented and informative site. It is one of the most supportive sites I have found. Be sure to visit each community's "Community Wall."

American Academy of Child & Adolescent Psychiatry, www.aacap.org   This organization provides important information on clinical research and mental health policies nationwide. Also provides regional organizations' information. English and Spanish!

NoStigma.org   A small but growing collection of news articles, submitted stories, and other clippings all part of the National Mental Health Awareness Campaign. This campaign debunks false myths about mental illness, and effectively provides hope for struggling youth and adult alike.

Special thanks to Meitar for sharing his experience, insight, and Web site: UPS AND DOWNS: A Personal Account of a Bipolar Teen. *www.danakama.com/ups_downs*

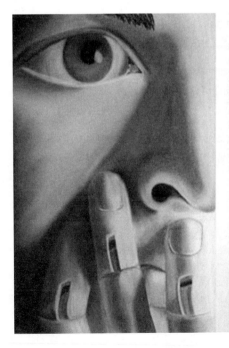

by Anna Petry

HITTING THE WALL

One of the more subtle, but critical passages of adolescence is the growing responsibility for your own actions and decisions. When possible, children are protected from danger and dangerous consequences. Babies are carefully watched. Young children are walked across the street. Children are legally restricted from using fireworks, or driving a car until they have been trained and reached an age when they are mature enough to make careful decisions and handle the physical and social dangers of these activities. With adulthood comes the full awareness and responsibility for our lives and our impact on others.

Eliza

Most people grow up a little at a time, but for some of us, it happens in an instant. One minute you're a child, laughing and playing and giggling about silly things. And the next minute, you have crossed the line and you are no longer a child; actions have consequences and you must face them as an adult. I never saw it coming because it seemed like something that only happened to other people or in the movies. I had been lucky and sheltered, all the while thinking my safety and innocence were guaranteed. The warnings of my parents and teachers seemed like typical adult paranoia, extreme and pathetic. Tragedy and accidents happened rarely and always to someone else. I wasn't stupid; I just felt invincible.

I have tried to piece together the details of that night, before the accident. I had a new pink tank top that I had bought especially for the party. It looked good with my black pants and light leather jacket. I remember feeling pretty and excited as I got ready. It was a Saturday in early October. We had just finished midterms and our football team was doing well. The weather had been warmer than usual and there was going to be a big bonfire at a favorite spot on the lake. I was the third teenager in my family, so my parents were pretty casual about where I went. They knew that there was beer at our parties, but expected me to use my judgment and not drink and drive or ride with someone who had been drinking. We didn't talk about it much, but it was an unspoken agreement in our family. I guess I had seen my dad drive after a couple of drinks, but he never seemed drunk or out of control.

When I came downstairs, my dad was finishing up the dishes and my mom was watering the plants—nothing special or out of the ordinary. I don't remember the exact conversation; I do remember my younger sister crying that my brother had hidden the remote control to the TV and my brother denying the charges. I was glad to be going out, away from the bickering and monotony of family life. I think we did the routine *"Where will you be? Who will you be with? Be back by 12:30"* drill. *"Out at the lake. I'm picking up Jennifer and Marsha—maybe Jo Anne. Don't worry, I am the designated driver—no drinking, just hanging out. Can't I stay out 'til 2:00? This is our last lake party and I'm the ride. Everyone else has permission to stay out til 2:00; it takes over an hour to drive home. . . ."* They gave me a hassle, but finally agreed to the 2:00 extension. *"Drive carefully. . . . No, I thought I would be reckless and drive the car into the lake. . . . Don't be funny. . . . Don't worry. . . ."* Nothing unusual. No foreshadowing. Nothing that made the night seem different from any other.

As I backed the car out of the driveway, I switched on the radio and fumbled for my new CD. The sound blasted through the car and canceled out the world I was leaving behind. I was a good driver—maybe a little fast, but I had never had an accident and only one minor speeding ticket. I loved to drive and knew every bump, speed trap, and shortcut in the area. I cut through a small subdivision to avoid the light on Pine Street and zipped around the cul de sac to Jennifer's house. I honked the horn and checked my makeup in the rearview mirror while I waited. Jo Anne was with Jennifer and they came out laughing and pumped up for the party. Jo Anne asked me to open the trunk so she could store her backpack, which landed with a clink, indicating at least two bottles for the party. Jennifer rolled her eyes and gave me a quick hug. Everyone was in a good mood. This was going to be a big party, the last one of the season before it got too cold to be up in the mountains. Jennifer said I didn't need to pick up Marsha—her boyfriend had come home from college for the weekend and was taking her out. We made a few jokes about that and headed out to the lake.

The lake was about an hour outside of town, up in the mountains. I had been going up there all my life, first with my family and church group and later with my friends. It was a winding but familiar ride. We got to the lake just before dark and helped collect more firewood. Only about twelve people were there when we arrived, but cars started pulling in and pretty soon the bonfire was surrounded by small, chattering groups of friends from my school—mostly juniors and seniors, but a few sophomores. Someone cranked up a boombox and the quiet night air was filled with squeals and laughter and rap music. Everyone was in high spirits. The air was crisp and the moon was rising up over the lake, a small crisp, crescent magnified by the water.

I was hoping that Paul would arrive with some of the other football players. Paul was a senior and I had had a crush on him for over a year now. Just recently he had seemed to notice that I was alive. We had a math class together and sometimes we would talk before class or on our way out. On Friday, I had casually asked him if he was coming to the lake party and he said "Sure, maybe I can see you there." That sounded promising, like he didn't mean "see" like in *pass by*, but "see" like *maybe we could spend some time together.* I was determined to make him notice me and hoped this would be the party to make it happen.

Someone had gotten a keg for the party and pretty soon the beer was flowing and there was a sweet smell of marijuana in certain circles around the party. Everyone was in a good mood and eager to celebrate the final end of summer before the winter snows began. The predictable ones started to get drunk and be a little rowdy, but most people were content just to relax and have a good time. We weren't a rave-type party group; no Ecstasy or uppers, just a lot of drinking and some pot. It wasn't that nobody ever tried anything else, but we didn't need a lot of extra stimulation when we got together. It was pretty mellow with couples walking by the lake and a few of us dancing on the lawn that spread out around the shore. I had just one beer, figuring it would be hours before I would have to drive and it would all be out of my system by then. I was having a good time, but still no Paul. I tried off-handedly to ask a couple of his friends if he was coming, but they were getting plastered and just gave me shit about why I wanted to know.

It was after eleven before Paul arrived and he wasn't alone. He walked over to the party with his arm around a sexy girl in a skimpy top and tight pants that I had never seen before. I overheard him introduce her as Ashley, his girlfriend from the dude ranch he had worked at last summer. The two of them had obviously been partying a little on their own; Paul was all over this Ashley person and she wasn't resisting. They were practically getting off right there with everyone around. After wishing all night that Paul would seek me out and get something going, I now only hoped he wouldn't even see me. I moved away from the football circle and started talking with a couple guys I knew vaguely from the yearbook. Inadvertently, however, I had moved directly between Paul and the keg and it wasn't long before he came over to get a beer.

"Hey, little math whiz," I heard him say as I tried to be invisible. "Whatsup?" All my clever and sexy responses had slipped out of my head when I saw Paul walk up with his arm around Ashley and his hands all over her. I tried to put a coherent sentence together, but it wasn't really necessary. He was stoned and focusing all his attention on trying to get the keg to work. He wasn't having much luck and I stupidly pumped the tank for him and he filled his glass. He then put his arm around me, grinned, and said "Hey, you're good." Going from the depths of despair to being in his arms in a matter of minutes caught me off guard and for a minute, I dared to hope that the party would turn out all right after all. Before I knew what was happening, his free hand slipped down past my waist and grabbed my butt. "Nice ass, too," he said and everyone around us started laughing. Paul laughed too and stumbled off to find Ashley.

I was mortified and miserable. The whole party suddenly went flat and colorless. I felt tears come to my eyes as the guys around me were saying things like, "Hey, let me have a feel too" and it registered what had just happened. "Don't worry about him," I heard a familiar voice say. "He's a jerk." It was Steven, a guy I had been friends with since third grade. He told the other guys to shut up and handed me a beer. "You look like you could use some cheering up." Relieved to have something to do besides burst into tears, I attempted a smile and took the beer. Steven took my hand and we walked off and sat next to the lake. I could always talk openly with Steven and he listened to my sad story while I drank the beer and tried to pull myself together. I only really thought about drinking one beer, but it was a long story and I think Steven refilled my glass from a bottle he had brought along. Steven always made me feel better and the beer was helping me forget the whole horrible evening. I was almost laughing by the time Jennifer found me.

"Hey, Liza," she called. "You have to come help me. Jo Anne is getting sick and it's almost one o'clock. We have got to clean her up and get home by 2:00 or my folks are going to kill me. They were pissed enough to extend my curfew to 2:00 and I *promised* I would not be late."

Steven and I went with Jennifer and we found Jo Anne puking in the bushes. "Oh sweet," I thought. "Just get it out of your system before you get in my car." Steven led Jo Anne down to the lake to wash up and we managed to get her in the car. It was after 1:00 by then and we would have to push it to get home in time.

Steven asked me if I was OK to drive and for the first time, I remembered that I had had that beer—or was it two beers? But I felt fine and there was no time to worry about that. It had been an exhausting evening and if anything, I felt tired. Jennifer fell over as she was helping Jo Anne into the car and sat there on the ground laughing. It was clear that no one else was in any shape to drive. I assured Steven that I was fine and kissed him quickly as I got in the car. "Thanks for being my hero," I said and smiled as I backed through the parked cars and seniors who were still going strong. They would probably stay out all night celebrating their last football season and their last high school lake party. I glanced over the crowd—Paul's car was still there, but he and Ashley were nowhere to be seen. My old jealousy and humiliation came back and I spun my tires in the gravel as I took off on the road home.

Jo Anne fell asleep in the backseat after about ten minutes and Jennifer climbed up front to keep me company. "Hey, I saw Paul with that sleazy girl. Sorry."

"Yeh, what a jerk," I replied and proceeded to tell her my whole sad woe story. By the time we got to the "nice ass" line, Jennifer was raging and we ended up laughing at all the revenge she was going to settle with him back at school. It felt good to be with a good friend who would always take my side and make me feel better. The road was dark and there was no other traffic so I went as fast as I safely could to try to get us home in time. All I remember was going around a curve and suddenly being confronted by two glaring headlights coming straight at us. I swerved sharply to miss them and could only hear screams and metal crunching as all the lights went out.

I vaguely remember being transported into an ambulance, but nothing else registered until hours later in the hospital. The lights seemed glaring as I tried to open my eyes and move my body. I hurt all over and felt some sort of board holding my shoulders in place. I vaguely saw my parents sitting anxiously next to my bed, and they looked terrible. My mom had obviously been crying and my dad looked pretty shaken. A third person appeared, and a smooth black face told me that I was going to be all right, not to worry. That was all I could manage for the moment and I fell back to sleep.

I don't know how long I slept or if I was really sleeping or just avoiding waking up. My whole body hurt and one of my eyes was swollen shut. People kept poking me and telling me to wake up, afraid that I would lapse into a coma or something. I could hear them, but I couldn't move myself to respond to them. It was night by the time I could gather enough energy to open my one good eye and survey the room. My mom was sleeping in the chair next to my bed and I couldn't see my father. The voice that had earlier told me that I was going to be all right spoke quietly. "So are you ready to wake up, baby girl? You got a bunch of folks here that sure want you to wake up."

My mother stirred at the sound of the nurse's voice and looked over to see me looking at her. Tears welled in her eyes and she quickly moved over to touch my hand. "Eliza, Eliza," she whispered. "My poor sweet baby." I tried to speak, but it was more effort than I thought it would be. All I could manage was a hoarse "Mom."

The nurse had gone to get a doctor and soon the room was bustling with activity as they checked my vital signs, shined a light in my good eye, and tried to get me to tell them who was the president of the United States. My dad came back in the middle of all this and I felt tears welling as he came over to gently kiss my forehead. "Oh Daddy," I managed to say, "what has happened?"

The lights that were coming at me as I drove around the corner were the headlights of a car full of juniors who were returning to the party to get a cell phone someone had left there. There were open bottles in the car and the driver, a boy I knew vaguely from the football team, tested .1, well over the legal limit for alcohol. I managed to swerve fast enough to avoid a head-on collision, but slammed us right into a large pine tree about twenty feet off the road. The other car had continued for almost a mile before someone in the car convinced the driver to go back and help us. My car was totaled and I hit the windshield. Luckily I had my seat belt on, but the air bag never inflated. I had hit my head, fractured my collarbone, and was bruised and cut all over. Jo Anne was caught in the backseat, but had been so drunk and asleep that her relaxed body escaped without any serious injuries. She was cut up and sore, but walking and checked out of the hospital by the time I saw her. Jennifer had never fastened her seat belt after she climbed into the front seat and was thrown from the car into another tree eight feet away. She never regained consciousness.

It took them a while before anyone would tell me that Jennifer had died. I guess no one knew quite how to say it or they were worried about how I would take it. At first, I was too overwhelmed with everything that was happening to ask. I couldn't imagine anything worse than what I already knew. When I was finally coherent enough to take stock of everything, I remembered the car and Jennifer and Jo Anne. When my dad first told me that Jennifer didn't make it, I wouldn't believe him. I was just talking with Jennifer; she was going to soap Paul's car in the parking lot on Monday; we were laughing and scheming. Jennifer was my best friend. We had been friends since kindergarten. We told each other everything.

"It wasn't your fault," my dad continued. "You did everything you could to avoid a head-on collision. She didn't have a seat belt on. The other driver has been charged with drunken and reckless driving and manslaughter. It wasn't your fault."

I sat there dumbstruck. *I had been driving the car that killed Jennifer.* In the shock of hearing that she was dead, I had temporarily forgotten my role in the matter. Now it rushed over me like a black cloud that would block out the sun forever. I couldn't speak or cry or move. I wanted to wake up and find this all a bad dream. How could I live with any of this? How could I face Jennifer's parents or the other kids at school? How could I ever forgive myself? I closed my eyes and tried to will myself to some other time and place. The voices and noises around me swirled into space and I disappeared.

For over a week, I stayed in some hidden part of my mind. I didn't want to see or hear anything. I remember people trying to get me to eat, but I wouldn't. I soiled my bed like a baby and refused to speak or listen. I kept a buzz going in my mind to avoid being part of the world outside of my head. Every now and then I would start to surface, but then I would remember and dive back under. Gradually, I used up my defenses and fell into a deep sleep, exhausted and overtaken by my body's need to rest. After this sleep, I woke up.

Nothing had changed. Having done my best to escape, I had to face it. My mother held me and we cried together. Jo Anne came and we cried. On the second day after I returned, Steven came to see me.

"Jennifer is dead, Steven," I said as bravely as I could.

"I know," Steven said, looking at his feet. "It wasn't your fault, Eliza. You did everything you could have done. The other car was driving all over the road. You could have all been killed."

"But I had been drinking," I confessed to Steven, the only one who already knew my secret.

"You only had about a beer and a half, Liza," Steven argued. "Your reflexes were good. You avoided a head-on collision that could have hurt a lot more people. You can't blame yourself."

"But maybe if I was totally clear, I could have avoided the car *and* the tree," I whispered, not wanting anyone else to know what I feared, what I had been avoiding in my mental and physical retreat.

"*What ifs* don't count," Steven insisted. "You saved your life and Jo Anne's life and probably the lives of six people in the other car. Jennifer died. That's all you can know and you just have to live with that. You did the best you could have done under the circumstances."

Under the circumstances. What part of that was fate out of my control, and what part did I contribute? Nobody ever blamed me or even questioned me; in fact, I was sort of a hero and people felt real sorry for me. Even Jennifer's parents told me not to feel responsible. I could just remember Jennifer consoling me and promising to stick up for me. I would give anything to hear her say that now.

But I'm not a child anymore and that is not going to happen. Jennifer's gone and I'm alive; I have to live with everything that happened *and* not having Jennifer to console me about it. All of the things that seemed so important the night of the party now seem so insignificant. I took a semester off from school and went on a three-month outdoor leadership course. I needed to test myself and have some time alone to think about the rest of my life. Every time I think I just can't live with all of this, I am left with the fact that I have to. No amount of begging or promising can change that. I sat out under the stars one night when I was on my solo—five days on my own on a tiny island off the coast of Maine. I felt so small and insignificant, and yet a part of a much larger puzzle at the same time. My life had changed in the instant that I went around that corner and I will always carry Jennifer with me. It was not the life I thought I would have, but it was mine, nonetheless. As much as I was responsible for that night, I am also responsible for the rest of my life. That has been the hardest part—no excuses, no second chances, no going back. As I looked out into the stars, I wondered if Jennifer had forgiven me and if I would ever forgive myself. I could feel her presence and she gave me a simple message: *You can't always control what happens, only how you run with it. Run for both of us.*

SADD's mission simply stated is:
To provide students with the best prevention and intervention tools possible to deal with the issues of underage drinking, other drug use, impaired driving and other destructive decisions.

CONTRACT FOR LIFE

A Foundation for Trust and Caring
This contract is designed to facilitate communication between young people and their parents about potentially destructive decisions related to alcohol, drugs, peer pressure and behavior. The issues facing young people today are often too difficult to address alone. SADD believes that effective parent-child communication is critically important in helping young adults make healthy decisions.

Young Person
I recognize that there are many potentially destructive decisions I face every day and commit to you that I will do everything in my power to avoid making decisions that will jeopardize my health, my safety and overall well being, or your

trust in me. I understand the dangers associated with the use of alcohol and drugs and the destructive behaviors often associated with impairment.

By signing below, I pledge my best effort to remain alcohol and drug free, I agree that I will never drive under the influence of either, or accept a ride from someone who is impaired, and I will always wear a seat belt.

Finally, I agree to call you if I am ever in a situation that threatens my safety and to communicate with you regularly about issues of importance to us both.

_____

Young Person

Parent (or Caring Adult)

I am committed to you, and to your health and safety. By signing below, I pledge to do everything in my power to understand and communicate with you about the many difficult and potentially destructive decisions you face.

Further I agree to provide for you safe, sober transportation home if you are ever in a situation that threatens your safety and to defer discussion about that situation until a time when we can both discuss the issues in a calm and caring manner.

I also pledge to you that I will not drive under the influence of alcohol or drugs, I will always seek safe, sober transportation home, and I will always remember to wear a seatbelt.

_____

Parent/Caring Adult

        SADD and all SADD logos are registered with the United States Patent and Trademark Office and other jurisdictions. All rights reserved by SADD, Inc. a Massachusetts non-profit corporation. Copying of this material is prohibited unless written permission is received. SADD, Inc. sponsors Students Against Driving Drunk, Students Against Destructive Decisions and other health and safety programs.
Students Against Destructive Decisions
SADD, Inc. PO Box 800 Marlborough, MA 01752   Tel. 508-481-3568
Toll Free   1-877-SADD-INC

Artwork:

Balinder Tara Singh
Kent School

Landi Guidetti
Mercersburg Academy

Mo Higby
Viewpoint School

Mo Higby
Mercersburg Academy

Anna Petry
Mercersburg Academy

Notes

[1] From *Positive Dyslexia Ltd.*, http://www.dyslexiacanada.com/fam.htm

[2] Do you know these famous dyslexics:

1. Leonardo Da Vinci, 2. Erin Brokovich, 3. John Irving, 4. Thomas Edison, 5. Joe Pantoliano, 6. President Woodrow Wilson, 7. Charles Schwab, 8. Albert Einstein.

[3] From *John Irving Uncensored* 2 <@randomhouse.com>

⁴ *The Wall Street Journal* [10/09/98] from the Action on Smoking and Health website, http://ash.org

⁵ From *Long Time Gone* by David Crosby and Carl Gottlieb, Doubleday Press, 1988, p. xi.

⁶ Ibid., p. xvii.

⁷ Ibid., p. 119.

⁸ Ibid., David Crosby, p. 301.

⁹ Ibid., David Crosby, p. 318.

¹⁰ Ibid., p. 427.

¹¹ Ibid., p. 466.

¹² Ibid., p. 475.

¹³ Ibid., p. 476.

¹⁴ www.doitnow.org/pages.mias.html

¹⁵ Monroe—alcohol/pills, Bogart—smoking, Hendrix—barbiturates, Joplin—heroin, Presley—speed, Belushi—cocaine/heroin, Moon—alcohol/pills, Bias—cocaine, Cobain—suicide, Hoon—heroin, Shakur—violence, B.I.G.—violence, Farley—cocaine/heroin

¹⁶ Kay Redfield Jamison. *An Unquiet Mind*. First Vintage Books, 1995, pp. 217–19.

¹⁷ Meitar Moscovitz. *UPS AND DOWNS: A Personal Account of a Bipolar Teen.* www.danakama.com/ups_downs

I think of the two major tasks of childhood as the development of competence and the development of connectedness, both of which contribute, in different ways to the over-arching goals of developing a sense of confidence and self-esteem. . . . What is connectedness? It is a sense of being a part of something larger than oneself. It is a sense of belonging, or a sense of accompaniment. It is that feeling in your bones that you are not alone. It is a sense that no matter how scary things may become, there is a hand for you in the dark. While ambition drives us to achieve, connectedness is my word for the force that urges us to ally, to affiliate, to enter into mutual relationships, to take strength and to grow through cooperative behavior. . . . These connections act as internal supports that pick one up from failure, disappointment, or rejection. The connected person can never fall very far because there are the lifelines of support to break the fall. The disconnected person, on the other hand, dangles precariously, held in place only by the strength of his own arm.

—From *Connections* by Edward M. Hallowell, M.D.

Chapter 4.

The Quest for Connections

Lessons from Geese by Milton Olson

1. *As each goose flaps its wings, it creates an "uplift" for the birds that follow. By flying in a V formation, the whole flock adds 72 percent greater flying range than if each bird flew alone.* LESSON: People who share a common direction and sense of community can get where they are going quicker and easier because they are traveling on the thrust of one another.

2. *When a goose falls out of formation, it suddenly feels the drag and resistance of flying alone and quickly gets back into formation to take advantage of the "lifting" power of the bird immediately in front.* LESSON: If we have as much sense as a goose, we will stay in formation with those who are headed where we want to go (and be willing to accept their help as well as give ours to the others).

3. *When the lead goose tires, it rotates back into the formation and another goose flies to the point position.* LESSON: It pays to take turns doing the hard tasks, and shar-

ing leadership—with people. As with geese we are interdependent on each other.

4. *The geese flying in formation honk to encourage those up front to keep up their speed.* LESSON: We need to make sure our honking from behind is encouraging, not something else.

5. *When a goose gets sick, wounded, or shot down, two geese drop out of formation and follow it down to help and protect it. They stay with it until it dies or is able to fly again. Then they launch out on their own, with another formation, or catch up with the flock.* LESSON: If we have as much sense as geese we too will stand by each other in difficult times as well as when we are strong.

POPULARITY

One thing that begins to develop in middle childhood and is usually in full bloom by adolescence is a sense of social consciousness—an awareness of where you stand in relation to significant groups in your life. As you grow up, your identity gradually shifts from being exclusively a member of a family to more immediately being a member of a larger, less homogeneous peer group. Gradually that shift will continue until you actually become an independent, adult member of both your family and your peer group. In the meantime, establishing your role and identity with people your own age takes on increasing importance. Friendships, social status, and popularity help you define your new identity outside of the family.

This is not always a simple or confidence-producing process, however. Not only are you occasionally feeling anxious and inadequate, so is everyone else. While confidence and security breed compassion, openness, and tolerance, insecurity tends to breed competition, awkwardness, and exclusion. Small groups may form which become closed to people not directly associated with the group. Individuals may be judged by what they wear, who they hang out with, and their physical appearance or social behavior rather than their personal qualities. There is safety in numbers, so many people spend their time trying to blend in or be the person they think everyone else would approve. To one degree or another, everyone else is doing the same thing, so it is difficult to know exactly who is approving of whom and who is setting the expectations.

UNTITLED *by Drew Walton*

Joe Cool

I have been working for two years now on understanding the essence of being totally cool. This is no small science because I have discovered that coolness changes with time and occasion, not to mention school, group, individuals, and whim. You have surely noticed that what freshman boys think is cool is rarely appreciated by sophomore girls, and what sophomore girls think is cool is often looked down on by senior girls. Cool dudes in California look, dress, talk, and act totally different from cool gang leaders or cool New England debutantes. What is seen as *way cool* at your rival high school is frequently quite dorky by your own school standards. In some places, to be "hot" is cool and to be "bad" is good. And we won't even go into what your parents look like when they are trying to be cool.

Hairstyles, clothing, music, slang, and what needs to be pierced all revolve in what I call a *coolish fad cycle*. Something is wildly cool for a certain period of time until everyone gets tired of it or something cooler comes along; then it is lame. Nothing stays cool indefinitely. I haven't been able to establish anything that cool fads have in common except that the cool people are wearing, saying, or piercing them. And sometimes, the really cool people can take a dorky look and make it cool. And really uncool people can make a cool fad passé. This is completely unfair since it makes it virtually impossible to pass from uncool to cool status by doing or buying cool things, contrary to what advertising may tell us.

That takes us back to the basic unanswered question of what makes a person cool or uncool. Looks help, but there are definitely some very funny looking cool people and some very attractive people that just don't make the cut. Being nice is nice, but it isn't always cool. Some cool people are real jerks. In some schools, it is cool to be smart, while in other schools, smart people are definitely uncool. Jocks are usually cool, but it can depend on the sport and how well your team is doing. In each of these categories, there are people who manage to be cool and others who do the same things without ever achieving coolness.

This brings up the old chicken and the egg question: Do cool people make things cool or do cool things make people cool? My observations suggest that cool people make things cool, but what makes the cool people cool in the first place? The only thing I can figure is that cool people confidently *think* they are cool. But does thinking you are cool automatically make you cool? To think you are cool when you are not can definitely get ugly. And does worrying about whether or not you are cool automatically make you uncool? Surely, even the coolest cool person occasionally doubts his or her coolness.

Movies sometimes represent cool people as shallow, stuck-up snobs while the hero is a decent, abused loser. That certainly appeals to the underdog in all of us, but it doesn't make high school any easier or coolness any less coveted. We are told what music is cool by top-ten charts, MTV, and radio stations, but then, the movies about the talented, but uncool recording stars explain that the media is pretty much bought by the production companies and we hear and buy what the agents have decided is cool. That doesn't seem cool.

Advertisers would have you believe that a cool person is anyone who buys *their* product and that you too can become cool if you do, but we have already decided that that is not true. No matter what you buy, even the people that sold it to you will announce that it is soon out of style—read *uncool*—and you must buy the new, improved model to be truly cool. That promise keeps cycling until you run out of money and are left broke and uncool.

This leads us to another strange pattern that I have studied. Cool people often seek out some obscure, unknown thing to be cool—something only the cool people know about. It is like a password or secret signal. Only cool people shop or eat at a particular little out-of-the-way place. Only cool people drive a certain car, listen to a certain kind of music, or wear a little known but marvelous (usually expensive) brand of clothing. Companies try to capitalize on signaling coolness by subtly pasting their name brand all over your clothes. The catch is, that when too many people discover that shop or music or activity or jeans, it is no longer cool. It has to remain privileged information. The cool people quickly move on to a newer secret coolness, leaving the rest of us trying to get the uncool labels off our T-shirts.

The one constant that I have noticed is that cool people hang out in groups. If you are not hanging out with cool people, it will be very difficult to be cool. There are always a few cool loners, but if your friends are not cool, you will have a hard time achieving coolness. It is also uncool to abandon a friend just because he is uncool, so this is a tricky situation. You are either somehow miraculously born into a cool group or you must somehow earn your way into a cool group without doing anything uncool to get there. In fact, it seems coolest to not care if you are in a cool group at all. People who are trying to be cool are definitely not cool, hence the ultimate uncool label, "wannabe."

And actually, I have not observed a great deal of switching between cool and uncool groups. I hate to be discouraging, but it appears to be easier for cool people to become uncool than the other way around. The encouraging factor is that with time, the boundaries seem to blur a bit. Seniors seem to be less worried about coolness than freshman, and I have heard that unless you are in a fraternity or sorority, coolness in the college scene is not that important at all. Some very uncool freshman seem to become very cool seniors without doing anything at all—and as Bill Gates is always pleased to admonish, "Be nice to the nerds; you will be working for one of them some day." Coolness appears to have no real long-term reliability or predictability.

All this reminds me of the Dr. Seuss story that I used to read when I was a kid about the Sneetches.[1] There were these funny looking Sneetches that hung out on the beaches, only some of them had stars on their bellies and some of them did not. The star-bellied Sneetches were the cool ones—they walked around the book with their noses in the air and wouldn't let the ones without "stars upon thars" come to their frankfurter roasts. I could never figure out why the Sneetches without stars didn't just have their own frankfurter roasts, but they just moped around feeling uncool. Then this dude called Sylvester McMonkey McBean comes into town with this big machine that can put stars on bellies, so all the uncool Sneetches pay him some money (sound familiar?) and get cool stars put on their bellies so they can be cool. But hey, what did I tell you, as soon as they get stars on their bellies, the star bellied Sneetches decide that stars are no longer cool. So Sylvester helps them take off their stars (for a price, of course) so that they can remain cool. Then it gets all crazy because the Sneetches keep putting stars on and taking stars off, Sylvester is getting rich, and nobody can remember who was cool and who wasn't—exactly the problem I was having coming up with what made somebody cool in the first place. Sylvester took off with all the money, thinking you can't teach a Sneetch not to be so gullible and superficial. But the Sneetches fooled him and stopped caring whether they had a star or not.

I can't see that happening in my high school in the near future. The only thing about coolness that I have figured out for sure is that truly cool people don't worry about the essence of being totally cool, so all my research has unequivocally put me in the uncool camp. Oh well, who knows, maybe someday being uncool will be the new cool thing to be.

GENDER

One group that everyone in the world belongs to is a gender group. You are either a male or a female, and there are many different expectations that go along with each of these roles. The first thing that we want to know about a little baby is the gender. Observation and research have shown that we then begin immediately to treat this baby differently. We actually hold boy and girl babies differently, talk to them differently, and use words like "pretty" or "strong" according to their gender. We surround baby girls with pink and yellow, colors that may actually stimulate verbal development. We tend to give boys action toys that encourage high activity and competition while girls receive dolls and homemaking toys that encourage nurturing and caretaking. Parents expect boys to be more active and aggressive and unconsciously tolerate more noise and competition from their sons than from their daughters. They are more likely to help their daughters when asked and encourage their sons to try harder and do it for themselves. Parents tend to tolerate "tomboy" behavior in girls, but react strongly to "sissy" behavior in boys. By age five, children have already developed clearly defined notions of what is appropriate behavior for women and for men. In school, teachers tend to encourage boys to speak out and learn to be independent, whereas girls are most often rewarded for being neat, well behaved, and cooperative.

It is difficult to be aware of the messages that we learn about being male or female because they are so ingrained in our social environment and upbringing. It is diffi-

cult to realize that our curriculum and expectations focus almost exclusively on a white, heterosexual, male perspective because that is the way it has usually been in our culture. While we tend to think of sexism as exclusively a problem for women, rigid gender stereotyping is detrimental to any individual. Males and females can be caught by the prejudices and expectations of gender roles, which specify and limit how they feel, what they do, or who they may become. Sexism is not strictly a matter of power, but also of personal freedom and expression. In the long run, the price that men pay for power in a patriarchal society may be as debilitating as the loss of personal power is for women. Both the women's and men's movements are attempting to help men and women be conscious of the limitations of rigid sex roles and envision more flexible ways of being and relating to each other.

"VICTORIA" *by Kim Kern*

Aisha

Let's Get Rid of "The Girl"
Wouldn't 1979 be a great year to take one giant step forward and get rid of
"the girl"?
Your attorney says, "If I'm not here, just leave it with the girl."
The purchasing agent says, "Drop off your bid with the girl."
A manager says, "My girl will get back to your girl."
What girl?
Do they mean Miss Rose?
Do they mean Ms. Torres?
Do they mean Mrs. McCullough?
Do they mean Joy Jackson?
"The Girl" is certainly a woman when she's out of her teens.
Like you, she has a name.
Use it. (Author unknown)

For three years, this poem has been proudly displayed on my best friend's wall, and every time I see it I have an extreme sense of pride in what is says about women and society. Even though there have been a lot of changes since the '70s, I am able to identify with this poem—as I am sure many women can—even today. Not only does it represent the struggle that the women in my family went through, but it also reminds me of the strength that they possessed and which I hope to adopt from them someday.

It links me to my history because I know how hard my grandmother fought in order to gain respect, not only as an African American, but also as a woman. Many times she has told me about her fight to be thought of as an equal in the work force. She had a problem getting her coworkers to take her seriously. They thought of her as an immature, emotional, dramatic girl, instead of a woman who was a wife and mother and professional who deserved their respect. This was especially hard for her because she was forced to deal with the lack of respect that came with her race at that time. When men called her "girl," she knew that it wasn't just because of her gender, but because she was African American. In her early years, even women called her "girl" while she scrubbed their floors. She told me about how hard it was to lift her head high while she shook with anger and frustration, but now she speaks of this with pride instead of bitterness.

The struggle raged on with my mother. It took a lot of strength to raise three children as a single parent in law school and for years after that. She had to rush home at night—not to relax, but to sell clothing at the mall until it closed. But it was something that she knew she had to do in order to become the kind of person she knew she could be.

I don't want to seem bitter in any way about the hardships that my family dealt with. Instead, I want to convey that this poem makes me feel strong and proud of the fact that these women would not settle for the status of a "girl" presented to them. They chose the harder route in order to be happy and satisfied with themselves.

I am still a "girl," but this poem reminds me of the shoes that I must fill. I need to be focused because even though the struggle has changed, I know that I want to adopt the pride, dignity, and determination that my mother and grandmother possessed.

—Written by Aisha Dawson, 1995

Katherine

When in 1969 I became publisher of the (Washington) Post as well as president of the company, my plate was fuller than ever. I had partly worked myself into the job, but not, except for rare occasions, taken hold. I had acquired some sense of business, but still relied on others more than most company presidents did. One article written about me that appeared fully five years after I'd gone to work said, "Mrs. Graham accepts her responsibilities much more often than she asserts her authority." That was true; I didn't always take charge or handle my relationships with people throughout the company in the coolest or best way. My expectations far exceeded my accomplishments. In fact, the years from the mid-1960's to the mid-1970's, rich and full as they were, were depressing for me in many ways.

I seemed to be carrying inadequacy as baggage. When I thought about my uncertainty and nervousness, a scene from the first musical comedy I'd ever seen, "The Vagabond King," kept recurring to me. There is a moment when the suddenly enthroned vagabond, appearing for the first time in royal robes, slowly and anxiously descends the great stairs, tensely eyeing on both sides the rows of archers with their drawn bows and inscrutable faces. I still felt like a pretender to the throne, very much on trial. I felt I was always taking an exam and would fail if I missed a single answer; a direct question about something like Newsweek's newsstand circulation would flummox me completely.

What most got in the way of my doing the kind of job I wanted to do was my insecurity. Partly this arose from my particular experience, but to the extent that it stemmed from the narrow way women's roles were defined, it was a trait shared my most women in my generation. We had been brought up to believe that our roles were to be wives and mothers, educated to think that we were put on earth to make men happy and comfortable and to do the same for our children.

I adopted the assumption of many of my generation that women were intellectually inferior to men, that we were not capable of governing, leading, managing, anything but our homes and our children. Once married, we were confined to running houses, providing a smooth atmosphere, dealing with children, supporting our husbands. Pretty soon this kind of thinking—indeed, this kind of life—took its toll; most of us became somehow inferior. We grew less able to keep up with what was happening in the world. In a group we remained largely silent, unable to participate in conversations and discussions. Unfortunately, this incapacity often produced in women—as it did in me—a diffuse way of talking, an inability to be concise, a tendency to ramble, to start at the end and work backwards, to over explain, to go on for too long, to apologize.

Women traditionally also have suffered—and many still do—from an exaggerated desire to please, a syndrome so instilled in women of my generation that it inhibited my behavior for many years, and in ways still does. Although at the time I didn't realize what was happening, I was unable to make a decision that might displease those around me. For years, whatever directive I may have issued ended with the phrase "if it's all right with you." If I thought I'd done anything to make someone unhappy, I'd agonize. . . .

When I first went to work, I was still handicapped with the old assumptions and was operating as through they were written in stone. When I started my job, I was "inferior" to the men with whom I was working. I had no business experience, no management experience, and little knowledge of the governmental, economic, political, or other matters with which we dealt. I truly felt like Samuel Johnson's description of a woman minister—"a woman preaching is like a dog's walking on this hinder legs. It is not done well; but you are surprised to find it done at all."

—From *Personal History* by Katharine Graham[2]

Malcolm

- *Every four hours, an American black child is killed by a gun.*

- *More young black men are murdered each year in this country—most of them by guns and each other—than were killed by lynching in all the inglorious years of its history.*

- *Youth violence takes more than twice as many American lives every year as cancer, heart disease, and car accidents combined.*

- *In 1990, there were 22 handgun deaths in Great Britain, 68 in Canada, 87 in Japan, and 10,567 in the United States.*

- *During the 1980s arrests for drug abuse among black juveniles rose by more than 150 percent.*

- *Well over half of America's black children live without a father in the household, twice the rate of 1970, twice the rate of Hispanic children, and more than three times the rate of white children.*

- *Nearly half of the black children in this country (46 percent) live in poverty.*

- *Every eleven minutes, a black juvenile is arrested for a violent crime.*

- *Of the black men between ages twenty-five and thirty-four who have dropped out of high school, 75 percent are in prison or on parole or probation.*

- *Although blacks make up only 12.4 percent of the general population of the United States, they constitute more than 50 percent of the inmate population. In the city jails in San Francisco, blacks outnumber whites by a ratio of fourteen to one.*

I hold tightly to the belief that inner-city teenagers can be taught and raised in such a way that they don't have to become part of the wantonness swirling around them. They can be persuaded to steer clear of guns when everyone else is packing M.A.C.-10s, to stay sober when everyone else is drinking forties; to stay clean when everyone else is either selling crack or smoking it, if not both. . . .

What makes this possible is the peculiar fact that the players of the urban game actually hate the game they play. Although few show it and fewer admit it, many of them inwardly despise the violence and the degradation that rule the neighborhoods and bring so much anger and pain to them, their families, and their friends. They join the game only because they can't beat it, or more to the point, because they *think* they can't beat it. Because it's all they see, they think it's all there is. . . . The homie does these things because, unlike me thirty-something years ago, he has no fortification against an environment that has escalated its attack upon him. He inhabits a different world than I did. He faces serious unemployment issues that discourage the legal work ethic it takes to compete in mainstream American society. He has to deal with weapons of war that have been literally dumped on the streets of America—AK-47s, Uzis, nine millimeters, glocks, M.A.C.-10s. But most of all, he has to deal with crack cocaine, the worst thing to hit the black American since slavery. Hell, crack is worse than slavery. Crack cocaine pulls young men into the illegal work ethic— some as young as age nine or ten—and most of them never manage to get out of it, ending up dead or in jail. But there is something even more pernicious, even more insidious, about crack. Crack has been able to do something even slavery couldn't do: It has stopped the African-American woman from mothering her child. Imagine that—a force stronger than motherhood. The effects of crack are nothing short of unbelievable.

So here sits the homie with a daddy he never sees, hardly knows, and deeply resents. Hell, Daddy's probably in prison anyway. Mom's home being both Mom and Dad, but too often now she's strung out herself, buried too deep in her own problems to worry about fixing snacks or checking the book bag when her son gets home from school. And dude's angry about that because he knows he's getting screwed. Other adults, meanwhile—the extended community—well, they're scared to death of him because he's been terrorizing them from the age of thirteen.

So the homie goes where people are there for him, at least ostensibly. He goes to the streets to hang out with the other brothers, who have nobody at home, either, and who share the same problems. As a group—a gang, a set, a clique, a posse, whatever you want to call it—the lot of them try to be for each other what they desperately need in their lives: men. Of course, they don't know how to do that because nobody's shown them.[3]

. . . Under these influences, I was impelled to do the most radical thing I'd ever done. I picked up a book about Malcolm X. Malcolm had been murdered early in 1965, and although the event had little effect on me, I was still curious about the man. All I knew of him was what I'd read in the newspapers, which depicted him as a raging, conflicted militant. I suppose it was all the commotion over Malcolm that intrigued me, and I figured that if I understood *him* a little, I might understand the times a little bit. What I hadn't counted on was that by understanding Malcolm a little, I would come to understand myself a lot.

I started out with *Malcolm X Speaks*. For me, that was Black Man 101. Through *Malcolm X Speaks,* I began to see that the public portrayal of Malcolm, by the press and policy makers, was completely simplistic, mainly erroneous, and grossly self-serving. I was exposed to points of view regarding Malcolm that I hadn't glimpsed through the mainstream channels, and it made me angry that the media had so distorted and shortchanged this great brilliant man. My response was to read *The Autobiography of Malcolm X*. With that, my life changed.

Traditionally, if you're a young black person in this country, you know that something's wrong, but you don't know exactly what it is. Malcolm showed me what it is. He explained the rage through the triumph and tragedy, the achievement and oppression, the dignity and degradation of black history. He explained it with bold, chilling logic. As I turned the pages of that incredible book, Malcolm showed me why it was that a group of black kids who didn't even know me had beaten me up over a baseball game when I was eleven years old. He showed me why the vice-principal at Layola High had virtually endorsed the football player's racist, verbal attack on me. He showed me why South Central Los Angeles was so menacing, even then, why kids who lived just a few blocks from me, who by all appearances were just like me—the same nappy hair and everything—scared the hell out of me. He showed me why none of my neighborhood friends joined me in college. *The Autobiography of Malcolm X* unlocked the door for me and flung it wide open.

After reading Malcolm, I realized that my Catholic education—which, in this respect, was no different from public education—had included absolutely nothing about me as a black man. I had never even heard of Booker T. Washington or Frederick Douglas or W.E.B Du Bois or Paul Roberson. The only black person mentioned in my history classes was George Washington Carver, the peanut doctor, and he was recognized, no doubt, because of his contributions to the mainstream (that is, white) economy. It was as if black history were of no real significance whatsoever, which implied, in turn that black people were of no real significance. Malcolm not only enlightened me about black history, but he turned me on to the fundamental fact that there *was* black history. More than that, he showed me how that great and scandalous history was still playing itself out in our homes and in our schools and in our communities and in our minds. From the tribal abductions to the planter's libido to the Klansman's hood to the brother's habit, he put it all in perspective—oh God, did he ever. Many of the things he wrote have since become so ingrained in my consciousness that they seem elementary to me now, but in 1966 I'd never read or heard anything like, for example, Malcolm's explanation of the black American's cultural emasculation, as described in part through his conversations in prison.

"I began first telling my black brother inmates about the glorious history of the black man—things they never had dreamed," he wrote. "I told them the horrible slavery-trade truths that they never knew. I would watch their faces when I told them that because the white man had completely erased the slaves' past, a Negro in America can never know his true family name, or even what tribe he was descended from; the Mandingos, the Wolof, the Serer, the Fula, the Fanti, the Ashanti, or others. I told them that some slaves brought from Africa spoke Arabic, and were Islamic in their religion. A lot of those black convicts still wouldn't believe it unless they could see that a white man had said it. So, often, I would read to those brothers selected passages from white men's books. I'd explain to them that the real truth was known to some white men, the scholars; but there had been a conspiracy down through the generations to keep the truth from black men. . . .

"It's a crime, the lie that has been sold to generations of black men and white men both. Little innocent black children, born of parents who believed that their race had no history. Little black children seeing, before they could talk, that their parents considered themselves inferior. Innocent black children growing up, living out their lives, dying of old age—and all of their lives ashamed of being black."

With my stomach growling for more black history, my next book was *Before the Mayflower*. I devoured it. There was my heritage right in my lap, like a lost chapter of the Bible. I was enthralled, and the deeper I plunged into my discovery, the more piqued I became over the white man's reconfiguration of history, over his systematic attempt to dupe me and my race, depriving us of knowledge that would make us proud of our culture. When I found out that George Washington had owned slaves, I thought, "You've got to be kidding." I had the same reaction upon reading that Abraham Lincoln had favored deporting blacks to Central America. . . .

In Richard Wright's *Native Son*, I found the rage of the black man searingly conveyed, but even so, it was Malcolm who explained to me, first and always, why the rage was there. The more I read, the more I realized that Malcolm's writings, Malcolm's lessons and logic, hit me harder than anyone else's and made the most sense. My father had taught me how to be a man, but Malcolm taught me how to be a black man.[4]

—From *Street Soldier: One Man's Struggle to Save a Generation—One Life at a Time* by Joseph Marshall, Jr.

Joseph Marshall is the executive director of the Omega Boys Club in Oakland, CA, based on the belief that young people of the inner city want a way out of the life they're in, but just don't know how to get out. The Omega Boys Club provides young black males with time, information, and strong male role models to help them imagine a different way and reclaim their heritage. For years, Joe responded to calls on a weekly radio program called "Street Soldiers," answering tough questions about gangs, drugs, teen pregnancy, and the many pressures of inner-city life.

"FACES" by Milee Uhm

RACIAL AND ETHNIC DIFFERENCES

As we begin to define who we are, our ethnic and racial background may play a surprising role in how we view ourselves and how others view us. In part, this is the way we look, the way we have been raised, and the music, food, and customs that we are accustomed to. The impact of how other people and our culture view us, however, can be more baffling. This has always been a part of our lives, but as we attempt to establish our independence and uniqueness, social stereotypes and expectations may seem contrary to what we know and believe about ourselves. As superficial as these definitions may seem, they define our reality in subtle yet appreciable ways.

Carol

I never really felt that I was a member of a "race." I was white and all of my friends were white and that seemed like a very normal thing to be. As a member of the majority in my world, I assumed that I was the norm and it was *other* people who had a race. I couldn't imagine how my race influenced and shaped who I was—I never even thought about it.

After I graduated from high school, I joined VISTA—Volunteers in Service to America, the domestic Peace Corps—and I moved into a black neighborhood near downtown Cleveland. Almost all the people I saw or spoke to or bought my groceries from or waited at the bus stop with were black. The people on the billboards were black and they were selling products for black skin or black hair. I stood out with my pale skin and blonde hair. People noticed me when I walked down the street—not because of what I was wearing or what I did, but because I was *white*. For the first time in my life, I was consciously aware of my skin. When I met people in the neighborhood, I discovered that most of them brought with them some preconceived notion of what I would be like—some version of white. I wasn't just a "girl" anymore; I was a "white girl." Some were suspicious of me; some wanted to hit on me; some couldn't look me in the eye; some wouldn't speak to me; some seemed like they felt sorry for me. I felt like I glowed. As I got to know a few of my neighbors more personally, my whiteness faded a little bit, but it would never completely go away again.

Cleveland gets hot in the summer and there was a city pool practically across the street from my house. I had avoided the pool because a bathing suit provided no cover for my white skin and the pool was full of strong, glistening black arms and legs and laughing children. I would most definitely be "the white girl." The day the temperature reached 100 degrees, I decided I could hold out no longer. So I was white . . . I had the right to swim too. I admit that I was nervous, but stubborn too. I walked across the street, paid my dollar and walked over to the pool, trying not to meet any of the bemused, curious, friendly, or hostile eyes that watched me. It was a strange sensation to do a perfectly normal thing and yet stand out so distinctly because of the color of my skin. I tried to smile and act like being white had nothing to do with anything. I puttered around, cooling off, trying not to lose my confidence.

Suddenly I felt someone grab my foot and pull me under the water and hold me down. I struggled and got free easily enough, but was totally unnerved, embarrassed, and furious. I turned around to watch a nine- or ten-year-old boy rapidly swimming away to a group of his friends who were laughing and high-fiving each other. Why would he do that and why did they think it was funny? I had done nothing and he knew absolutely nothing about me—except that I was white. Or did it have anything to do with being white? What else could it be? How could anyone hate or mock me just because of the color of my skin?

It was the first time that I grasped how it felt to be an anonymous member of a "race" and how profoundly it determined the assumptions that some people attached to who I was. And that part of being white had been the luxury of being oblivious to my own skin.

Jose

At my old school, I was president of the student body. I gave my nomination speech in Spanish. My English is good, but the speech was a point of pride and solidarity among the students. Most of us were Mexican. Most of the teachers and administrators were not. I did well in school and my principal said he thought I should consider going to a private school. It would be a great opportunity to get a good education and get accepted at a good university. My parents were very proud. They do not speak much English, but they have worked very hard to make sure that my brothers, sisters, and I have all the good American opportunities. My grandmother wept and said I did not need a gringo education; I would forget my family and my culture and be lost to them. My friends laughed and made fun of me. Why would I want to go to the rich boys' school? Just to chase the rich white girls? I would become a *malinchista*, a traitor to my culture.

I guess I went to please my mother, but also because I could. I wanted to see what it would be like. I want to go to a good college. I want to show everyone—even me—that I can do it. I guess I get along OK. I do well in my classes and have made friends with many people. When other guys make jokes about Mexicans, they punch my arm and say "Not you, dummy. You are different." Sometimes I am embarrassed and laugh along with them. Other times, I am embarrassed that I don't stand up and say, "No, I am NOT different." Other times I am afraid that I am *becoming* different. I am proud of my race and my people, but I am not making speeches in Spanish any more.

Tiffany

My body looks Korean, but my life has been American in every way that I know. I was two months old when they flew me from Korea and I was adopted by my American family—the only family I have ever known. I have never seen Korea nor do I know my Korean parents or any other Koreans, really, except a family at the Korean restaurant in town. I never thought anything about it when I was little. It was just my family and my life. I love my family and they always taught me that being Korean was special and that they were very lucky to have me in their family. I remember when I was a child, I used to make up a language and tell my parents that it was Korean. I taught it to my dolls and translated for my parents—my private world of imagination and wonder.

I think it was when I went to school that I felt different for the first time. It surprised me—I felt just like everyone else in my class, but some of the other children seemed to be curious about the way I looked. One day, a boy on the playground called me "slanty eyes." I didn't know what he meant, so I asked my mother when I got home. She was so angry. I didn't feel angry; I just thought it was funny that I looked different to some people from who I was—like wearing a costume on Halloween. It seemed funny that it fooled other people. When I got to be older, occasionally even my good friends would comment that they thought I looked irritated or angry. I never understood what they meant until I realized that it was that my eyes were shaped differently from theirs—to them it looked like I was upset. Fooled again. I even met a Korean girl at camp who had cosmetic surgery to change the shape of her eyes to look more "American." I think I know how she felt, but it seemed superficial and unsettling that she would have surgery in order to fit in.

Most of the time, I don't think much about it, but my appearance is a real part of my life, just like being a blonde or tall with freckles. Most of my friends are Caucasian Americans and we have been friends so long that none of us think much about the way we look. We all giggle when we meet a stranger who tells me I speak such good English or asks where I am from. When Korea comes up in the news, I am interested, but I don't really know much more than any other American. When it is a negative story or event, I feel a confusing mix of shame and defensiveness, though I don't really know why. I am just a regular daughter, niece, and grandchild in my family even though nobody else looks like me, but it doesn't really matter. I sometimes think about who I will marry and what my child will look like—I almost think he or she will come out white.

I sometimes wonder what it means to be Korean. Is there something in my blood that will pop out and make me Korean? Are there ethnic traits or talents that are lurking in my genes? Sometimes it all seems so foreign and superficial; other times I try to search my mind and heart to find my Koreanness. Mostly, I feel just like my American-looking friends—except that people don't expect them to be Korean.

Someday I want to go to Korea and see what it is like there. I wonder how I will feel.

Billy

I had a great childhood. My family owns a large avocado and lemon ranch in southern California and I had 400 acres to explore and run around. The Mexican workers were always very nice to me and let me steer the tractor or catch a ride in the back of a truck. We lived way out in the country, but there were always about twelve families who lived on our ranch behind the orchards, so there were plenty of children for me to play with. Salvador and Pepe were my closest friends. We built a big tree house back in the old orchard that had real glass windows and a ladder we could pull up to keep the animals and girls out. Sometimes our parents would let us spend the night there and we would listen to the coyotes and tell scary stories to each other. Salvador was the oldest and he would tell stories of his parent's village back in Mexico. He told us about the Day of the Dead and how all the families would gather and spend the day picnicking and telling old stories in the graveyards of their dead family members. I was scared even to walk by the old graveyard near the ranch, so Salvador's stories seemed pretty brave to me.

In the late summer, the migrants would come to help us pick. Salvador, Pepe, and I would take charge of all the children. We staged battles and adventures and felt like kings of our empire.

Then the summer of my twelfth year, everything changed. One day, my dad called me in to his ranch office. He told me the old story of how my grandfather first settled this ranch and how one day I would be in charge of taking care of the land and carrying on the family name. I knew this old story by heart, but I still loved to hear it. He talked about the responsibility of running this ranch and taking care of the land and all the people who depended on it. He told me that I must work hard in school and go to a good college to learn the business of it. That I must always be fair and appreciative of all the people who worked here so that they would honor my leadership—I was given the opportunity by blood, but I must earn their respect through hard work and fairness.

Then he told me that I was too old to be playing with the Mexican children anymore. One day, Salvador would grow up to be our ranch manager and he must learn to respect my authority as his boss, not his little friend. I could not argue with my father, but I knew this was silly. Salvador was two years older than me and we would always be best friends, no matter what our jobs were.

But after this talk, I noticed that Salvador and Pepe were too busy to play and when I called out to them, they glanced down and pulled away. Had my father spoken to them too? Could they believe that I would actually do what my father said? Why did they suddenly treat me like a stranger? I tried to talk to them, but they just shrugged and said they were busy.

The next year, I went away to boarding school. Salvador dropped out of school and now works full time at the ranch. My dad says he is a good worker and learns quickly. When I am home on vacation, I hardly ever see him. One time I went back to the cabins where the workers live to get someone for my father. When I walked away, I heard the older boys laugh and make a joke in Spanish. I caught Salvador's eye, but he just shrugged and looked back to his friends. How could everything between us disappear? I never thought he would mock me or betray our friendship. But now he is Mexican and I am white. I guess my dad was right.

Kimberly

I was born in North Carolina where my father teaches at the University and my mother works for an insurance agency. We go to the Presbyterian church and have lived in the same town for two generations. I have a strong southern accent, which always surprises people because I am Japanese American. We are the only Japanese Americans in my town and most of my relatives live in New York City. Sometimes the kids in my school would tease me because I looked different, but mostly they were used to me. We grew up together.

I have always wanted to be a pediatrician and work in some of the Appalachian areas where they don't have many doctors. I work hard in school and am applying to colleges that have a premed program. I am ranked second in my class, play two varsity sports, volunteer at the local retirement home, and am a National Merit Scholar honorable mention. I have always done well in school and worked hard to write a good college application and essay. The school I want to go to has a really good premed program that practically guarantees that I will get into a good medical school. In my college interview, the representative was very nice and said that while my application was strong, I should apply to other schools as well because it was an especially difficult school to get into for Asians—they had many Asian students apply each year and had to limit the number that they would accept so that the school did not become overbalanced with Asian students.

I didn't know what to say. I felt angry and confused. I am just an individual person. It seems so strange to have this cultural label suddenly have such power in my life. People look at me or see "Japanese American" on my application and think they know who I am.

Lorenzo

Because I have been able to withstand the pressures of attending boarding school far from my home, I have always thought of myself as being independent. I developed the notion that I was a lone person in my educational and emotional battles, relatively unconnected or unaligned to anything other than myself. This summer, an impromptu trip to a place I'd known all my life made me realize how wrong the perceptions I had of my life really were. Though I am proud of my independence, that day I also realized how proud I am that I have taken part in a long history that, in many respects, is now disappearing.

As I rode in the gray, compact car my father had rented, I looked forward to seeing *El Salao* again. During the trip, I recalled my childhood images of the small pueblo town, perching lazily on a dry, dusty, and otherwise unremarkable bluff on the southern plains of Colorado. It is called *El Salao* because of the creek that runs through it. I recalled the story my grandfather once told me, in which he referred to it as the "black creek," partly because a nearby oil refinery had dumped its flowing entrails into it years ago, but also because he once experienced a great loss there. When he was near my age, his five-year-old brother was pulled into the watery depths of the black creek; my grandfather tried his best to swim against the current to save him, but he couldn't. This was why my mother had insisted that I learn to swim at an early age.

My father and I were going to *El Salao* from a nearby city to drop off a gift for my aunt and we were only going to be there for about ten minutes. As the car pulled to a stop in front of my aunt's house, I opened the door and walked toward the river, my eyes resting on the hill in the distance. It was crowned by three telephone poles that called to mind images of Golgatha. While my grandfather called the river the black creek, most everybody else called it *El Salao,* for the tears that the Indian women cried as their babies were thrown into the raging arms of the river, in retribution for Ute attacks on settlers. On the knobby hill called "the Ute," my great-uncle had found two babies' skeletons while digging holes for the telephone poles that were later to go in. Those three poles now stood solemnly, marking the small graves, which everyone in the town regarded as sacred.

These stories never scared me or angered me. They merely provided a quiet backdrop for a town that held for me many intimate memories. My eyes wandered from place to place as I thought about each of the town relics. From the unsightly bottle-ridden dirt field that I stood in, where years before my grandfather had played baseball (and more recently I had played football) to the nearby church, haunted by a piano-playing ghost called *El Cowboy* who refused to leave the saloon his home had once been. To my right was the gaping entrance to the underground tunnels where thieves' treasure was supposedly hidden. I recalled my first fights, loves, games, small triumphs, and friendships made there—in a town that I knew was dying.

Only two families live there now; the rest have gone off to the cities, to find better jobs and homes. I was invaded with a deep sense of loss at this, my town—that even through the tears of its beginning, had managed to live. I felt the undying human need to be connected to something greater than myself. As I got back into the waiting car, I felt as if every ghost in *El Salao* was looking at me, and as I shut the door, I wondered if I was the only one who felt the loss of this place.

It was sunset when we passed the old cemetery. I kept my eyes on the rose bushes that framed its boundaries. The Aztecs believed that tears, wars, poetry, and flowers were all part of the same cycle of life. Life was all one thing: continuous, yet dying every day. I recalled the Nahuatl poem, written by an Aztec prince as he saw his city razed. *In otin ihuan in tonaltin nican tzonquica.* "Here ends the road and the days." That day was a beginning for me, the beginning of the realization that I was not just my independent self; I was a part of a history that was more ancient than I ever could be. As we drove away from the town, I was struck by how young I had been and how completely old I felt.

—Written by Lorenzo Moreno, 1996

"SELVES" by Claire Min

TO LIVE IN THE BORDERLANDS MEANS YOU

Are neither hispana India negra Espanola—
Ni gabach, eres mestiza, mulate, half-breed
Caught in the cross fire between camps
While carrying all five races on your back
Not knowing which side to turn to, run from;

To live in the Borderlands means knowing
That the india in you, betrayed for 500 years,
Is no longer speaking to you,
That mexicanas call you rajetas,
That denying the Anglo inside you
Is as bad as having denied the Indian or Black;

Cuando vives en la frontera
People walk through you, the wind steals your voice,

You're a burra, buey, a scapegoat,
Forerunner of a new race
Half and half—both woman and man, either—
A new gender;

To live in the Borderlands means to put chile in the borscht,
Eat whole wheat tortillas,
Speak Tex-Mex with a Brooklyn accent;
Be stopped by la migra at the border checkpoints.

Living in the Borderlands means you fight hard to
Resist the gold elixir beckoning from the bottle,
The pull of the gun barrel,
The rope crushing the hollow of your throat.

In the Borderlands
You are the battleground
Where enemies are kin to each other;

You are at home, a stranger,
The border disputes have been settled
The volley of shots have shattered the truce
You are wounded, lost in action,
Dead, fighting back.
To live in the Borderlands means
The mill with the razor white teeth wants to shred off
Your olive-red skin, crush out the kernel, your heart
Pound you, pinch you, roll you out
Smelling like white bread but dead.
To survive the Borderlands
You must live sin fronteras
Be a crossroads.

—From *Borderlands/La Frontera: The New Mestiza* by Gloria Anzaldua

FRIENDSHIP

Men Have Buddies, But No Real Friends

My friends have no friends. They are men. They think they have friends, and if you ask them whether they have friends, they will say yes, but they don't really. They think, for instance, that I'm their friend, but I'm not. It's OK. They're not my friends either.

The reason for that is that we are all men—and men, I have come to believe, cannot or will not have real friends. They have something else: companions, buddies, pals, chums, someone to drink with and someone to wench with and some one to lunch with, but no one when it comes to saying how they feel—especially how they hurt.

Women know this. They talk about it among themselves. I heard one woman describe men as the true Third-World people—still not yet emerged. To women, this inability of men to say what they feel is a source of amazement and then anguish and then, finally, betrayal. Women will tell you all the time that they don't know the men they live with. They talk of long silences and drifting off and of keeping feelings hidden and never letting on that they are troubled or bothered or whatever.

If it's any comfort to women, they should know that it's nothing personal. Men treat other men the same way.

For instance, I know men who have suffered brutal professional setbacks and never mentioned it to their friends. I know of a guy who never told his best friend that his own son had a rare childhood disease. And I know others who never have sex with their wives, but talk to their friends as though they're living in the Playboy mansion, either pretending otherwise or saying nothing.

This is something men learn early. It is something I learned from my father, who taught me the way fathers teach sons to keep my emotions to myself. I watched him and learned from him. One day we went to the baseball game, cheered and ate and drank, and the next day he was taken to the hospital with yet another ulcer attack. He had several of them. My mother said he worried a lot, but I saw none of this.

Legend has it that men talk a lot about sex. They don't. They talk about it only in the sense that it is treated like sports. They joke about it and rate women from one to ten. But they almost never talk about it in a way that matters—the quality of it. They almost never talk in real terms, in terms other than a cartoon, in terms that apply to them and the woman with whom they have a relationship.

Women do talk that way. Women talk about fulfillment, and they admit—maybe complain is the better word—to nonexistent sex lives. No man would admit to virtually having no sex life, yet there are plenty who do.

When I was a kid, I believed that it was men who had real friendships and women who did not. This seemed to be the universal belief, and boys would talk about this. We wondered about girls, about what made them so catty that they could not have friendships, and we really thought we were lucky to be men and have real friends.

We thought our friendships would last forever; we talked about them in some sort of Three Musketeer fashion—all for one and one for all. If one of us needed help, all of us would come running. We are still friends, some of us, anyway, and I still feel that I will fight for them, but I don't think I could confide in them. No, not that.

Sometimes I think that men are walking relics—outmoded and outdated, programmed for some other age. We have all the essential qualities for survival in the wild and for success in battle, but we run like hell from talking about our feelings. We are, as the poet said in a different context, truly a thing of wonder.

Some women say that they have always had this ability to confide in one another, to talk freely. Others say that this is something relatively new, yet another benefit of the woman's movement. I don't know. All I know is that they have it, and most men don't, and even the men that do—the ones who can talk about how they feel— talk to women. Have we been raised to think of feelings and sentiment as feminine? Can a man talk intimately with another man and not wonder about his masculinity? I don't know. I do know it sometimes makes the other man feel uncomfortable.

I know this is a subject that concerns me, and yet I find myself bottling it all up, keeping it all in. I've been on automatic pilot for years now.

It would be nice to break out of it. It would be nice to join the rest of the human race, connect with others in a way that makes sense, in a way that's meaningful— in a way that's more than a dirty joke and a slap on the back. I wonder whether it can be done.

If it can, it will happen because women will insist on it, because they themselves have shown the way, come out of the closet as women, talked about it, organized, defined an agenda, set their goals and admitted that as women—just as women— they have problems in common. So do men. It's time to talk about them.

—By Richard Cohen, reprinted with permission by *Minneapolis Tribune,* January, 1980

This article raises some interesting questions about relationships, but it was written over twenty years ago. Here are some contemporary male reactions to the article and how men at different ages today related to the ideas in the article.

Yaseen, 21

Much truth is hidden between the lines of this man's statement. I can still remember much of my childhood being raised among four women and without a male figure ever there to teach me the countless lessons I had to learn. NO, my parents were not divorced. My father was present through it all. Physically, yes; emotionally, though . . . no.

It seems as if the only advice my father could ever provide me was virtually similar to what his father provided him. "If you're going to have sex, make sure the woman's a virgin. You don't want other people's leftovers. Ha-ha. . . . What do you mean you don't like to play sports? Are you gay or something? All men play sports, my son. You'll find the one you're good at. . . . I don't want my son to learn how to cook and clean like Martha Stewart." Basically, all I had to take in was baseless and useless tidbits of information my father collected over the years and he felt I, too, had to hear.

In grade school, I envied how all the girls use to get all together to play jump-rope or the latest version of "Who's got the cooties?" On the other hand, the male friends I had only liked to play boxing matches with one another or the sporadic game of basketball, usually ending with rock fights over who cheated and who actually won.

Here I am, a twenty-one-year-old male in college having big dreams about where I am and where I want to be. Yet with whom can I actually share these deep and provoking thoughts? True, like the writer, I have many male pals and buddies to whom I can call upon for answers to the last homework assignment or a workout partner at the gym. But can I truly confide in them my innermost secrets or desires? Should I finally tell them that I'd rather be reading a good book or magazine than going to the club and staring at scantily clad women I may never have a chance with? I don't know.

It is a commonly held misconception that "it's a man's world out there." If so, then why aren't men displaying signs of true happiness today? Locked within every man are countless thoughts, ideas, and confusions that they would like to bring to the surface so they may bring new meanings to their lives. Yet who can actually be there to listen—besides a woman, of course? Women seem to be the only beings on this earth who possess the qualities to hear a man out.

Nate, 22

I *do* have male friends, but only a few. I agree that a good majority of men do not share their feelings, or, if they do, it is only with women. But that stereotype is beginning to change. My fiancée tells me that I am very good at sharing my feelings. In fact, she admits that I do a better job of describing my emotions than she does. But she is not the only person I share with. I have two male friends that I share with on a regular basis. Just the other night, I had a four-hour conversation with a friend about relationships and spirituality. It definitely broke the surface and was deeper than rating girls between 1 and 10.

I haven't ever had this kind of discussion with my father, so I'm not really sure where I picked it up—maybe from hanging out with a lot of girls in high school. But when it comes to talking about sex, I'm not only uncomfortable talking about it with guys, but I'm also uncomfortable talking about it with girls. Except for the very shallow surface of the topic, I only discuss sex-related topics with my fiancée, the person to whom I am closest. That may be a "guy thing," but I'm not worried about it.

Dillon, 22

Whoever this dude is, he's not a man. I was born in 1980 so I'm not familiar with the way things were then, and even today I'm not really familiar with anyone else's experience but my own, but the guy who wrote that article is ridiculous. He overanalyzes masculinity. You can't do that. A man is a man, no questions asked. That's the golden rule. Thou shalt not cast judgment. "Men Have Buddies, But No Real Friends"? That's absurd: A man has no friends only when he questions whether the people around him are his friends. Otherwise all men are friends. My father and I know each other so well that if (god forbid) we didn't say one word to each other for ten years, we could come back and pick up right where we left off . . . one tilted grin, one word, one handshake, and we'd both know what it meant. Many of the women I've known know nothing about this. If I don't talk about my feelings, consider that it may not be an inability. Maybe it's because I have respect for the pain and choose to store it. I hate dwelling on the things that go wrong, so sometimes I just try to cope. I'm proud to say that I'm completely autonomous and have no need to lament the pitiful doubts that Richard Cohen proclaims.

Henry, 25

Recently a friend of mine lost his father. His father was fifty-one years old, not a drinker or a smoker, just your typical midwestern father. At the funeral I hugged my friend, asked how he was, and then sat quietly next to him. What do I say? How can I make him feel more comfortable? Women are golden in these situations, not missing a beat and always comforting, but more important, always real! Eventually my friend said he wanted to go outside and get some air, relax or at least try. It was drizzling and cold, but we walked for at least a mile. During this walk I told him how sorry I was and that I truly did not know what to say. He smiled and said, "It's all right, I don't either."

Before I left, I grabbed some cold cuts, drank some water, and gave my respects to his family. On my way out, my friend shook my hand and said, "Give your father a hug"; I replied "Of course." As I began to turn, my friend grabbed my arm and said, "Don't shake his hand, give him a hug." I pondered this for two weeks. Have I ever given my dad a hug or him me? I came to the conclusion that there was one time when I hugged my father, when I moved out at the age of eighteen. Since then we have not hugged. This scared me. I not only hug, but also kiss my mother, my sister, grandmas, aunts, female cousins, female friends—all of them get hugs. Anyhow, I have yet to hug my father and have seen him four times since my friend said, "Don't shake his hand, give him a hug."

Fred, 41

I think things have changed for males' sensitivity and relationships over the past twenty-five years, but I think the real test will be how the *next* generation of men thinks and behaves. Most of my "boomer" male friends relate stories very similar to mine: almost all of us had Dads who didn't show their emotions, express their fears, or do much hugging and kissing. Intriguingly, many of my relationships with males have been very deep, very open to the sharing of emotions. I think that this is in part due to the fact that the young women we grew up with and went to school with were more liberated than their predecessors—this meant that many of us young men were able to form strong friendships with women. Like many of my closest male friends, I spent hours and hours talking with women, learning along the way how to listen, to empathize, to allow my vulnerable side to show. For many of us, our wives truly are our best friends. I think this impacted my friendships with men. I've talked through the night with male friends, I've hugged my closest male friends, and I've arranged to be on days-long bonding adventures (like sea kayaking) with them. Most of us have wonderfully strong relationships with our wives. And most of us have sons who have seen the strength in our sensitivity.

I'm looking forward to seeing how my sons grow in their friendships. I can already see that many of these nineteen- or twenty-year-old men have formed very close bonds with male friends and even more friendships with women than my generation did. I'm not saying that these young men (or my older group of male friends) don't fit some of the old stereotypes—I think in the end men are "hard-wired" for less talking and sharing than our female counterparts—but I think the next twenty-five years will see women adopting more and more "male" behaviors and men adopting more and more "female" behaviors. I hope so, because both sexes have so much to teach each other! Don't worry about us guys and our friendships; I feel like I've formed my closest friendships in my adult years, and actually in the last ten years or so I've learned more than I ever dreamed I would about being a good friend.

Ed, 53

I agree with a lot of what the author says about men and their levels of relationships. But . . . I'm one of the lucky ones. I have a friend—a damned good friend. Mike and I have known each other for more than twenty years. He's fifty-six. I'm fifty-three. We have helped each other through a failed marriage and terrific remarriage, the challenges of raising our kids, Vietnam (we were both conscientious objectors), coming to terms with drugs (Mike is chemically dependent and has been sober for more than twenty years), and we share a love of reading, music, and spiritual questioning.

Mike and I have been through a lot—with other people and in our own relationship—but we truly love and care for each other. We know that each of us will always be there when needed. We know that we can talk about the most personal crises and speak frankly about choices we have to make in our personal and professional lives.

And we laugh . . . God, how we laugh. Our minds race along during our conversations as we attempt to match and then outdo each other's witty remarks, puns, and non sequitors (that really do end up relating). We made an agreement several months ago that our relationship meant too much to not see each other more. Thus, we try and schedule a breakfast or happy hour every week so we can exchange wisdom, and whatever else shows up.

I feel lucky because Mike is my friend, and I know he feels the same way. I know we may be the exception, but it can happen more frequently. Men just need to see how wonderful and fulfilling it is to have someone be there to care about what you say and do—and to care for them too.

Terry, 58

It's hard to believe that article is over twenty years old. It stands almost timeless. If friends are defined as those to whom you can and do talk with about topics beyond the weather, sports, and the stock market, I'd have to saw that virtually all my friends are women. Quite frankly, I have always been alternately amused and disgusted when men talk about women sexually. And yet women have been able to ask me about lovemaking.

I have a lot of interaction with men, as I am active in sports, I play in two card games, and along with my wife entertain and go out a fair amount. I really enjoy my sports, play hard, compete to win, and have a few beers when the games are done. I enjoy the entire experience with almost everyone I play with and will actively continue this pursuit. But they are not my friends. I have played squash with one fellow virtually every week for twenty years. We have partied together. And I would not even dream of discussing my feelings with him.

When I lost my job, I found a lot of men and women I could talk to. I got good professional advice, heartfelt and sincere. But the men didn't ask me how I felt. I believe they thought they knew how I felt, and yet the women took the time to ask and probe and actually show emotional concern beyond the course of action of "what do I do now." I didn't resent the men for missing this, as I was trying to avoid thinking about it as well.

I believe that men are more prone to be innately competitive, and hence unwilling to show weakness or fault. I really enjoyed writing this down, even though I didn't like reading the article. It's no fun learning you are missing something you didn't know about. But when your best friend is your spouse, you actually have it all in one package, and that is probably all I need.

Al, 62

I can only speak for myself. I have two close male friends. We pretty much talk about everything—yes, our feelings, our disappointments, jealousies, failures, worries, sex lives, sexual inadequacies, fears. The one thing we don't talk about is how much money we have and where it is and how we feel about it. That is the real taboo subject among men.

I attribute much of my comfort with unloading things to my friends without much fear of being seen as being weak or deficient or weird to the fact that I was a member of a wonderful men's group for about four years when I lived in Syracuse, New York. What I learned from the men's group was how wonderfully funny, sensitive, artistically sophisticated, adventurous, loving, and idiosyncratic men could be. There was much sharing about sex, marriage, relationships with women, failures, fears, etc., but again, no sharing about money.

I believe enough in sociobiology to believe that some of this reluctance to open up to each other and to expose weakness and deficiency has to do with a primordial fear of being taken advantage of, a fear of showing weakness because others will move in on one's territory or somehow do harm to one. This obviously means that the key requirement before men will open up to each other is TRUST—BIG TIME WITH A CAPITAL "TRUST."

Women, Stress, and Friendship

Women respond to stress differently than men do. Fortunately, we also have a better way to fight against it: each other. Friendships between women are special. They shape who we are and who we are yet to be. They soothe our tumultuous inner world, fill the emotional gaps in our marriage, and help us remember who we really are. But they may do even more. Scientists now suspect that hanging out with our friends can actually counteract the kind of stomach-quivering stress most of us experience on a daily basis.

A landmark UCLA study suggests that women respond to stress with a cascade of brain chemicals that cause us to make and maintain friendships with other women. It's a stunning finding that has turned five decades of stress research—most of it on men—upside down.

"Until this study was published, scientists generally believed that when people experience stress, they trigger a hormonal cascade that revs the body to either stand and fight or flee as fast as possible," explains Laura Cousino Klein, Ph.D, now an assistant professor of biobehavioral health at Pennsylvania State University in State College and one of the study's authors. It's an ancient survival mechanism left over from the time we were chased across the planet by saber-toothed tigers. Now the researchers suspect that women have a larger behavioral repertoire than just "fight or flight." In fact, says Dr. Klein, it seems that when the hormone oxytocin is released as part of the stress response in a woman, it buffers the fight or flight response and encourages her to tend children and gather with other women instead. When she actually engages in this tending or befriending, studies suggest that more oxytocin is released, which further counters stress and produces a calming effect. This calming response does not occur in men, says Dr. Klein, because testosterone—which men produce in high levels when they're under stress—seems to reduce the effects of oxytocin. Estrogen, she adds, seems to enhance it.

The discovery that women respond to stress differently than men was made in a classic "aha!" moment shared by two women scientists who were talking one day in a lab at UCLA. "There was this joke that when the women who worked in the lab were stressed, they came in, cleaned the lab, had coffee, and bonded," says Dr. Klein. "When the men were stressed, they holed up somewhere on their own. I commented one day to fellow researcher, Shelley Taylor, that nearly 90 percent of the stress research is on males. I showed her the data from my lab, and the two of us knew instantly that we were onto something." The women cleared their schedules and started meeting with one scientist after another from various research specialties. Very quickly, Drs. Klein and Taylor discovered that by not including women in stress research, scientists had made a huge mistake: The fact that women respond to stress differently than men has significant implications for our health. It may take some time for new studies to reveal all the ways that oxytocin encourages us to care for children and hang out with other women, but the "tend and befriend" notion developed by Drs. Klein and Taylor may explain why women consistently outlive men. Study after study has found that social ties reduce our risk of disease by lowering blood pressure, heart rate, and cholesterol. "There's no doubt," says Dr. Klein, "that friends are helping us live longer."

In one study, for example, researchers found that people who had no friends increased their risk of death over a six-month period. In another study, those who had the most friends over a nine-year period cut their risk of death by more than 60 percent. Friends are also helping us live better. The famed Nurses' Health Study from Harvard Medical School found that the more friends women had, the less likely they were to develop physical impairments as they aged, and the more likely they were to be leading a joyful life. In fact, the results were so significant, the researchers concluded, that not having a close friend or confidante was as detrimental to your health as smoking or carrying extra weight! And that's not all: When the researchers looked at how well the women functioned after the death of their spouse, they found that even in the face of this biggest stressor of all, those women who had close friends and confidantes were more likely to survive the experience without any new physical impairment or permanent loss of vitality. Those without friends were not always so fortunate.

—Reprinted with permission from Building Green, Inc.
122 Birge St. Ste 30, Brattleboro, VT 05301
802/257-7300 ext. 102

UNTITLED *by Mo Higby*

OUTSIDERS, BULLIES, AND BYSTANDERS

Nick

Somehow, I never really know what to say with people my age. Everyone else seems pretty relaxed and accepted, but I don't think I have ever felt that way. When I was little—actually, when I was *young;* I was never very little for my age—the other boys would laugh at me and push me and tease me. The girls would whisper to each other and then giggle as they watched the boys knock me down or taunt me. I never knew exactly why; I was just an easy target and seemed powerless to resist or defend myself. I was always saying things that other kids found stupid and I was never very coordinated or interested in the same things the other boys found appealing. I would rather sit in the playground and watch a colony of ants build their network of highways and storehouses than race around and throw balls at the others. The other boys would stomp on the ant fields and knock me over and call me names. In first grade, that would make me cry, but crying only fueled the bullies even more, so I learned to be on guard and ignore them and fall farther to the edges of the playground. After a while, they got bored and left me to sit by myself. As I got a little older, I realized that I was big and could frighten the more persistent bullies by standing up and threatening them. They still took some cheap shots, but I learned how to use my size to protect my distance. Even I could see that I was an amusing freak to most of the others.

The classroom was a different problem. It was harder to hide and I found myself drawn to the lessons and questions that the teacher presented. I read easily and loved to sit quietly by the back windows and read anything I could get my hands on. This sometimes got me into trouble, but most of my teachers seemed to like me in a funny sort of way. I didn't always finish my homework, but I learned quickly and could spend endless periods reading or observing something we were studying. I was fascinated by science and nature. I didn't know how to relate to the other children in the class, but spent every free moment teaching the class mouse tricks or just watching him order his little caged home. I admired his relaxed friendliness and imagined that he felt the same way I did, trying to go about his business with everyone staring at him.

It felt good to be smart and know the answers, but that didn't help my social standing. My classmates laughed at my questions and groaned when I pointed something out that even the teacher had not thought of. Sometimes I would find my lunch scattered in the coatroom or smashed in my coat pocket. I sat alone in the lunchroom, trying to avoid the knocks and shoves as people walked by me. One day, the class mouse was missing— we searched everywhere, but at the end of the school day, I found it dead in my coat pocket. The teacher seemed to understand that I had not killed it, but I was devastated. I held its small, stiffening body in my hands and felt responsible for its death—not by my own hands, but by my awkwardness and alienation. From then on, I decided to be as quiet and invisible as I could be. I was still the brunt of jokes and teasing, but my silence bored the bullies, and I no longer stood out in class. A couple of my teachers tried to draw me out, but I had learned not to respond to anyone. New teachers saw my high test scores, but never saw any evidence of my ability in the classroom. Being smart drew too much attention, so I just kept to myself and daydreamed.

Home was my sanctuary. My parents accepted me and were proud of everything I did and said. I was an only child. Our conversations rarely condescended to my age and I adapted. I watched the evening news with my mom and dad, and we went bird watching and camping and traveling together. My parents read to me since I was a baby and I had stacks of books and a trunk full of Lego's and Playmobile characters. I would build for hours and create my own fantasy worlds. When I was ten, my dad helped me build a shortwave radio and I kept a map of all the locations I had contacted. It was easier to talk to these people around the world than it was to my own classmates. It felt safe to be in my own room and gradually I grew more confident and outspoken again.

But junior high was a nightmare. All the bullies that had tired of me seemed to gain new interest—the locker room and showing off for girls provided new incentive for harassment. My size still gave me some protection, but a couple of the boys suspected that I wouldn't really fight back and started pushing me. Usually they weren't completely sure I wouldn't fight, so they kept their distance as they heckled me. One afternoon, however, five guys jumped me on my way home. I was too surprised to put up much of a fight. They broke my glasses, threw my books around, and punched me pretty soundly; but mainly they destroyed the bravado that had kept me safe. I knew I would have to stand up for myself in some way or be chased for the rest of the year. I knew I was big enough, but I just didn't have the heart for fighting. I stayed home sick for a few days, hoping everything would pass. My parents were worried and suspected something had happened, but I kept it to myself. The year passed miserably. I managed to avoid another big fight, but every day I worried and watched over my shoulder. The solitude that had been my only protection growing up now began to feel remote and lonely. I watched the groups of friends and heard about the parties and activities and felt my isolation.

For ninth grade, my parents decided to send me to a private school. I think they suspected how miserable and lonely I was and my testing indicated that I was smart enough to get a good scholarship at a local day school. While I didn't think things could get much worse, I dreaded breaking in to a whole new group of people. The boys weren't as threatening, but I still didn't know how to make friends and felt awkward and shy. One big break was that, at this school, it was a plus to be smart and I gradually began to relax and participate in the classroom again. The classes were small and I found myself speaking up—and people didn't laugh. I worked hard on my homework and soon was doing well in all my classes, an accomplishment that gave me an identity and respect at this new school.

My academic success, however, was slow to impact my social life. I covered up my awkwardness by keeping busy and avoiding most social situations. Even when someone approached me casually or for help with some homework, my ease vanished and I could never put the appropriate sentences together. I would end up saying something stupid or nothing at all. If it was a girl, I was hopeless. I think I probably seemed pretty rude and most people didn't try to approach me twice. A few people made jokes about me, but most people just gave up and ignored me. Except Wyatt.

Wyatt was the last person you would ever have expected to try to get to know me. In fact, on the surface, he was a lot like the boys who had bullied me in elementary school. He was a jock, very good looking, and popular—he always seemed to have girls chasing him. He had a BMW and his parents were very rich and influential in the community. His great-uncle had been a well-known politician and his last name always caused somewhat of a stir. The only thing he and I had in common was that we were both quiet. He had lots of friends, but seemed to stay to the side of the group. They were more with him than he was with them, if you know what I mean. We had a philosophy class together and every now and then I would catch him watching me. I really liked this class and often argued and questioned the issues we were studying. Wyatt didn't speak up very often, but his ideas were always thought-provoking. I don't like to prejudge people, but it seemed out of character with his rich, social image. I found myself wondering who he really was.

One day, we were supposed to work in pairs to argue the pros and cons of a particular philosophical position. Before I could worry about how to deal with this situation, Wyatt approached me and asked if we could work together. Rather than try to figure out what to say, I simply said, "Sure." This was the beginning of the most unlikely friendship. We met in the library to research our position, but ended up talking about everything—from Kant to politics to families to school cliques. I had never had such an interesting conversation with anyone my age. I found myself telling stories and laughing and listening to Wyatt tell about his life. He was interested in what I had to say and seemed to understand what I couldn't quite put into words. To everyone's surprise, we became friends. I can only imagine what it must have looked like in the beginning—this big clunky guy walking around with one of the most popular boys in school. I felt comfortable with Wyatt alone, but it took a while to relax and be myself with his friends.

At one point when we were talking about school and friends, I asked Wyatt what it was that made me seem like such a sideshow. Wyatt laughed. "Well, my friend, you are a bit certifiable." I winced. "You say what you are thinking without thinking about it. No tact; you just speak your mind. You don't even seem to notice when you say something outrageous." By now, he noticed my growing discomfort and embarrassment.

"But that is what I admire about you," Wyatt continued. " I have spent my whole life thinking about what I say and being polite and restrained. My family does all the right things and we know all the right people—though sometimes I don't think I really even know my family and I know they don't know me. Nick, I never know if people like me or if I got into this school because of me or because I am a Roosevelt. I would never dream of just blurting out what I am thinking like you do—except when I am with you. Sometimes, I don't even know what I think, just what I have been taught to think. With you, hey, I always figure you will tell me the truth and you don't even care who my family is. When I see you off in your own world, I know just how you feel. Only my world is all polished and refined, so it looks like I'm connected. But it's just a game. I don't know how to be real with them any more than you do. I just know how to look like I do. We all have our own loneliness, Nick."

I thought a lot about what Wyatt said. Though I never got much better at small talk, I made some good friends, and, as we spent more time together, more people seemed to appreciate what Wyatt had seen in me. Wyatt and I stayed best friends all through high school and we kept in touch at college. He gave me the confidence to laugh at myself and when we were together, Wyatt was even occasionally known to say something outrageous. I'm still sure we made an unlikely pair. Some people still laugh or exclude me, but it doesn't make me feel bad like it used to. Wyatt always seems to know just the right thing to say and do—I admire that in him and it is hard to imagine that he admires me because I don't.

SELF-PORTRAIT *by Julia Hopkins*

ALL KINDS OF FAMILIES

Families throughout the world are the basic social unit, but they come in many shapes and sizes.

Kyra

While we all live through the function and dysfunction of our family structures, my story is somewhat unique. My life has been a bit of a soap opera with surprises at every turn. My experiences have caused me to define family loosely. My family, as I define it, includes anyone, related by blood or not, who shows up to engage in a relationship of love and support—be that emotionally, financially, or through shared experiences.

My story begins with Bruce and Kate getting married in 1980. At a beautiful fall wedding on a mesa high in the Rocky Mountains, two very different families gathered to share in an unconventional, outdoor ceremony. Kate was the only daughter in a family with four full brothers and three foster siblings. Kate's father died of cancer when she was just four and her mother was a hardworking single mom for the majority of Kate's childhood. Penny, Kate's mother, was the first person in her family to go to school beyond the eighth grade. At that time she was a nurse with a B.A.; she later went on to receive her Ph.D. in sociology. Bruce, on the other hand, came from a family that, on the outside, resembled *My Three Sons*, a middle-class family with three boys. Bruce's dad, Ted, served in World War II and then became a teacher and a coach. His mom, Gus, was the typical at-home mom. Both Bruce's parents had college degrees. Their values were progressive for the time; they were a family that would rather go camping together than go to church.

At age twenty-six, Bruce had attended some college, but found his calling in the outdoors. He became a NOLS/Outward Bound instructor. Kate, at only nineteen, was halfway through college. Kate and Bruce were really in love and happy to be getting married, but they had a little secret—Kate was three months' pregnant. I was born six months later, in a one-room cabin in Colorado. Penny, my maternal grandmother, delivered me. In a few months, Bruce and Kate moved to this little ski town where there was an opportunity for Bruce to manage the nordic ski center. Kate was busy finishing college, taking care of a new baby, and managing the town bakery. It didn't take long for the stresses of life to take a toll on their marriage. When I was only two, they decided to separate. Less than a year later, while riding his bicycle, Bruce, my papa, was hit by a drunk driver. After spending almost two years in a coma, his system turned septic and he died. I had not yet had my fourth birthday. This first experience of family was a little rocky, to say the least.

My mother remarried a man named Kent and they had my little brother, Matt. After completing her college degree, my mother taught school, and Kent did construction. They built a beautiful house together in Telluride. For the next ten years, I would experience what it was like to be part of a "nuclear" family, to live a middle-class lifestyle in a rural mountain resort town that was almost completely white and increasingly wealthy. I experienced many things that were unique to that environment. Seeing Hollywood celebrities or locals being filmed in national commercials was a common occurrence. Physical education was a half-day of skiing during school. Vacationing at the beach was what everyone did the day the ski area closed. This was clearly a life of great privilege.

At a young age, I was able to recognize that things within my family were becoming a little rough. I later found out that "a little rough" meant that Kent was having an affair with one of my best friend's mothers, who also happened to be my brother's preschool teacher. Upon return from a family vacation, my mom and Kent separated. Kent and I decided that just because he and my mother were getting divorced, our relationship did not have to change even though there were no longer any legal bonds between us. In other words, he was still my dad.

After my mom and Kent separated, I faced many significant changes in my living circumstances. Two of my mom's brothers had recently moved to town. They needed a place to stay and there was room in the family house. Her brothers are not your typical relatives. Mac, her youngest brother, spent a good decade of his life in and out of jail, on and off of drugs, and had recently found a spiritual path. Marshall, my mom's oldest brother, is a genius, but has his own definitions of how family should be in relation to each other. And he doesn't really care if your definition matches his. Somewhere along the way, my mom had introduced Mac to her best friend, Sabina, and they fell for each other. So, for about a year, we all lived together—me, Kate (my mom), Kent (my stepdad), Matt (my stepbrother), Marshall and Mac (my uncles), and Sabina (my mom's best friend). Each of these adults participated in the care of the children.

This shift from a two-parent household to one where many adults played significant roles in my life was similar to some more tribal ideas of family. Like the Australian aborigines and the Zinacenteco of Mexico, we all lived together. I could certainly recognize how people were related to me, but their titles, dad or uncle, had nothing to do with the role they were playing in my life.

My mom was now single, really for the first time in her adult life. She found that she had some major soul searching to do. Her mother, Penny, had gone back to college when my mom was young. My mom had sworn she would never do that to her kids, but one day, she announced that she was moving to Boulder because she was going back to school. I spent a year and a half living alone with my mother while she was fully immersed in studying the psychology of gender equity and female leadership. By earning a Ph.D. in psychology, my mom increased her social status, but temporarily decreased her economic status. She was over forty thousand dollars in debt.

Kent, my stepdad, had never been the kind of person to be alone. He quickly got into a relationship with Sharon. Sharon and her son, Elliot, who was seven years old, were living together. After about a year, they invited Kent, Matt, and me to live with them. So we moved in, and I got another mom, brother, and education in religion—they were Jewish. Kate, having finished her Ph.D., moved back to town and we rented a small apartment. Once again, all my family was close. Sharon, Kent, and Elliot in one house, Kate and I in the other, while my brother, Matt, went back and forth.

My mom had racked up a great deal of loans during grad school, and money was really tight. We lived in a tiny apartment built as employee housing for the ski area. Many Mexican immigrants, legal and illegal, also lived here; it was the least expensive living arrangement you could find in town. We were also receiving financial assistance from the housing authority to be able to pay rent. This was really hard for me. Just across town, the other half of my family lived in a beautiful house, regularly ate at fine restaurants, attended grand parties, and enjoyed frequent vacations to my dad's house in Cabo Pulmo in Mexico. Money was never really discussed. Living this contrast made me a poor little rich girl, but it also taught me how to be comfortable with all sorts of people, regardless of economic circumstances.

The last big change in my family structure came when I was a freshman in college. My mom had called to tell me that she was in love. "With whom?" I asked, not having heard any names recently. "With the woman who answered the phone," was her reply. Wow. The shock of that news settled in and the tears began to run. I hung up the phone and ran to my best friend's room. People talk about the significance of coming out to relatives and what a big event that can be in a person's life. What they don't discuss is the way it feels to be on the other side of that closet. With time, I adjusted to the idea, and I could hear how happy my mother was. I was blessed with an opportunity to open my mind to yet another idea of family and welcome my mother's partner into my life and our family.

In contrast to the very alternative structures my immediate family has taken on, my paternal grandparents, Gus and Ted, have a marriage that has stood the test of time. I spend a week with my grandparents every summer. I am their only grandchild and they spoil me terribly. When I visit, I often ask lots of questions about my father's life and theirs. I have a need to understand the other side of my family that I never really knew and they are my only connection. After all of my experiences, I still have some fantasy that I could meet the man of my dreams, get married only once, and we would be in love forever. This summer, I had the privilege of spending my grandparent's fifty-fourth wedding anniversary with them. At seventy-eight and seventy-four years of age, they are still very much alive and in love. It is inspirational. I asked if there was ever a time they thought it wouldn't work. I saw a tear in my grandmother's eye as she looked at my grandpa and said, "True confessions for you." My grandpa just replied, "There were times that were not easy, but never did I think of divorce." My sense was that there was more to that story, but I was never going to hear it. I am learning that every family has secrets, some which never get told.

In my life, my family has taken on a spectrum of different forms, from very traditional to very alternative. What I have learned is that family can be anyone who cares deeply, regardless of whether they are blood related or not. I started life with one mom and one dad and have acquired three moms, two dads, two brothers, as well as an elaborate extended family. I have lived a life mostly of great privilege, but I have also seen poverty first hand. The greatest lesson I have learned is how important it is to have people in my life who are willing to show up and love me. Love may be one of the only constants in my changing, chaotic family, but it has been abundant and never once have I questioned if I was loved.

Written by Kyra Ryan, 2002.

Art Work:

Drew Walton
Mercersburg Academy

Kim Kern
Viewpoint School

Milee Uhm
San Domenico School

Claire Min
Newark Academy

Mo Higby
Mercersburg Academy

Julia Hopkins
Mercersburg Academy

Notes

[1] Dr. Seuss. *The Sneetches and Other Stories.* Random House, copyright 1953.

[2] Katharine Graham. *Personal History.* First Vintage Books Edition, March, 1998. Random House.

[3] Joseph Marshall, Jr. *Street Soldier: One Man's Struggle to Save a Generation— One Life at a Time.* Delacorte Press, Bantam Doubleday Dell Publishing Group, Inc. 1996, pp. Xiii–xxii.

[4] *Ibid.,* pp. 11–14.

If sex is such a natural phenomenon, how come there are so many books on how to do it?

—Bette Midler

Chapter 5.

Sexual Quandaries and Questions

FAMILY VS. PEER VALUES

"MEMORIES" by Jennifer JungEn Shim

MERCEDES

My father and mother came to New York City with he was eighteen and she was sixteen—they were just married in Puerto Rico and my *abuela* cried and wailed to watch them leave their family and their homeland to make their fortune in the big American city. My uncles told stories of drugs and gangs and young girls losing their virtue in the fast-paced streets of New York. My papa countered with stories of success and riches for anyone who would work hard and contribute their talent and dreams to the city. I was not yet born, but I have heard the two versions of this story over and over any time something good or something bad happens to my family in New York. Each side is eagerly watching for evidence that they are right. It has always been known to me and my brother and sisters that we are to provide proof that my father's hopeful version is correct and warned sternly never to do anything that might give my uncles the slightest satisfaction. This provided a very narrow walk and we were guarded by a loving, but vigilant hawk.

My father and mother moved to the very Upper East Side of Manhattan, Spanish Harlem, brimming with Puerto Ricans. You were more likely to see a billboard or hear music coming out of the cars and windows in Spanish than in English. While I visit my relatives in Puerto Rico every summer, Spanish Harlem is like Puerto Rico to me—an extension of New York City cornered off by my people, my food, my music, and my friends. Like me, most of my friends were born here, but we were strictly supervised by our parents and churches, which both still had one foot back on the Island. Spanish Harlem is like a stray islet of Puerto Rico that is connected to New York like a glamorous tiara on the head of a bull. My father started out working two jobs—in a kitchen during the day and a garage at night. He wanted to go to the local college so that he could get a good job and capture the American dream. At first, he refused to let my mother work; it was his job as a man to provide and protect his woman and family. Money was tight, but he was stubborn. My mama was stubborn too, so she and a friend in the same building started taking in sewing and mending without their husbands' knowing. It was the American way, they told themselves. Women could make good money here in the United States. My mama was always good with sewing and another woman in the building worked for a wealthy family who lived on the Upper East Side, so she could transport the work without my mother ever having to leave the building. Word got around that Mama was good, and soon she had more work than she could keep up with alone. She found two or three other housebound wives who had good skills and soon started her own secret business.

My papa was always the strict, loud, but softhearted, boss of our family, and it was three years later, after I was born, before he knew about my mother's work. Mama handled it perfectly. After three years of working and saving, my father was still $500 short of the money he needed to attend the community college and the deadline for registration was coming up. My birth had taken quite a bit of his savings and he was about ready to give up on his dream of an American education, feeling his vulture uncles circling in their triumph. That night, at the parking garage where Papa worked, one of the regular customers mentioned that his wife had been particularly impressed with some tailoring that my mother had done for her. Papa managed to smile at the customer, but, boy, was he boiling when he got home. He would never hit my mother, but he yelled and threatened and told her she had shamed him in his new country. My mama had been expecting this day for a while and was perfectly prepared to handle it. She cried and apologized; she pointed out he had cared for her so well that she had the time to work quietly in her own home to help the family; she flattered him and boasted of his courage to come to the United States where a wife could help her husband, that he was not an old-fashioned Island man like his uncles, but a New York City man who was making something of himself and she was proud to be at his side. This was all working very well and the clincher was when my mother handed him the $500 that he needed for his college. I was just a child, but this story is often told, in quite different versions, by the women and by the men whenever they get together to tell their stories.

The result was that my papa was able to enroll in the local community college, give up his kitchen job, and my mama now had the freedom to openly expand her tailoring business. She took on four more seamstresses and, by word of mouth, was soon the trendy new place to get your sewing done—even the mayor sent his family tailoring to my mama. In the meantime, my brother and two sisters were born, and my papa earned honors in his college work in business management. When Papa graduated, he surprised my mother by buying a small shop for her business and proceeded to expand the business until we had three shops in different sections of Manhattan, employing over twenty seamstresses. Even one of my aunts from Puerto Rico came up to manage one of the shops. This was a particular pleasure for my father as his grumbling uncle came in tow. By the time I reached high school, my parents had realized their teenage dream and we lived a busy, but happy life surrounded by strict family obligations, salsa music, and love.

During all this time, we never once missed Mass. My parents are devout Catholics and we kept our religion in the same way we kept family and our Spanish culture. My brother and sisters and I are perhaps less devout than my parents, but honor the church and would never think of missing Mass or letting our parents down. It is more than a religion in my family; it is a faith that honors our heritage and holds our family together.

I had done well in school, modeling my parents' hard work and high expectations. My English was excellent and I found the schoolwork easy and *simpatico*. My papa's struggle to get an American education taught me not to waste mine. At the end of eighth grade, I graduated at the top of my class and was offered a place in the city-wide Honor Academy. The Honor Academy was across town and provided special educational opportunities for the top students from schools all around the city. My papa was very proud of me; sent telegrams to my uncles back in Puerto Rico and held a big party in my honor. My mama was proud too, but I could tell that she was worried. *"You will go too far from your home. You will forget things and the city will become more complicated for you."* I assured Mama that I would be home every night and nothing could ever complicate the family that I love so much. She smiled and gave me her blessing, but I could tell she was still worried.

In the fall, I left my safe Spanish Harlem and traveled a subway and two buses to attend the Honor Academy of New York City. I had to leave before seven in the morning and did not get home until after six at night. The work was hard, so I spent most of my evenings and weekends studying— I did not want to let down my papa and the opportunity that had been given to me. My friends were surprised at first; they did not think that attending a different school would make such a big difference in our relationships. I guess I was surprised too, but I kept focused on what I needed to do to be successful in this new school. I came home each night, but gradually my mind seemed to be somewhere else—in my books or at my new school.

The new school was brand new and polished, the other extreme from my school in Spanish Harlem. We wore uniforms, which my mother thought was very appropriate and which kept me from looking like an outsider. My mother tailored my uniform beautifully, so that I always looked a little more fitted and neat than most of the other students. My figure was starting to develop and, in a moment of female solidarity, she tailored my uniform so that it flattered my new form in subtle, but attractive ways. I arrived on the new campus looking quite beautiful and proud of myself. The students came from all over the city—a racial mix of whites, blacks, Asians, Africans, Europeans, Middle Easterners, and Hispanics like I had never seen in one place. We were the chosen students and entered with a peculiar mix of arrogance, excitement, and shyness. The classes were small in shiny new rooms with the latest lab equipment and teachers especially chosen to work with the brightest students in the city. We felt like an exciting experiment in social education and were determined not to fail.

This was not an easy road—we came from so many backgrounds and schools; the expectations were so high that each of us felt repeatedly threatened by the gaps in our skills and upbringing. It wasn't really until the third year that we began to feel safe and worthy of the honor that had been given us. Our deficiencies had evened out and with the addition of new younger students as we matriculated, we felt older and wiser, confident in our position of seniority.

It wasn't really until my senior year that my mama's worry interrupted my education. I did well in school; I was on the student council and elected secretary of my class. I had many friends from all over the city. I loved getting to know their families and their neighborhoods—so different from my own—and to show them my home and family. My grades were good and the school counselor was encouraging me to apply to Ivy League colleges, sure that I could get a good scholarship. My mama kept saying things like, "You never have time for your old friends" and "Why do you want to go all over the city when your family is right here?" But I never missed Mass and Sundays with my family, so I didn't really understand what she was talking about. My younger sister told me I was getting *loco*—I talked funny and laughed about things that nobody around home thought were funny. My uniform was strange enough, but she considered my other clothes preppy and out of style. She thought my friends from school were nice enough, but insisted that they didn't really fit in. They seemed self-conscious and not like us. I knew what she meant, but it wasn't true when I was with them at school or in the city. They liked me and I fit in with them just fine. In fact, sometimes I felt like I fit in better with them than I did at home. Mama was right. It was getting complicated.

In my junior year, I fell in love with David. He was clever and funny and always made me laugh. He was a serious space cadet, but he was also a good student and we could argue for hours about any subject—I think we both taught each other as much as the teachers did. David was from the Upper West Side. His parents were divorced and he lived with his mom who was an artist. His dad worked on Wall Street and lived out in Greenwich, Connecticut, with his stepmom. They had money, but David was totally unpretentious. If it weren't for the uniform, he would have looked a lot shabbier than I would. He respected my parents and easily won over my younger sisters and brother. He and my brother, Alfonzo, played basketball together and David taught Alfonzo how to play chess, which became his new obsession. David seemed comfortable in Spanish Harlem, though I never liked him walking alone and always arranged to be there with him or send my brother. I was OK in his neighborhood, but he escorted me too. I really liked his mom—she was as free-spirited as David. We roasted hotdogs in the small apartment fireplace and painted one whole wall with handprints of everyone who came to visit. David's dad would invite us downtown for dinner in a fancy restaurant and talk of sports or school or the economy. Our families could not have been more different, but we all tolerated and liked each other. David and I laughed at both our family's idiosyncrasies and warned each other when they were coming.

Amazingly, it was all working out pretty well until we hit the big impasse—sex. It wasn't really a problem for David and me. Our physical attraction was hot and while it was sometimes hard to keep our hands off each other, sex was just a part of such an amazingly full relationship, that we enjoyed our physical relationship without rushing or feeling a lot of pressure to have intercourse. I carried a lot of strong messages from my family about being a virgin—my mama and aunties would warn me about the importance of protecting the virtue of my womanhood and Papa simply said he would shoot anyone who violated his daughter. Pretty simple, old-fashioned, and un-American, but they were my family and there was no arguing. As David and I spent more and more time together, I could see a warning look in my mother's eye, but no one took the relationship that seriously (he was not our kind) nor could they imagine that I would violate such a strong family taboo. Good Puerto Rican girls do not have sex before they are married.

I *was* a good Puerto Rican girl, but I was also a good American girl. I was smart and responsible—I would never be promiscuous or have unprotected sex—but I also felt the pressures and desire to take our relationship to a more physical level. I was almost eighteen years old and we had been dating for over a year. That was almost unheard of among my American friends. There were a couple times when we had almost gotten carried away and that scared me. I didn't ever want to be in a position where I might get pregnant or expose myself to a disease. We either had to decide firmly that we would not have intercourse and have the discipline to be sure we didn't, or we had to be realistic and responsible, making a conscious decision to have sex and protect ourselves. After a lot of thought and talk, we decided we were ready to have intercourse and needed to take the responsible steps to protect ourselves. It was easy for David to get condoms, but to be absolutely safe, we decided I should take some version of the birth control pill.

That is when discussion turned into reality and I felt the disapproval of generations of Catholic Rodriguez women looking at me in shock and disapproval. *Mia cara, how could you think such things?* To be a responsible

American woman, I had to turn my back on my family's traditional values. I was ready to have sex with David, but I was not ready to get married the way my parents had. They were having sex at my age. My world is different—I want to go to college and establish a career for myself, but that does not mean that I don't love or have sexual feelings like they did. Their world is good and I love and admire both of them, but it is different for me. David listened, but could not really understand how I was feeling. His mom thought we were being very responsible and talked openly with us about birth control. David respected my parents, but his attitude was, "If it is just going to upset them, don't tell them." I knew what he meant and it sounded logical (and much easier), but I had never secretly violated my parents' trust like that. I was an independent, American woman, but my training and respect for my parents would not let me sneak around their back. I could disagree and make an adult decision about my sexuality, but I could not lie to them.

As noble as that may sound, telling them was quite another thing. Two scheduled doctor's appointments came and went unattended as I procrastinated. The more I hinted to my mother, the more she turned a deaf ear to any discussion. My papa was oblivious, treating David as an odd, but potential son-in-law with no idea that David might be so bold as to consider sex with his daughter. *Ay carumba*. How could I speak to such narrow-minded monarchs? How could I make them understand this was neither Puerto Rico nor like when they were my age? I silently complained and delayed until one night our lovemaking came dangerously close to violating both my parents' restrictions and my own good sense. This was stupid. Fearing my parents' values and not honoring my own was putting me in an irresponsible and dangerous place. I needed to either speak up for myself or honor my parents' expectations. As it was, I was not respecting either.

I decided to speak to my mother—she would know how to break it to Papa and while she was the tougher critic, she was also a woman and knew something of the American ways. I found a time when we were alone and she was absentmindedly mending my brother's shirt. I spoke bravely, telling her that David and I were in love and respected each other and had controlled our passion for each other in the many months we had been dating. Without looking up from her sewing, my mother said, "Good." I went on about how I respected her and Papa and understood the values they had taught me, but that this was not Puerto Rico. In America, young people do not just get married when they are sexually attracted to one another. They have to prepare themselves with an education and independence, which means they do not get married until they are older and established. Still not looking up, Mama said, "This is true." But they still have sexual feelings, I continued, and sex is still a part of a mature, caring relationship. I took a deep breath. David and I were ready to have sex as a part of our relationship and wanted to be careful and responsible about it. We had studied birth control methods and decided that a combination of a condom and the Depo-Provera shot would be safest to protect us against pregnancy and STDs. This was our careful and thoughtful decision as responsible young adults, and I wanted her blessing.

The room was filled with an expectant silence as I held my breath and Mama stopped wordlessly at her work. After the longest minute, she continued her mending and quietly said, "No."

"But Mama," I wailed. "Please understand. I am trying to respect you and be responsible to myself. I am not a child. This is not an impulsive decision. David and I have thought long and hard about it. Most of my friends have sex without ever thinking about these things and never tell their parents. Just because I am being responsible and respect you and Papa, you act like a tyrant, like I have no right to make this decision for myself. You brought me to America and expect me to live in Puerto Rico. I am a grown, independent woman; you have taught me to be smart and think for myself, and now you treat me like a baby."

Mama looked quietly at me and waited for me to calm down. I was caught somewhere between tears and anger and wanted her to rescue me with her comforting words as she always had when I was a child. Finally she spoke. "*Mi hita.* I understand that this is a very difficult decision for you and I can see that you have thought of many things. To speak to me and ask my blessing is a courageous thing and shows respect for your papa and me. You are almost eighteen years old—I was married two years at your age. Yes, you are a grown, independent woman and you have made a decision for yourself. Now you must take responsibility for that decision and not ask my blessing. You know I do not agree with this choice. It is not in my upbringing, nor do I think it wise. Being independent means that you consider my wishes and opinion and decide for yourself. Being a mother means that I give you limits and advice as you make these decisions. You are not a baby and I cannot control your life. You have asked and I have answered. Now it is up to you."

I was stunned by the ambiguity of her reply. I could neither rebel nor acquiesce. She spoke as my mother but respected me as an adult—leaving me with the autonomous responsibility of my choice. There was no question how she felt about my decision, but it was clear she was not going to either prohibit or approve my choice. It was mine to make and accept responsibility for. As I left the room, I had no idea what I was going to do.

COMING OUT

One of the most emotion-laden and confusing aspects of sexuality is a person's sexual orientation. Throughout recorded history and in every known society, some people have been sexually attracted to members of the same gender. In Kinsey's study, only 4 percent of males and 2 percent of females in the United States reported being exclusively homosexual, but also only 63 percent of males and 72 percent of females were exclusively heterosexual. The other one-third of males and one-quarter of females were somewhere on a bisexual continuum between homosexuals who had some heterosexual feelings or activity and heterosexuals who had some homosexual feelings or activity. Homosexual individuals, both known and "closeted," have contributed significantly to every area of human endeavor—Dag Hammershold, Tennessee Williams, Gertrude Stein, Alexander the Great, Tchaikovsky, John Maynard Keynes, Leonardo da Vinci, Elton John, Rock Hudson, and Willa Cather, among others. Some gay men and women choose to "stay in the closet," or conceal their sexual orientation, because of strong and sometimes violent reactions from the straight community. While it is always unfortunate for anyone to have to hide or feel threatened by a part of who they are, the question of coming out is up to each individual. Some gay activists believe that if more gay people "came out," homosexuality would become more accepted and comfortable for everyone. Many gay people resent "living a lie," and find that the fear and deception eats away at their self-esteem and dignity. Other gay people believe that important jobs or relationships would be threatened if they were to come out. Some gays feel that their sex life is private and should not be anyone else's concern. Homosexuality is just a small part of a person's identity, but when it is known, it can overshadow other qualities or relationships. Coming out, like any act of independence and self-affirmation, may require personal strength and courage. In a culture that can be very critical about homosexuality, this can be a lonely and confusing decision. As many as one-third of all teenage suicide attempts are by gay or lesbian adolescents. Individuals who are questioning their own sexual orientation should find a safe and caring confidante to explore their feelings and questions. The unconditional love and support of families and friends can make this decision much easier.

Harvey

In 1977, Harvey Milk was elected to the board of supervisors in San Francisco. He was the first openly gay city official in the United States.

Harvey Bernard Milk was born on May 22, 1930 in Woodmere, Long Island in New York. He was the second son of middle-class Jewish parents. Harvey was an average student, well liked, and known for his practical jokes. After college, he went into the navy and then returned to New York and took a job on Wall Street as a stock analyst. Harvey had realized that he was gay when he was fourteen years old, but it wasn't until the 1960s—over fifteen years later—that he dropped out of Wall Street, became involved in a Broadway theater production, became an activist in the Vietnam anti-war movement, and "came out" as a gay man.

He and his partner moved to San Francisco in the early 1970s where he opened up a small camera shop and became involved in local politics. Between 1973 and 1976, he ran for office—and lost—three times. Harvey was a clear and outspoken representative of the growing gay and lesbian population in San Francisco, but he was also a strong voice for the many disenfranchised groups in the city—minorities, immigrants, the disabled, senior citizens, and working-class people. Each election, he gathered more recognition and support, and in 1977, he ran for the board of supervisors from District 5—the Castro district—and won.

This was a new board of supervisors under the leadership of Mayor George Masconi, who had encouraged involvement and respect for all factions of the city by redesigning district elections so that supervisors were elected by their district rather than citywide. This redistricting plan not only gave Milk the votes he needed, but gathered an eclectic group of individuals that represented the diverse ethnic and political groups of the city—the first Chinese American, the first black woman, the first liberal feminist representative—and a middle-class fireman named Dan White. Harvey Milk consistently spoke up on people issues—public transportation, rent control, senior citizens, handicapped access, voting machine—that could be used and understood by older and immigrant citizens. He was an excellent speaker and a smart politician and he never forgot the importance of his role representing gays and lesbians. In a speech after his election, Milk said:

> *Somewhere in Des Moines or San Antonio, there is a young gay person who all of a sudden realizes he or she is gay and that if his parents find out, he may be tossed out of the house and his friends will taunt him. . . . That child has several options—to stay in the closet or suicide. . . . Then one day that child opens a paper and reads "Homosexual Elected in San Francisco," and there are two new options . . . to move to California or to stay in San Antonio and fight.*
>
> *Two days after I was elected, I received a phone call from Altuna, Pennsylvania. The voice was quite young and the person just said*

"Thanks." . . . *We have got to elect gay people so that young child and the thousands upon thousands like that child will know that there is hope for a better world; there's hope for a better tomorrow. Without hope, not only gays, but those blacks, the Asians, the disabled, seniors. . . . The "us's" . . . the "us's" . . . without hope, the "us's" give up. I know that you cannot live on hope alone, but without it, life is not worth living. You and you and you have got to give them hope.*[1]

In his first months on the board of supervisors, Milk sponsored the Gay Right's Bill, which protected gay employees from being fired if they "came out." The board of supervisors overwhelmingly passed this bill, with only one dissenting vote, from Supervisor Dan White. The backlash, however, gave birth to a statewide initiative, Proposition 6, introduced by John Briggs, to deny gays the right to teach in public schools. It was a heated and uncertain battle, but on November 7, 1978, the initiative was soundly defeated by a vote of 59 percent against to 41 percent in favor. This was an important victory in California and for gay rights initiatives around the country. Harvey had fought hard to defeat Proposition 6 and had become a much-loved leader and representative for gay rights.

Four days later, under personal and political strain, Supervisor Dan White unexpectantly resigned from the board of supervisors. A week later, White changed his mind and decided that he wanted his position back, but the city attorney advised Mayor Masconi that White could not rescind his resignation and that it was up to the mayor to choose a replacement. Masconi considered reappointing Dan White, but decided against it. On Monday, November 27 at 10:45 a.m., Dan White went to city hall to speak to Masconi. They argued and White pulled out a gun and shot Masconi three times in the head. He then went to the other side of the building to Milk's office and shot and killed Harvey Milk too.*

The city was in shock—thousands and thousands of gay and straight citizens marched in a silent candlelight procession from the Castro to city hall; the newspaper headlines read "The City Weeps." Many prominent doctors, teachers, and businesspeople "came out" to their employers, neighbors, and families in support of what Harvey had stood for. Harvey believed that as more gay and lesbian people came out, the myths, stereotypes, and fears about homosexuality would be shattered.

---

*Four months later, Dan White was tried for two counts of murder. After only eleven days of trial and deliberation, the jury found him guilty of voluntary manslaughter, a reduced charge that carried a four- to eight-year sentence. White was released on January 7, 1984, after serving five and a half years in prison with no psychiatric treatment.

One year earlier, Harvey Milk had tape-recorded a will.

> *This is to be played only in the event of my death by assassination. I fully realize that a person who stands for what I stand for, an activist, a gay activist, becomes the target or potential target for somebody who is insecure, terrified, or afraid, or deeply disturbed. Knowing that I could be assassinated at any moment or any time, I feel it is important that some people know my thoughts. I stood for more than just a candidate. I have never considered myself a candidate. I have always considered myself part of a movement . . . part of a candidacy. I wish I had time to explain everything I did; almost every thing was done through the eyes of the Gay Movement.*[2]

Joey

I think I first figured out that I was gay in junior high and I cannot imagine a more nightmarish place to make this discovery. The discovery itself wasn't all that bad—it was more like an "aha" moment when my feelings about girls and guys and me all clicked and it felt true and right. Like my whole self came together and made sense for the first time. It didn't take long to realize that everyone wasn't going to be as thrilled about this insight as I was—I mean, eighth grade is not the most enlightened place for a young gay male to gain validation and encouragement. The word "faggot" is tossed around meaning everything from a friendly put down to a damning epitaph—usually nothing to do with sex, but you get the point. The guys especially were so worried about their masculinity that they were constantly talking about sex and getting it on with girls . . . they wished! I was a good athlete so I don't think many people suspected that I wasn't a "macho guy," but I still had to sit through all the homophobic bullshit. The nonathletic guys—most of them straight—were teased and excluded. It was like everyone thought being gay was contagious or that if you liked someone who wasn't macho maybe you weren't that macho yourself.

Looking back, it all seems pretty pathetic, but at the time, I felt completely alone and intimidated. I can't explain why I didn't think being gay was as lame as all my friends did, but I did have some doubts. I mean, how could I be OK when everyone else seemed so sure that being gay was terrible? It's a sin; it's gross; it's unnatural. I was raised with all those same prejudices, and, at times, I guess I believed them. What was wrong with me? Why did I feel this way? Why couldn't I be like everyone else? I was confused and ashamed. I hate admitting that and even then, I couldn't figure out what I had done to be ashamed of, but I guess being different in any way in junior high is a major catastrophe. After the initial relief of understanding my sexuality, I spent the next three years trying to hide it from everyone else.

My parents were always "liberal" about homosexuality, but I couldn't quite imagine my dad dealing with it. I didn't ever think he would disown me or anything, but I just thought some how I would be letting him down. I was in tenth grade before I first felt brave enough to talk about it with my older sister, Linda. She was a senior and pretty open-minded, and she usually stuck up for me. I tested the water a few times just to see what she thought about a movie that had a gay guy in it or a news article about gays being harassed. Linda seemed OK with it, so one afternoon when we were watching Oprah and pretending to do our homework, I just came out and said, "I think I'm gay." It seemed so strange to hear those words out loud after keeping them a secret for so long. The silence was crushing as I waited for her to say something. "Yeh, right," she quipped, "and I'm a transvestite." I almost lost my courage in the joke of it, but I knew if I backed off, it would be years before I got up my courage again. "No, I'm serious. I think—no, I *know* I'm gay."

Something in my voice must have gotten through to her. Linda looked up from her homework and stared at me with a questioning look on her face. "You *are* serious," she said. "Shit, are you sure?" *Make a joke. Toss it off. Take it back.* I withered under her question, but something forced me to say, "I think so." I would have turned and run if I weren't frozen to the spot— desperately wanting her to understand and say it was OK. Suddenly I wasn't sure at all. Maybe I was just imagining. Maybe if I just went with a girl, I would find out what everyone was so excited about. Maybe my hormones just hadn't kicked in yet. I was surprised at my vacillation and surprised at how much I wanted Linda to understand.

Linda watched me quietly for what seemed like forever; then she said "That makes sense." I didn't know what she meant by that or why it made sense to me either, but I suddenly didn't feel so alone. Somebody else knew and that person thought it made sense too. True to form, Linda started asking me all these questions such as when did I figure it out and what was it like and had anyone given me a hard time about it. She is a very detail-oriented person and, for some reason, it was comforting to have someone take such a matter-of-fact approach to the whole thing. I told her about school and hiding and worrying—even about doubting myself and feeling ashamed. She brushed that aside like it was the silliest thing she had ever heard—"Like eighth grade boys know anything about anything," she said in her long-suffering senior way. "Joey, you are who you are. This doesn't change that; it's just a part of it. Anyone who doesn't get that isn't worth the time."

Just having Linda in the same school with me made it easier to begin to accept and be myself there. She never changed or treated me differently, but I knew she would always be there when I doubted myself or needed to talk. I didn't really come out to anyone else that year, but I was less in the closet, less uncomfortable, and less worried that someone might find out. I didn't say I was gay, but I didn't pretend to be straight either. I was just myself and my sexual orientation wasn't a determining part of that.

When Linda graduated, I felt a real loss. Even though we seldom hung out together in school, just knowing she was there gave me confidence, made me feel safer. We had a long talk about it that spring and, in addition to her telling me she was always only a phone call away, she suggested that maybe it was time to let someone else know, so I wouldn't feel so alone. I had lots of friends, played front line on the basketball team, and was pretty well respected at school. Linda thought if anyone could pull it off, it would be me.

I wasn't so sure. I had visions of friends being shocked and guys avoiding me in the locker room. I was a little surprised to find that part of me believed that my friendships and popularity depended upon me being straight. When I thought about it that way, it made me feel like an impostor. It made my friendships and accomplishments seem like a sham. Linda came to the rescue once again. "These people like you because of who you are; they have known and liked you for years. You have earned their respect because of who you are and what you have done. If anyone changes the way they see you just because they find out you are gay, that just makes them smaller, not you." When Linda said it, it made sense. Coming out didn't change me; it just changed people's perception of me, and that was theirs to deal with.

That summer, I came out to Irene, a good friend of mine. She didn't miss a beat, gave me a hug, and said "No duh. I was wondering when you were going to get around to telling me that." We both laughed and continued our conversation as if nothing big had happened. I asked her how she had known. Did I "act gay"? She laughed again and asked me what I meant by that. I didn't know. I just thought it had been my secret. Irene hugged me again and said, "Joey, we are best friends. Don't you think I know you? You don't act gay, whatever that means; you just act like Joey. But I figured any guy as good-looking and popular as you are who was never interested in all the girls who kept flirting with him must have other interests. And you don't do those dumb guy sex things around me. We can just be friends. It is totally cool."

Wow. I didn't know these things about myself. I had been so absorbed in figuring out who I was to me that I hadn't really thought about how I came off to others. I asked Irene if other people knew and she said, "Oh, probably some do. Most people probably just haven't thought about it. It's not like a question you routinely ask yourself about your friends." I knew not everyone would be as accepting and honest as Irene, but what she said made sense. Being gay was mine to figure out and understand. Everyone else's opinion and reaction was theirs. I couldn't control it or even predict it, but it also didn't define who I was, only who they were.

Over the next two years, I didn't really *come* out, I *became* out. I told a few people, ones I could really trust, and most of them handled it really well. I found that as I became more honest and comfortable, it was easier for other people to be comfortable. There was one guy who I had been friends with since second grade that just couldn't deal with it and that hurt. I knew it was his thing, but it made me angry on the outside and hurt on the inside. How could he just give up our friendship like that? I was no more gay now than when we were friends. Girls were easier with it than straight guys and there were a few guys who said some pretty mean stuff, mostly behind my back. I was lucky to have a lot of friends who stuck up for me and I think probably protected me from a lot of it.

Being out, I came to know most of the other gay kids at school—those who were out and those who either questioning or hiding. I had a couple of relationships, but mostly we were all really good friends. Some of us chose to be out and some didn't. That was a personal decision. We were all totally different—some theater people, a couple jocks like me, some really brainy, some goof-offs, some partiers, and some straight (as in drugs)—but being gay gave us a sense of camaraderie. We each knew what it feels like to overhear a joke or put down about gays. We knew what it feels like to doubt yourself. We knew what it feels like to have someone get nervous when you are alone with him (or her; two of my best gay friends are lesbians). What it feels like when someone is threatening and homophobic. What it feels like to wonder if someone treated you a particular way or if you weren't selected for something because you were gay. What it feels like to tell your parents.

In spite of all the pressures at school, it was actually hardest for me to tell my parents. I knew they loved me and would support me no matter what, but all my old fears and doubts about what it meant to be gay kept getting in the way. I was afraid I would disappoint them; that they would be supportive, but secretly be ashamed of me. I guess I projected my deepest, darkest fears on to them. Linda quickly pointed out that that was all *my* stuff. I needed to deal with it, but I shouldn't project it onto our parents— I wasn't giving them a chance to react for themselves. She told me that they could probably deal with just about anything except me being scared to tell them—*that* would make them feel bad. I knew she was right, but I kept wanting to protect our relationship, to keep being gay out of it. But it was getting harder and harder to keep being gay out of any of my life. *Who are you going to take to the prom? What are you doing this weekend? Any special girls at school this year?* They were innocent, normal questions, but I couldn't answer them honestly.

I finally told my parents during the fall of my senior year. It was around the football prom and I was seeing a guy named Todd. We weren't going to go to the prom—too much hassle—but had decided to go down to a jazz club that we both liked and make a big evening of it. I could tell that my parents wondered about it even though they didn't say much. The idea that they might already know, like Irene had, bothered me. So one evening when we were alone, I decided to tell them. Even after I had decided, I couldn't figure out what words to use. "I'm gay" didn't seem big enough to explain it. To be honest, I don't really remember what I actually said. I was so intent on how they would react that it kind of blurs up to that point. I just remember sitting on the blue chair in the living room, staring at the floor, and trying to get some hint of what they were thinking and feeling. The silence was deafening. After a few minutes, my dad was the first to speak. He quietly said, "OK." There was something in his voice that seemed sad, confused, surprised, but really OK. Like when I had figured it out, things had suddenly slipped into place and he understood. I knew it would take him a while to come to terms with the whole thing— look how long it took me—but I also knew he was going to be OK with it.

My mom is always more expressive than my dad, but, for once, she was the last to speak. Her words finally came out in a torrent. "Now Joey, you're too young to know that for sure. Lots of guys aren't interested in girls until college. I'm sure this is a stage. Don't make any hasty decisions. You're just too busy with everything to have time for girls right now. . . ." Then she stopped talking. She knew, probably had known for a while. There were tears in her eyes when she finally spoke again.

"I'm sorry, Joey. I know this has got to be hard for you and I am just making a scene. I think I already knew somehow. I just want to protect you from it, from anyone hurting you, from you having to live with all the prejudice and small-mindedness people have about homosexuality. I just want you to be happy and safe. Just give me some time to figure this all out."

That was fair. When I thought of all the feelings and fears that I had worked through over the past five years, I could only imagine how my parents were feeling. But I knew for sure that they weren't ashamed, just feeling vulnerable and worried. Those were familiar feelings and I could help them with those. Now that I wasn't afraid to tell them, we could help each other. And as they came to understand and champion me, I became able to face my own last fears and shame, and champion myself.

Being yourself is never easy. We all have secrets and feelings that we are afraid to share with others. I think that being gay has forced me to deal with that and be true to myself in spite of what anyone else may think. I have had to come to terms with my own attitudes and fears and I have learned not to take on others'. I have been lucky. My sister, my friends, and my parents have all come out with me—facing their own doubts and prejudices. It is not easy, but I think we are doing just fine.

SELF-PORTRAIT *by Hana Tuskamoto*

ABSTINENCE AND VIRGINITY

Sex is often thought of as a romantic, spontaneous part of a relationship, but each individual should make a thoughtful and self-affirming decision about when, how, and if sex is a good and healthy part of their relationship. Pressure may come from many sources, including your own body, but it is a decision you must make by yourself and for yourself.

Ramona

When people say that I don't look like a virgin, I just laugh. Just what do they think a virgin looks like? Like a nun or someone too ugly to get a date? I am president of our class at school, I am a model, and I work out regularly to keep my figure. Some guys don't believe that I'm a virgin, but I am and I don't care who knows it. I don't have a boyfriend right now, but I date and, when I was a sophomore, I went with one guy for almost a year. I have too many things in my life right now to get tied down with one guy. I want to be a photojournalist and I spend a lot of time working on my photography skills and trying to build a portfolio. Last year, I won a special scholarship to a three-week photography workshop in Scotland—I was the only person under twenty-five. It was a blast. I want to travel a lot and work for *National Geographic* someday.

I do go to church and my church teaches abstinence, but that doesn't stop some of my friends, and I don't think it is the only reason why I decided this is important to me. Just between you and me, I don't think premarital sex is a sin—I just think it is too important to take lightly. I have watched friends experiment with sex and it almost always screws up their relationship and makes them feel bad. Guys get a lot of pressure to lay a bunch of girls and then they act like jerks and girls believe them or are afraid to lose them. Then things get ugly. A guy drops the girl after they have had sex and acts all innocent and the girl feels all hurt. Then pretty soon everyone is acting like they don't really care and can have sex with anyone without getting involved or getting hurt. No thank you. When I finally do have sex, I want it to mean something *and* I want my partner to genuinely care about me and my feelings—not just at the moment, but for a long time.

When I turned fourteen, my mom and dad both sat me down and told me they knew that a lot of my friends would start thinking about having sex and they wanted me to know how they felt about it. My dad was embarrassed and I could tell he just wanted to say he would shoot anyone who touched me, but they told me how precious I was and that I should never treat myself like anything less. They said that sex was a whole lot more than a physical act—it was trusting and sharing and allowing another person into my most private, most intimate life. My mom said that before I let a man inside of my body, I needed to feel completely ready and confident of my choice—and that meant being safe, feeling comfortable with my body, and being in an honest and committed relationship. By this point, I was getting pretty embarrassed myself, but you could tell my parents were not going to quit until they had their say. My dad told me that guys weren't insensitive, but they could get pretty competitive with other guys and sometimes that involved girls. He said guys also got a lot of pressure to express their masculinity, so they had to prove themselves. He told me that no matter what a guy said, guys respect a girl who respects herself—and use a girl who doesn't. I can't remember all they said, but it was clear they didn't want me having sex. I don't think my parents really know what it is like for me and my friends, but I do know they love me and I have thought a lot about what they had to say.

A few of my girlfriends have told me they wish they had not lost their virginity the way they did—it wasn't the way they wanted to remember their first time. Most of them feel that they "gave in" and did it to please the guy. I ask them if they enjoy sex and most of them say not really, but the guy does. I don't understand that—girls take all the risks about getting pregnant and taking the pill and protecting themselves from AIDS and STDs and they don't even enjoy it? What a racket. Blowjobs are all the rave these days and some girls say it's not really sex and it is safer. They don't like doing it, but guys love it and it is sort of expected. Why do girls put up with that? Some of the guys I go out with say it is nice not having to worry about having sex since they know where I stand. My mom says that with the right guy and the right relationship, sex can be really great for women, but I don't see many of my friends having such a great time. As far as I can tell, it's the guys that are scoring and the girls are just putting out. Not my idea of great sex.

You know, I am only seventeen and I have my whole life to figure all this stuff out. Sure, I get hot and enjoy kissing and being with a guy, but I'm not ready for all these complications. I am still trying to figure out who I am on my own and what love means and what things I want in my life. I don't know if I will wait until I am married, but I do know that I will be a lot more sure of myself than I am now and I will be in a relationship with somebody that I know and can trust completely before *we* decide to make a sexual commitment. And I will never let someone pressure me or make that decision for me. Sure, some people give me a hard time, and a couple of my friends don't think I will be able to resist the pressures—but you know, it really isn't that hard if you think about it. I can wait.

MALE SEXUALITY

"JUSTIN" *by Robyn Strumpf*

Brett

All you ever hear about is girls and their precious virginity. Guys are objectified as sex-crazed idiots looking for action like males were some kind
of primitive hothouse of hormones with no feelings or a brain. Even Robin
Williams said, "God gave me a penis and a brain, but only enough blood to

run one of them at a time." Sure, some guys are jerks, but all this macho press objectifies guys just as much as girls. Especially when it comes to sex.

People say that the media represent women as super-thin, dimwitted sexual objects and this makes girls have a bad body image and sense of their own worth. Well, take a look at the men in those same shows. We are either a bumbling, hen-pecked sit-com pseudo-male, or "Bond . . . James Bond." Given the choice, most guys would rather be James, but James Bond is a pretty daunting role to fill. James Bond is never scared, lonely, boring, undesirable, nervous, unsure of himself, or without a clever reply. He is physically strong and athletic without ever working out and can jump out of moving cars without getting his hair messed up. He is always cool, calm, and collected, quickly outthinking any villains or women that cross him. Women can't wait to get him into bed and he never lacks the interest or stamina for marathon, unemotional sex. He gives and takes physical violence without a flinch or second thought. He drives fast, sleeps around, fights, and takes life-threatening risks without ever getting hurt. He is rich, suave, and detached. James Bond is the center of the movie and everyone in it, but he has no obligations or vulnerabilities. That adds up to a pretty hard act to follow.

James Bond didn't create the male mystique; he is the composite picture of all the subtle and flagrant fantasies about manhood that boys *and girls* grew up with. Strong, calm, independent, unemotional, violent, impenetrable, and inexhaustibly sexual. And for many guys, the male media model is the only one we have. I know more about women—real women—than I know from experience what a *real man* is. My mom did most of my raising and almost all of my elementary school teachers were women. My dad works long hours and is usually tired and somewhat preoccupied when he is at home. I have never seen him cry or look scared. He is the disciplinarian in our family and while he is fair and I know he loves me, he is still a little intimidating and distant. We talk about sports and political stuff, but I don't have any idea what he thinks about sex or love. We did a quick version of the birds and the bees when I was 14, but it was mostly about don't get a girl into trouble. He seems more uncomfortable talking about that stuff than I am. All this adds up to what I know about being a sexual man.

That's not to say I don't talk about sex. As you may have heard, guys talk about sex all the time. We make jokes and rate girls and talk about getting laid. What we don't talk about is when you are madly in love with a girl and she dumps you. Or being a virgin. Or worrying about getting an erection at a bad time—or not getting an erection at a good time. I don't want to sit around and talk about this stuff *all* the time, but there isn't anyone I can seriously talk to about these things *ever.* I am guessing that other guys worry about girls and performing sexually, but, for all I know, I might just be the only one. I can get drawn into the macho sex talk like anyone else; in fact, most of my talk is to convince others that I *don't* worry about that stuff. Half of what I say is bullshit and I expect that is true of other guys as well. Only with them, I don't know which half. I think most of the big talk that guys do is to impress other guys, not girls.

And then there is all that pressure not to be gay. Girls can act and dress masculinely and get away with it most of the time, but if a guy acts "feminine" in any way, people wonder about his sexuality. If you don't like sports, if your voice hasn't changed, if you like art or theater, if you don't talk about sex and girls all the time, or, God forbid, if you cry when something is sad—all that puts you on the suspect list. And since in early adolescence none of us knows for absolute sure that we aren't gay, this produces a lot of swagger. I know one guy who gets teased mercilessly just because he doesn't look and act macho enough. I have no idea if he is gay or not, but hey, who needs the hassle? It is easier to exaggerate all that wonderful James Bond maleness than put up with homophobic bullshit.

Height is a big deal when you are a guy. I don't care what they say, girls don't like to go out with guys who are shorter than they are. Men are supposed to be tall, dark, and handsome. And as much as girls criticize guys for being attracted to a girl's looks, girls are just as bad. Except girls are allowed to use makeup and clothes that accentuate their looks; guys are just supposed to look good naturally. Try to cover up a pimple and you will hear about it forever. Check out the guys in advertising—they are just as much of a travesty as all the female models. You have to be buff in a certain kind of off-handed sexual way. Don't let your voice squeak. Shave even if you don't have a beard. Make sure your muscles are well defined, shoulders broad, butt tight, and size may not matter during intercourse, but it sure does in the locker room.

A lot of this is in competition with other guys, but if it is a contest, then girls are the prize. That sets up problems right from the start—girls don't like to be objectified any more than guys do. Now, don't tell me that girls don't go after guys who will give them social status; they do it too. But with guys, there is an added sexual element. Not only do you have to be seen with a good-looking girl, you have to be scoring. Or at least say you are. This ignores two questionable assumptions. One, it assumes that all men are unequivocally competent and confident in their sexuality, and two, that all male relationships with a girl are exclusively sexual. James Bond strikes again.

Guys may have strong sexual feelings, but that doesn't mean we are always experienced or confident. Physically, you may have noticed, we occasionally don't have complete control over our "manhood." Wet dreams are just the tip of the iceberg. Somebody said that the brain is the largest sex organ. Seeing or imagining someone or something that turns me on can give me a hard-on, time and place not withstanding. Girls may get turned on by a situation, but it doesn't show. And the opposite is also true. Girls can fake an orgasm, but it is rather difficult to fake an erection. So, girls can pretend to be aroused and go through the motions whether they are or not. Guys can't. Now, if it were true that guys are the sex maniacs they are made out to be, that wouldn't be a problem. But the truth is that sometimes guys aren't in the mood or don't want to have sex or just plain can't get it up. Not only can guys not fake it, this lack of inexhaustible sexuality may reflect negatively on our self-image. Even if the girl or other guys don't mind, we have been brainwashed to question ourselves. *What is wrong with me that I don't feel like having sex? Why can't I get an erection? Am I gay? What will the girl think of my masculinity?* Girls may worry about that kind of stuff, but they aren't in a position to have to be constantly proving themselves.

In addition to all of the physical performance demands, we are also put in the position of always being the one in control. We have to make the first move whether it is asking a girl on a date or attempting the first kiss. If you don't think that guys worry about rejection when we do this, you have been watching too much James Bond. Girls may feel impatient waiting for us to make a move, but they don't risk getting turned down cold. And no matter how inexperienced or nervous a guy might be, he is supposed to be confident and worldly. Watching James Bond can only get you so far and even pornography doesn't usually provide much resemblance to my sex life. I may have the hormones, but they didn't come with operating instructions. It is part of the male sexual myth is that we always know just what to do. I have the basics of my own body down, but the female body is an amazing mystery. All the talk about foreplay and the clitoris and multiple orgasms is pretty intimidating. As long as I am pretending that I know what I am doing—and a guy is not supposed to need to ask—it is hard to figure it all out. I am usually comfortable talking with girls, about most things, but even with girls I am expected not to need to talk about sex. To admit doubts or ask questions just doesn't fit the image.

And then there is the matter of reading a girl's mind. There seems to be some kind of female code about playing hard to get and a guy is somehow supposed to know when it is a game and when it is for real. No means no—but sometimes girls say no because that's part of the game. And sometimes girls act like they mean yes even though they are saying no. As a guy, how are you supposed to figure out what a girl is really saying?

Girls don't always own up to their sexual feelings—who knows why?—and then expect the guy to keep pressuring them until they do what they really wanted to do in the first place. I am not excusing any guy for raping a girl—that is inexcusable—but it does get confusing. Girls need to say what they do and do not want and not play games. I think guys should just back off until girls get the courage to admit to their feelings and take equal responsibility for having or not having sex.

The other problem with boundless male sexuality is that it assumes that every male-female relationship is sexual. Don't get me wrong, sex is great and I do think about it and I do get turned on. But that is not all I am looking for in a girl. Guys have feelings and I sometimes think when a guy really falls for a girl, he can be more emotional than a girl is—inside. I have a friend who was depressed for months after he broke up with his girlfriend. I know another guy who is so crazy about this one girl that he doesn't dare approach her and get rejected. I have had sentimental crushes on girls that would embarrass Hallmark. The thing that makes this so hard for guys is that it doesn't fit the James Bond image, so we either have to hide these feelings or feel hopelessly emasculated. The typical male reaction to rejection is anger or indifference. Girls are supposed to be lovesick; guys are supposed to be sexual.

Girls complain about this, but they also reinforce it when they act like we don't have any feelings. *"All guys ever think about is sex."* I have seen some girls treat guys really terribly, using them to get invited to a dance or make someone else jealous. If a girl knows that a guy really likes her, she may manipulate him—and then drop him because he isn't macho enough. Some girls tease guys sexually and then act surprised when the guy comes on to them. It's like they use their sexuality to make a guy crazy; sort of a sexual power trip. Pretending that relationships are only sexual, not personal, can be just a way us guys develop for protecting ourselves.

Maybe guys do think about love and sex differently—frankly, I can't imagine being in love with a girl without having sexual feelings for her. And I can also have sexual feelings that don't have anything to do with love. I think of these as two very different experiences—maybe the James Bond male thing and the real relationship thing. I definitely have James Bond feelings, partly hormonal and partly socialized into me. But to define male sexuality as strictly *search and conquer* is simple-minded beyond belief. The more we are trapped into this model, the less fully masculine and sexual guys can be. We buy into it, guys trap each other into it, girls label us with it, and the media love to define male sexuality as some sort of contest. As long as guys or girls are defined by this superficial sexual mythology, it's not sex; it's just masturbation.

PREGNANCY

Samantha

I was no dummy. I knew what birth control was, and I knew where and how to get it. I knew I should be using it. Unfortunately, it just simply wasn't on my mind. My boyfriend and I had several discussions on the subject. We would decide we shouldn't have sex anymore until we got some protection. But passion was more powerful than logic. We just never got around to using a reliable method on a regular basis. Our situation was not unique. We stayed together the entire year. He graduated in the spring.

We spent a lot of time together that summer. In late June, I found out I was pregnant. After months of taking chances, I was finally caught. Needless to say, I was devastated. I decided to have the baby. My boyfriend was going away to college, and regardless of good intentions he may have had, he was basically out of the picture.

I was faced with the decision of whether or not to return to school. Within a few months, my pregnancy would be apparent. My friends, my support system, my future was at school. I decided to return that fall and live in the dorm. Later that summer, my parents and I met with the headmaster to discuss my condition. Although shocked, and perhaps uncertain of what lay ahead, the administration and the board of trustees allowed me to return to school. I don't think they could actually have stopped me, but it was considered.

Everyone knows that teenage girls get pregnant and have babies, but as far as I know, it doesn't usually occur at reputable boarding schools. After a long summer, I returned in September to begin my senior year, three months pregnant, but not yet showing. Although only some of my friends knew, in a school of not many more than several hundred students news travels fast. I decided to return to school because I couldn't imagine myself alone at home with a tutor, or in a home for unwed mothers, from September to February. I belonged at school. I was a good student, and I had a lot of friends there. I wasn't sure what was in store for me. To put it mildly, this was the beginning of a very difficult year.

As I mentioned before, at first not everyone knew I was pregnant. Baggy jeans hid the weight I was gaining. One day in the cafeteria, I remember a guy joking, saying: "That shirt really makes you look pregnant," He had no idea until I answered, "I am." It was a pretty embarrassing situation.

As nature took its course, it wasn't long before the entire school knew. At first, I felt like everyone was walking on thin ice around me. Eventually, they got used to it. I think a lot of people had a very difficult time knowing what to say to me. Some tried to act like everything was the same, but it wasn't.

Being seventeen, a high school senior, and pregnant was not a lot of fun. Besides the physical pain, I think one of the things that made me suffer most was my inability to participate in many activities that were important to student life. During my first three years of high school, I was a great athlete. I loved playing field hockey and lacrosse. Being pregnant, varsity hockey that fall was out of the question. I missed being on the team. I watched them play and cheered them on at home games. It was heartbreaking knowing that I should have been out on the field with them. Certainly, my social life also suffered. No boy dared ask me out, and I couldn't blame them. I heard about parties, but was never invited. I probably wouldn't have gone anyway. At a time when peers were so important, I felt I didn't belong anymore. I would have given anything to be able to fit into a pair of jeans and go out on a Saturday night. Instead, I was wearing maternity dresses and practicing my breathing. I did have fun shopping, going to movies, etc., but I could no longer participate in a lot of typical high school fun. Since the father of the baby was far away, I felt very alone. Besides that, I felt fat and ugly. It was a nightmare. Nonetheless, I was glad to be at school.

I did consider going to a home for unwed mothers, but after visiting it, I knew I couldn't. I wanted to be with my friends. I wanted to take classes at my school and most of all, I wanted the senior status that I had waited for so long. I tried to do everything as normally as possible. At the time, I felt that by leaving school I would have been copping out, running away and hiding. I was in a sheltered environment. Even the people who worked in the kitchen got to know me and made sure I was eating well enough "for two."

I was lucky to be in such a nurturing environment. Not once did I hear an insulting or derogatory remark. More than once, I was complimented on my courage in both direct and subtle ways. I had a group of very close friends. Although I'm sure that many people may have been uncomfortable around me, eventually I blended in. Both teachers and other students approached me and offered support. At times I welcomed it, and at other times I just wanted to forget everything. At times I felt so alone, so distant, so depressed that I just couldn't take it anymore. I felt as if my deepest, most intimate secrets were all out in public. But I was never completely alone, and I learned to deal with it.

In one sense, I was very lucky. There was one person I could not have survived without, my adviser. A woman with a child of her own, she was my backbone, available to me twenty-four hours a day. I spent many hours talking, crying, and just hanging out and relaxing in her apartment. From her I learned not only good exercises and ways to make the pregnancy more comfortable, but also how to stop worrying about everyone else and concentrate on taking care of myself. Her insight, patience, and caring held me together. We became very close. She took care of me and protected me. Without her support, I never would have made it. She stuck by me through it all. My friends tried very hard to be supportive; I think they became frustrated at times. They didn't quite know what to do or say. I was a constant reminder of what could happen to them if they weren't careful.

Like every other senior, I was applying to colleges for the coming September. Because I was pregnant, I chose not to have interviews with any prospective schools. The seniors from my class went to the local public high school one Saturday to take the necessary standardized tests. I can't remember if it was the SATs or the Achievements. Being pregnant, it was strenuous to sit and take these tests, any tests. Despite everything happening in my life, I managed to keep up my grades. I did miss some classes, but not enough to put me significantly behind. I was accepted at three out of the five colleges I applied to and was determined to go.

As time went on, school became more and more difficult. I lived on the third floor of my dorm. It was tiring walking up two flights of stairs. I loved having friends nearby, but dorm life doesn't offer a great deal of privacy. I was embarrassed to be seen in the bathroom, getting in and out of the shower. I wasn't much for staying up late and talking. For at least a month, I cried myself to sleep every night. One of my best friends lived in the room next door. I later learned she could hear my crying, but didn't know what to do or say. It was tough to get up in the morning and face school. Getting there by eight thirty, after spending a sleepless night, was a strain. I was jealous of every other girl there. It was hard not to be depressed. Physically, I was uncomfortable. I felt scared, guilty, tense, angry, impatient, lonely, frustrated, and confused.

Classes at my prep school were small; I couldn't hide. Sometimes, I just didn't have the energy to pay attention. One day during class, I felt the baby kicking. I was very excited and very happy. A friend sitting next to me asked to feel it also. Although it was a happy moment, it was a pretty strange thing to be doing during math class. The fatter I got, the more uncomfortable it was to sit at those desks with the attached chairs. I could barely fit behind them. Somehow I managed to keep up with my work. My teachers didn't give me extra leeway in terms of assignments until close to the baby's due date. I respected them for treating me like everyone else. After all, I was in school to learn.

I delivered a baby boy late in February and returned to school in March. The baby was adopted five days after he was born. I loved him. After spending six months of my senior year at school pregnant, I was back. Everything was not exactly back to normal, but I was working on it. I talked a lot to students who had been adopted, and also faculty members who had adopted children of their own. I can never repay the love and support I was given by many. Although my experience was painful, it was a chance for me to learn a great deal about myself. I wouldn't wish it upon anyone, but it is possible to be pregnant, go to school, have a child, and still be able to go to college the next year. I am not advocating teen pregnancy. I am simply showing that when faced with one of the most challenging experiences of my life, I was able to successfully finish my senior year. No one was happier than I was at graduation.

I believe I touched the lives of many people that year as well as being touched by them. I did become distant from some friends and closer to others. I know my "situation" made some girls think twice before having unprotected sex. In a letter I received after giving at talk to the entire school about my experience, my adviser wrote: "Another milestone, another opportunity for us to confront your courageousness: another opportunity to simultaneously experience such deep sadness and great joy. You were beautiful, composed, and honest. I and many others feel it was an honor to have you speak to us. . . ."

I tried to think back and remember if any type of sex education, birth control, etc., was ever discussed. I could remember only one gathering that dealt with these issues. It was during my sophomore year. I do remember frequent attempts made by the faculty and administration to educate the students on the danger of drug abuse. Our sex lives were not a hot topic at that time. I don't know if the faculty were simply unaware that sex occurred on campus, or they chose not to deal with it. If as much emphasis is placed on contraceptive use as it is on drug use among students, they would learn how important it is. Granted, for most teenagers, sex is still an embarrassing, but infinitely intriguing, topic. Candid advice about sexual relationships and contraceptives should be available. And, it should be available again and again and again. In a situation such as a boarding school, where many teenagers are together in a close extended way, the faculty and administration have a responsibility to teach not only mathematics and English, but life's lessons as well. Maybe then, students would be more compelled to think realistically before engaging in sexual relationships.[3]

UNTITLED *by Katie Mullet*

ABORTION

In the United States, about 30 percent of all abortions are performed on teenagers; 45 percent of all teenage pregnancies end in abortion. Abortion is the most controversial option for dealing with an unwanted pregnancy. Pro-life advocates decry the murder of a human life. Pro-choice marchers protest the government invasion of a woman's rights over her own body. Congress and the Supreme Court grapple with the limits of legal decisions and personal rights. "Nothing like it has separated our society since the days of slavery," said Dr. C. Everett Koop, former surgeon general of the United States. Abortion clinics have been bombed and doctors performing abortions have been threatened, even murdered. Protesters on both sides have been threatened and attacked. Both pro-choice and pro-life advocates feel very strongly and emotionally that their position is right and just. Each decision about abortion is complicated and raises difficult personal, ethical, and legal questions.

Melissa

This is a really hard story for me to write because I don't talk about it easily and I want you to really understand, not just project your own ideas on what I am going to say. If you are pro-life, you probably already think that I made an irresponsible, selfish decision and, if you are pro-choice, you probably think it was my right and no big deal. Both of you are wrong. It was the most serious and difficult choice I have ever made—I thought long and hard about it when we made the decision and I still think about it. The whole experience was very complicated: My feelings were not simple or unambiguous and it was not just about me. Please try to put your assumptions or judgments aside and really hear me.

I guess it all starts with Mike and me. We had been going together for almost three years. He was my best friend and my confidant. Neither of us were angels, but I think we were good for each other. Mike could always make me laugh and we would spend hours talking and listening to each other. We had gone through some tough times together—Mike's parents had gotten a divorce two years ago and it had been a hard time for him. Sometimes the fighting would get so bad that he would sneak out and come stay with me. He was worried about his mom and wanted to protect his younger sister, but he felt so helpless. He was angry, confused, and scared. My parents had divorced when I was eight so I knew some of how he felt. I did my best to comfort him and let him talk. I was having trouble with my stepmom and Mike was always there for me too. But it wasn't all serious, for sure. We always had a good time together whether we were with friends or just on our own. We enjoyed the same things and just felt comfortable and happy together. I admired Mike and saw things in him that other people didn't recognize. He always made me feel pretty and special and important.

We started having sex after we had been going together for almost a year—it was just about the time Mike's parents were splitting up. We had always been physically close and knew that sex would be a part of our relationship at some point, but we wanted it to be deliberate and special. The openness of our relationship allowed us to talk openly about sex and we explored our feelings and bodies in caring and playful ways. We were always careful—Mike never resisted using a condom and I used a spermicide for good measure. We laughed a lot and learned about sex together, talking and learning what pleased each other and honestly sharing our doubts and questions. We weren't in any position to parent a baby, but in every other way, we were responsible, loving, and comfortable in our sexual relationship.

So how did I get pregnant? I have gone over that in my mind a hundred times. Did the condom slip when Mike was withdrawing? Was it a sperm in the pre-cum when we were just messing around? Was it just the luck of the draw? We never had unprotected sex, but that "human error" variable must have gotten in there somehow. When my period was late, I wasn't really even worried because I *knew* I couldn't be pregnant. Not only had we been careful, but also I must admit I couldn't imagine really being pregnant. I was still getting used to all the changes in my body—the idea that I could actually carry a real live baby inside of me was just a fantasy.

But by the time I was two weeks late, I started to get nervous. I had been pretty regular for a couple of years now and this was definitely unusual. When I told Mike, his face went pale and he asked if I was sure. I never remember the exact dates of my period, but my last period had been the weekend that we had gone sailing with his dad, so I could trace it exactly. That was six weeks ago. Mike gave me some money to buy a pregnancy test—he felt embarrassed buying the test at the drugstore with me, but he wanted me to know we were in this together. In less than an hour, the little spot turned pink. I didn't believe it. When Mike called first thing in the morning, I told him I hadn't taken it yet and went out and bought a second test. Pink again. Mike picked me up after school and he could tell right away by the look on my face. I cried and Mike held me, but he looked like he was about ready to cry too. We looked for all the possible ways that it might not be true. We tried to figure out how it could have happened. We didn't really blame each other, but I knew we were both looking for someone to blame, someone else to take responsibility and make it all go away. Gradually the truth sank in and we were faced with this new reality—and big decisions.

Mike very gallantly said that he would respect my wishes and that he would do whatever I needed him to do. Timidly, he offered to marry me if that was what I wanted. I loved Mike and had often fantasized about being married to him, but I was just seventeen and he was only eighteen, working for a year in order to save money for college. We both had dreams and plans. I would have to drop out of high school. We had no money or resources to raise a baby. I had a two-year-old stepsister and I knew how much time and work babies required. My dad would go ballistic and my mom would be so worried. Mike couldn't even imagine telling his folks. His dad was in and out of the picture and his mom was pretty seriously depressed—he worried this would be too much for her to handle. We felt so alone and frightened. It seemed that this pregnancy affected so many people and yet we were the only ones in the world who knew about it. I must admit that even then it was hard to actually associate the word pregnancy with a real baby. I didn't look or feel any different and the "miracle of life" seemed more like a catastrophe—there were so many things to think about that the actual baby was an unreal eventuality.

I guess I had always been pro-choice, in a sort of mindless, rational way that most kids my age thought about abortion. *Of course* a woman should have the right to make this personal decision about her body and her life. But personally faced with the decision, I quickly realized what an overwhelming right and responsibility that was. For the first time, I fully understood that pro-choice didn't give any answers; it just asserted a woman's right to struggle with the questions. And there were no simple or easy answers. I was in no way ready to be a mother, but I had cocreated an embryo that could become a baby—our baby. Mike and I were devoted and careful lovers, but an early marriage and baby would most likely wear out that love and leave all three of us without a family. I don't think we were very realistic about financial factors, but even our naive projections came up short. We should take responsibility for our actions, but would we just be punishing a baby by bringing him or her into a life that provided no stability or security? Was it better to end a pregnancy before it became a real baby—or was it already too late for that?

I was lucky to have Mike to talk all this through with. I knew of other girls who had never told the father or fathers who had just walked away from the situation. Mike was careful not to pressure me; at the same time he tried to be honest and express his own feelings and opinions. Luckily, he was as distraught as I was. After four days of talking, crying, vacillating, and trying to come to terms with all the considerations, we decided to go to Planned Parenthood to talk with one of their counselors. We met with a woman named Brenda who was really nice and easy to talk to. She walked us through all the options—keeping the baby, adoption, and abortion—and let us ask questions and talk about the pros and cons of each choice. I always thought that Planned Parenthood was kind of an abortion clinic, but I quickly learned that they stress responsibility and careful, personal decision making, not abortions. Brenda gave us some materials to read over and set up an appointment to come back and talk with her in two days.

In the meantime, I decided to talk with my mother. We had always been pretty close and I think she knew that Mike and I were sexually active. I was uncomfortable telling her—I didn't like admitting I had screwed up. Also, it was my problem, and I didn't want her to take over and treat me like a child. But I needed to talk to someone besides Mike, someone else who loved me and would support me. I wasn't sure how Mom would react, but I knew she would support me. She was definitely taken by surprise, but I give her a lot of credit. She didn't yell or cry or make me feel bad—she was quiet for a few minutes and then came over and held me and said, "I'm so sorry, baby." Even calling me her baby, it was clear that she understood that I was facing an adult situation and there was nothing she could do to protect me or resolve it for me. I cried a little and told her everything that Mike and I had discussed and what Brenda had told us. I think part of me wanted her to wipe away my tears and make it all better, but she just listened, asked questions, and told me that I had to think deeply about what I would most feel right about. My decision affected other people, but I had to be true to my own sense of what was the best thing to do. None of the answers were easy or obvious.

When Mike and I went back for our second appointment, we had decided to have an abortion. Neither of us wanted to bring a baby into a situation as fraught with insecurity and limitations as the one we could provide. Brenda questioned us carefully and made sure that we had arrived at our decision from a place of thought, not desperation. My mother supported our decision and we made an appointment for the next Tuesday at 9:00 in the morning. The time passed in a blur and while I was scared, I felt in my heart that we had made the right decision. Mike said that he couldn't completely empathize because he wasn't the one who was pregnant, but he too felt it was the best thing to do.

At 9:00 on Tuesday, Mike and I arrived at the clinic. Mom was waiting at home for me and would be by the phone if we needed her. The receptionist was very helpful and gave me some paperwork to fill out. She was very careful not to use last names or say why anyone was there. I glanced around the room to see my company as I filled out the forms. There were a couple of girls my age and several women in their twenties and thirties; Mike was the only guy. I wondered who these other women were, why they were here, and what they were thinking and feeling. I turned in the forms and was told to wait until they called me for an ultrasound. Mike stared at a magazine and I held his hand while we waited. After about twenty minutes, a nurse called me in while Mike had to stay in the waiting room. The nurse explained that the ultrasound gave the doctor specific information about my uterus and clinical information about the pregnancy and fetus. She inserted an ultrasound probe into my vagina and slowly moved it around to see where the yolk sac was located and determine exactly how far along the pregnancy was. It wasn't much larger or more uncomfortable than a speculum and the technician talked with me and explained what she was doing the whole time. It only took about five minutes and then I got dressed and went back into the waiting room. Mike squeezed my hand and asked me how I was doing. For the first time, it really hit me how different this pregnancy was for me than it was for Mike. I suppressed a twinge of resentment and said, "OK so far."

It was another forty-five minutes before I was called in for a one-on-one consultation. Mike could join me in a few minutes, but Brenda wanted to talk with me alone first to make sure that I was comfortable with my decision and no one was pressuring me against my will. I assured her that both Mike and my mom had been great and I had considered all my options carefully. Brenda then called Mike in to join us—he looked relieved to be included, but uncomfortable being the lone male in this sanctuary of women. Brenda went over our options once again and asked us how we felt about our decision. We both felt confident that we were making the right choice, but admitted that it was all a bit overwhelming. Mike said that he felt helpless and detached watching me go through all this while he sat outside. Brenda explained that no one was allowed in the back rooms of the clinic in order to protect the women's privacy and security, and assured him that his support was very important. She told Mike that I would probably be hungry after the procedure, so bringing me some food, getting a heating pad for cramps, and maybe renting a couple of movies to watch tonight would all be very helpful. Mike seemed to be grateful for something concrete that he could do to help me.

Brenda asked if we had read the materials she had given us and described in detail everything that would be happening. She asked if we had any religious objections to abortion and who we could talk with about our feelings and thoughts. She was glad that I had talked to my mother and would have her as a support person. She gave us a list of counseling referrals if we encountered feelings we didn't expect or know how to deal with. Brenda answered all of our questions and seemed comfortable with our answers and how we had arrived at our decision. She said that it was normal to be nervous and even sad; an abortion was a complicated and very personal decision.

Mike then went back into the waiting room and Brenda accompanied me to the lab where a nurse took my temperature and blood pressure and drew some blood to make sure I wasn't anemic. The nurse explained that they used "conscious sedation"—either an IV or oral medication to help me relax and relieve the cramping—but I would be awake throughout the procedure. I don't like needles, so I chose the pills. The nurse said everything looked good, gave me the medication, and sent me back to the waiting room. I could tell that Mike was getting restless and asked the receptionist if we could take a short walk. She said we could walk outside, but not to go far—the medication would start to make me a little spacey within about twenty minutes and we should come back in when I started to feel it.

It felt good to be outside and feel the air against my face and the sunshine on my back. The day seemed so dazzling and vivid. Mike and I didn't have much to say—we walked along, holding hands, each of us in our own thoughts. I thought about how simple things had been only a month ago; how I never thought I would be in this situation. That seemed naive and yet I wished I could be back in that uncomplicated, childish place. I thought about babies and college and how vulnerable and public my body felt. Mike asked me if I was OK and I asked him if he was OK. He put his arm around me, gently kissed me, and whispered, "I'm sorry."

Back in the waiting room, it was another hour before the nurse called me back. She told Mike that the actual procedure only took a couple minutes, but that it would be an hour including preparation and time in the recovery room. She suggested that he go get something to eat and come back in an hour. Mike looked at me and I told him to go, that I was fine. He looked hesitant, but relieved. I gave him a hug and told him to be sure to bring me back something to eat. As he walked out the door, I wanted to run after him, but turned and followed the nurse into the room. It looked just like any gynecologist's office with that disagreeable table and its cold metal stirrups on one side of the room and a vacuum machine about the size of a large TV on the other. I undressed from the waist down and settled onto the table with its trusty stirrups. The doctor came into the room and introduced herself and asked how I was doing. By now, the medication was working and I said I felt fine. The doctor reviewed the procedure with me once again and checked to make sure that I felt comfortable with my decision. She felt around my abdomen to feel the position of my uterus. She inserted a warmed speculum and felt my cervix. I was feeling vague and detached, like I was watching the whole thing. I heard the doctor say something about dilating the cervix and felt a twinge of an injection and some cramping as she inserted some increasingly wide rods to dilate the cervix. The nurse stood by my head and kept saying reassuring things. I tried to listen, but kept getting lost in my own thoughts, occasionally being pulled back by a cramp or instruction from the doctor. She explained that everything looked good and she was inserting a plastic tube from the suction machine and it would all be over in a couple minutes. I heard the machine turn on and felt a pulling, cramping feeling in my abdomen. The doctor moved the tubing around gently, vacuuming out the lining of my uterus. It seemed like less than a minute and the noise stopped and the tube was withdrawn. The doctor explained that she was going feel the uterus to make sure all the lining had been removed. She then told me that everything looked fine; I should rest for a few minutes and then the nurse would take me to the recovery room.

The recovery room? After all that deciding and all that waiting, it didn't seem real that the abortion was over and I could go to the recovery room. As I lay there on the table, I took an inventory of my body. The pain reliever and Valium were still in effect and I felt a general numbness throughout my body. My vagina felt sore and stretched and there was a vague emptiness and cramping in my abdomen. Otherwise, I felt relaxed and OK. The nurse brought me a sanitary pad and said that the bleeding would come and go for a couple days. She escorted me to another small room with four padded chairs, each with a heating pad. Two other women were sitting there with heating pads on their stomachs. One was trying to read a magazine and the other was staring out the window—I thought I saw a tear on her face. I thought about my own personal struggle and wondered about the journey that each of these women had taken that had brought them to this room. Odd, disconnected questions crossed my mind. I wondered if they were scared, who their partner was, if they had used birth control, if they had been raped, if they had thought about keeping their baby or putting it up for adoption. I wondered how they were feeling and I wondered how I was feeling. All I knew for sure was that I was starving.

After about forty-five minutes, the sedation was wearing off and aside from the bleeding and occasional cramping, I felt pretty normal. My companions and I devoured the crackers and juice provided and made small talk about sanitary pads, the strength and burdens of women, and how we were never going to have sex again. The nurse gave me some instructions on the birth control I had chosen and an emergency number to call if I had extra-heavy bleeding, strong abdominal pain, or a fever over 101 degrees. I got dressed and walked out to the waiting room where Mike was waiting with an armful of yellow roses.

All this happened four years ago. No one, except Mike, my mom, and my best friend knew about it and I drifted back into my senior year as if nothing had happened. Physically I was fine after a few days, but my thoughts and feelings hung over my head for a long while. I wondered whether it would have been a boy or a girl. I knew it was just an unrecognizable gob of cells vacuumed off my uterus, but the reality of its potential settled in my imagination. I had periods of sadness on and off during that first year and I still find myself with a melancholy feeling around the time the baby would have been born. It is not regret, actually; I still believe we did the right thing and strongly guard my right to make that choice in a safe, thoughtful manner. It is all so deeply personal and complicated, no one else can fully understand or dictate my decision. What I feel is more like grief; grieving for the possibility, for the child that might have been, for a creation of my body and my relationship with Mike that was never realized. I think I also grieve a part of my innocence—a realization that no matter what my intentions or precautions, accidents happen and they have real consequences that I have to accept and live with. There is no inconsequential solution to an unplanned pregnancy. Each choice carries its scars and changes who you are.

Mike and I drifted apart about six months later—I never could figure out how much the strain of the abortion contributed to our breakup. As much as we worked through it together, it felt like a wedge between us. Mike could never completely understand how I felt and how it changed me. Though we were both responsible, I felt like I had to carry the heavier physical and emotional burden and Mike could just be a bystander. That wasn't Mike's fault and I know he felt awkward about it, but it separated us nonetheless. Sex carried this memory and threat for me that made our physical relationship tense and uncomfortable. On some level, I blamed sex and Mike for everything I went through. That wasn't fair but, unconsciously, it kept creeping into our relationship. Little things seemed to bother me and I kept finding fault and blaming Mike.

After I graduated, I looked to college for a fresh start and putting all this behind me. Mike was a reminder. I think this must have been pretty confusing and painful for him. We have talked about it since then and while our relationship will never be the same, we are good friends again. I am in a serious relationship with a wonderful guy right now and I know that I will have to come to terms with all my feelings about the abortion before I can feel safe and comfortable again in a sexual relationship. This has been an important discovery for me as I continue to grow and take responsibility for my life. I don't believe that my decision to have an abortion was either a sin or an entitlement. It was a deeply personal and significant choice. We didn't have a baby, but I think I became an adult.

AIDS

The AIDS epidemic was first identified in 1981 and named by the Centers for Disease Control in 1982 as a new disease that destroys the body's immune system—acquired immune deficiency syndrome. The virus that causes AIDS was isolated in 1984 and named the human immunodeficiency virus or HIV. Half of all people who currently acquire HIV become infected before they turn twenty-five and typically die of AIDS-related complications before their thirty-fifth birthday. AIDS is the sixth leading cause of death among fifteen- to twenty-four-year-olds and the second cause of death among people twenty-five to forty-four. The stakes for AIDS are high. It is fatal and, as far as we know, everyone who has been infected with HIV will eventually develop AIDS. The only 100 percent way to protect yourself from AIDS is to not have intercourse or use injection drugs or share needles of any sort, even for tattoos or piercings. Consistent use of a condom for both intercourse and oral sex will significantly reduce the risk, but abstinence or monogamy with an uninfected partner is the only way to be sure. The biggest danger of AIDS is not a lack of information or random infection. About 98 percent of teens know how AIDS is transmitted, but only 1 percent consistently practice safe sex. Less than 20 twenty of the college students surveyed reported using condoms more than half the time. The more sexual partners a person had, the less likely he or she was to use condoms. Passion and romance have never been particularly rational and in the heat of the moment, many throw caution to the wind. Some get away with it; some don't.

Carie

It was 3:00 in the morning. Scott was freezing. He had no body fat to keep him warm. He was shivering and his teeth were chattering. I put another log on the fire. My husband had been sick with AIDS for months. Taking care of him had become routine. I knew how to treat the big, red, blotchy bedsores. I knew how to massage his joints when they became so painful he screamed. I knew what to do if he had another seizure. I was afraid he might live in this condition for years. He was in a great deal of pain, but he said he wanted to continue living. He wasn't ready to leave me.

Scott was skin and bones. It was difficult for me to sleep next to him because the protruding bones were so sharp against my body. He used to weigh 170 pounds. He wasn't a classically handsome man, but I thought he was cute. His face used to be round. He had straight, baby-fine blonde hair that he wore long. His eyes were blue and sparkled with a hint of mischievousness. Scott was friendly and outgoing with a sense of humor that bordered on shocking, but he had just enough charm to get away with it.

The man I was living with was barely recognizable as the man I'd married three years earlier, but I still loved him with all my heart. I loved him so much that sometimes I wished he would die. It was heartwrenching to see him like this. His face and eye sockets were sunken in. He looked more like a skeleton than a human being.

Tonight, I was worried. It had been three weeks since he'd been able to keep down a meal. I couldn't even get him to take a bit of food anymore. Normally, I would have slept in the bedroom alone, and Scott would sleep on the couch. It was the only way I could get enough sleep to be able to get up and go to work in the morning. Tonight, I knew I needed to be out in the living room with Scott. He didn't look right. I couldn't pinpoint why I felt so uneasy. Was it something in his eyes? Or his speech? I sat in the living room next to the bed and watched him drift in and out of sleep.

Then it happened. I knew something was wrong. His arm flew up in the air involuntarily. He woke up and looked at me. Then it happened again. It was like the other seizures he'd had, but on a smaller scale. Every few seconds, he lost control of his arms. He was aware of what was going on, but was unable to stop it. I called his nurse immediately. Even though it was the middle of the night, she arrived within fifteen minutes. The mini seizures continued and Scott began to lose consciousness. By the time the ambulance arrived, he was in a fetal position with his eyes rolled up in his head. The paramedics gathered him in his bed sheet and lifted him onto the stretcher. I followed behind the ambulance on the five-minute ride to the hospital. While in the ambulance, Scott was given an injection of glucose, which revived him. His blood sugar level was dangerously low due to his lack of food intake.

I was relieved that Scott would be admitted to the hospital. It was getting scary taking care of him at home. I never knew what might happen, and the stress was wearing on me. Scott was hooked up to a glucose drip, which helped him maintain his blood sugar level. Within minutes of being in the hospital, he looked much better. The color was back in his face and that dazed look I had been noticing was no longer apparent. I stayed in the hospital with Scott for seventy-two hours straight. Luckily, there was an empty hospital bed in his room for me to sleep in. I didn't get much sleep, though. He needed help going to the bathroom every hour, more water, more ice chips, more pain medication, warm blankets. It was a constant struggle for him to have everything he needed to be comfortable for a few minutes.

The third night in the hospital, Scott started throwing up violently, only there really wasn't anything in his stomach. He still hadn't been able to eat much, and he had refused intravenous feeding. He was given a shot of Finnegan, an antinausea medication. It stopped the dry heaves, but he started hallucinating, a side effect of the drug. He couldn't function. He kept trying to pull the IV out of his arm and get out of bed. He thought there was a fire in the hospital. I could calm him down for a short time, then he would get anxious again.

At one point, he took a sip of water but panicked when he realized he couldn't remember how to swallow. I said, "Just spit it out" and he did. I was afraid he was going to choke on it. I kept him calm by repeating, "You're going to be okay. We're just waiting for the drug to wear off. I'm here. You'll be alright." Finally he fell asleep. Peace at last for both of us.

Scott woke up with a start.

"I'm having trouble breathing," he said.

"I'll get a nurse."

It was 2:00 in the morning and there were two nurses at the nurse's stations. The older nurse with the warm smile and caring eyes followed me back to room 101 where Scott was gasping to get enough air into his lungs. She cranked on the oxygen and slipped the tubes over Scott's head with two prongs in each nostril delivering the much-needed oxygen. He said it was better but not enough. The nurse turned up the oxygen until Scott said he could breath easily. Scott fell asleep quickly. I crawled into the spare hospital bed and fell asleep to the sound of Scott's breathing.

At 6:00 a.m., he woke up. He was still a little confused.

He asked, "Carie, are you alive?"

I said, "Yes, honey, I'm here."

Then he asked, "Am I alive?"

I said, "Yes, you're fine, you're going to be okay."

"I thought we died last night," he said. "Am I going crazy?"

"No, honey. It was that injection they gave you last night. It made you hallucinate. You're okay now."

"I'm still seeing things, but I know they aren't real. There is an older lady with red hair standing here next to the bed, and there are two men standing at the foot of the bed. I can see them, but I know they aren't really here."

"I think the drug is still wearing off. It shouldn't take much longer," I said.

I got into Scott's hospital bed with him, and he put his thin, bony arms around me. I lay on his chest listening to his heartbeat, hoping it would never stop. Unable to imagine what I would do if it did. I cried silently. My tears fell onto his chest.

"Don't cry, " he said. "I'll make it."

I fell asleep in his arms, praying for the first time in my life. Praying to a God I didn't even believe in. It was all I could do. Hoping, wishing, praying my husband would live.

A couple of hours later, Scott and I woke up. Dr. Troll had come into the room. He was our favorite doctor. He'd been out of town since Scott came into the hospital. We had both been hoping Dr. Troll would know what to do. Scott and Dr. Troll had grown quite fond of each other over the past year. Scott loved listening to Dr. Troll tell stories about his college days when he jammed with the Grateful Dead and roomed with Richard Alpert aka Ram Dass. There was no sign of the jovial doctor now, though. Dr. Troll's face gave away his deep concern. It was bad news. Scott was bleeding internally. All of his lab work pointed to the fact that his systems were shutting down. There was nothing more they could do.

Scott spoke first. "I'd like to be as comfortable as possible. Can I get some morphine?"

Scott had been addicted to drugs and alcohol for ten years before I met him. He had been through a residential drug treatment program and had stayed clean and sober for six years. I knew it was difficult for him to ask for morphine. He had told me he wouldn't take morphine unless he knew he was dying because of how addictive it was.

Dr. Troll left the room and sent a nurse in to give Scott an injection of morphine. I sat next to him in a daze. I had not fully absorbed what Dr. Troll had said. "There's nothing more we can do." I didn't believe it. Scott would be okay.

Five minutes had gone by. Scott said the morphine was helping but he needed more. I found the nurse. She got orders from Dr. Troll, and Scott was given a second dose intravenously. He was very relaxed now. He said it was easier to breathe.

Five more minutes went by.

"Honey, tell them I need one more shot of morphine."

Again, I found the nurse and asked for another injection. She came back to the room with me. She inserted the needle into Scott's IV and slowly administered the morphine Scott had asked for. Within seconds, Scott's body tensed suddenly and then relaxed. The nurse ran from the room and paged Dr. Troll who was in another wing of the hospital. It was obvious Scott was dying. I held his hand and watched him take his last breaths. Each inhale was followed by a long pause and then an exhale and another pause and an inhale and . . .

They say your life flashes before your eyes as you die. As I held my dying husband's hand, my own life flashed by . . .

I see Scott and I on our first date. I am wearing a short yellow dress. The Florida sun had bleached my hair blonder than it'd ever been and my skin is a gold tan. After a month in Washington, D.C., I had traveled down to Florida on a Greyhound bus. That's where I met Scott.

We are at a casual restaurant on the beach. Scott orders a club soda and I have a Coke.

"I don't drink alcohol," he said. "I used to have a problem with drugs and alcohol."

"Oh," I said, trying to hide my surprise so he could feel comfortable talking about it.

"I spent thirty days at the Care Unit Rehab Program. I've been clean and sober now for two years, and it feels great."

We talk for hours. Sharing the stories of our struggles and triumphs. Then he begins to talk about his spiritual beliefs. He believes in life after death; he believes in a higher power that can be called upon for help and strength; he believes all things happen for a reason even when he had no idea what the reason is. He is so sure of himself. He speaks with confidence and a sense of peace with himself and the whole world. It is the first time I had heard someone talk about spirituality without using the word God. I am able to put aside the only image I had of God, a man sitting on a cloud watching us. Finally, I am able to hear the possibility of some universal order. A force that can actually help me, is actually a part of me.

My heart beats fast and I can feel the excitement in my stomach when I realize this was what I am looking for. That was the moment I fell in love.

. . . Another scene flashed before my eyes. I am in the waiting room at the Downtown Doctor, a walk-in health clinic. It is Scott's day off work and I have come in with him to pick up some antibiotics. He had bronchitis again. I sit in the empty waiting room flipping through an outdated issue of *People* magazine.

I hear the door to the exam room open. The first thing I notice when I look up is how pale Scott is.

"I really recommend you get tested as soon as possible," the doctor says.

Scott's face is expressionless as we walk out the door. I follow behind him, and before I can ask, he says, "They think I have AIDS."

"That's ridiculous." I say. "No, you don't."

"The doctor thinks I have some early symptoms. He asked me if I ever used a needle for taking drugs. I did a few times at parties. We shot up co-caine, but that was years ago."

. . . I see our wedding day. We're in Connecticut in Scott's parent's back-yard. The grass is green and the water in the swimming pool is a dazzling blue. It's hot today. It'll probably hit 90 degrees. The guests are dancing, swimming, eating, drinking, laughing, and mingling. I can't believe how many people came—aunts, uncles, cousins, and old family friends. Most people I've never met and Scott barely remembers. We're having a great time though.

We dance to our song "Stand by Me" by Ben E. King.

"When the sky is dark, and the clouds are gray. Won't you stand, stand by me, stand by me. Oh I won't be afraid, no I won't be afraid, just as long as you stand, stand by me."

Scott is holding me tight; our cheeks are touching. It's the happiest day of our lives. The beginning of the rest of our lives. But we know something that no one else knows. The seventy guests see only a happy couple with a bright future ahead of them. We know Scott is HIV positive. Neither of us expects him to live another five years. We're going to make the best of it, though. We are going to live and love and enjoy each other while we can. It's the happiest day of our lives.

. . . I see myself in another waiting room. I'm here for myself this time. Scott couldn't come with me. He's at home. They think he might have pneumonia. I'm here for the results of my HIV test. I'm nervous. I've already tested negative twice, but from the day we found out Scott was positive, I worried that I'd eventually test positive also.

I look around the room and wonder about the other people waiting to be called in for their results. How many of them are positive, I wonder. They all look like normal, healthy people to me. But then again, I remind myself, so does Scott.

"Number 77532."

"That's me."

I stand up.

"Follow me, please."

I follow the social worker into a very small room with two chairs and a desk. The walls are white and bare. The desk is completely empty except for a file with 77532 written on the tab.

I noticed the social worker's name badge. Her name is Lynn. I conclude from the dark circles under her eyes that she is tired and probably overworked and underpaid. I wonder if she's ever been tested for HIV. Without looking up at me, she opens the folder with my code number on it and takes out a small piece of paper.

"Your results have come back positive," she said. She still doesn't look at me. She's looking down at the lab slip. "Would you like to talk about it?"

I know she doesn't really want to talk about it. She doesn't even want to look at me. I hate her. I hate her for telling me this news, and I hate her for not being able to look at me.

I'd already been collecting information for two years. I was sure she couldn't tell me anything about HIV that I didn't already know. Hell, I probably knew more about it than her, I thought.

"I have all the information I need." I stand up and leave. I walk down the hall as fast as I can, holding back my tears. I get to my car and jump into the driver's seat. I quickly start the engine and speed away before, finally, allowing myself to cry. I couldn't believe it. This was not supposed to happen to me. I pound the steering wheel with my fist. I start to feel sick to my stomach, and I want to scream at the top of my lungs, but I know that won't change anything. I can scream and cry and swear. I can get hysterical, but nothing I do can change the fact that I have this fucking virus inside of me.

. . . I am back in room 101 at Natividad Medical Center. These glimpses of my life had happened in an instant. Scott's hand is still warm. His face and chest have begun to turn an ugly shade of gray. His heart is still. He has taken his last breath. Scott had always believed in the existence of the soul. I wanted to believe it, but I didn't have the faith and convictions to be as sure as he had been. I begin to talk to Scott just in case he can still hear me. In case some part of him survived the death of his body.

"I love you, and I want you to know that I'm going to be okay. Don't worry about me. It is okay for you to go. You are going to be fine."

I stroke his soft, blonde hair and run my fingertips down the side of his face. His skin is soft. I kiss him lightly on his forehead, then remove his eyeglasses and the diamond earring that he wore on his right ear. Moving slowly, I pack up his personal belongings.[4]

—Written by Carie Ford Broecker, 1998

A Journey into Healing

Carie Broecker feels good. And that's saying a lot.

The thirty-six-year-old Pacific Grove resident eats right, exercises frequently, and takes herbs and supplements, as many of us do. In her case, it's more than life enhancing—it's an absolute necessity.

More than 15 years ago, Broecker was diagnosed as HIV-positive, which was at that time virtually a death sentence. As the years have gone by, she has traveled the path from grim awareness to radiant optimism.

Her viral load—the prime indicator of the presence of HIV in the body—is currently zero.

Although many diagnosed with the AIDS virus are living longer these days, thanks to new drug therapies, Broecker's story is different. She's held onto her health using alternative medicine in combination with a bare minimum of immune-booting drugs . . .

Living with HIV was not something Broecker had planned on. In fact, she expected to be dead a few years after that test in 1987 came back positive. Carie met her first husband, Scott Ford, in 1986. They fell in love and married, even though she was aware he had been infected with HIV, the virus that causes AIDS. Ford died in 1991 and Carie was a widow at age 24.

In the wake of her grief, she began working for the Monterey County AIDS project as a support group facilitator. Although the work was challenging and stimulating, it was also stressful. Three years later, she left the organization, and not long after that, threw away the AZT and other anti-AIDS drugs she had been taking.

Her doctors argued with her—told her she was committing slow suicide. Yet she was convinced that true healing lay elsewhere.

She had taught herself to meditate not long after Scott Ford's death, inspired by a book by Ram Dass sent to her by a friend. After leaving MCAP, she began to explore new territory with the help of several psychic healers.

Broecker admits she was skeptical of such things at first, but she could feel healing taking place as they worked with her. They also encouraged her to be patient and to trust in her body's ability to cure itself. She was coached in meditation and visualization techniques, where she would picture herself walking on a path of light toward a future where she was happy and healthy. She also spent time in nature, walking on the beach and working in the garden, something she'd never done before.

A new love bloomed into marriage, and she joined her life with that of Scott Broecker in 1994, in a ceremony on Carmel Beach.

"He's absolutely wonderful—my biggest supporter," said Carie. "He's the most positive person I know."

She also found a deep connection with animals, something that has bloomed into her work with the nonprofit organization Animal Friends, for which she is treasurer and a board member. In addition to her own pets, she takes in foster animals until they can be placed.

In addition to her self-care, she also keeps the books for her husband's business, looks after her 14-year-old niece, who came to live with them earlier this year, and works at Practical Magic, the Pacific Grove store she co-owns . . .

Her book, Reach for Your Soul, *grew out of journals she has kept over the past 10 years. People asked her for copies of the manuscript so frequently that she decided it was easier to get it published and have it readily available. "People have* read it and told me it's been meaningful to them," said Broecker. Her intent, however, is not to lecture people on what they should do or must do.

"I try to tell people to follow their own path, and their own heart," said Broecker. "They have to listen to their inner voice. Don't listen to mine. Everyone has a different journey."

Broecker began running in 1997, and still runs several times a week with a friend. She also works out with "hot yoga," in which the room is heated to 105 degrees. She meditates every day, and if she doesn't, she feels the difference in her body and mind. Broecker still visits a psychic healer once a year, and has regular "raindrop treatments" in which a naturopath applies essential oils to her spine, which Broecker said boosts the immune system.

Although at one point, Broecker went off all drugs, she has since swung to a more moderate point of view. She occasionally does take medications working closely with her doctor to pinpoint the precise times that she needs such things. Her intent, however, is to use them sparingly.

"I'm trying to heal as naturally as possible," she said. "I don't want to be on medication forever. They're hard on the liver and the heart."

After all, she's planning on living a long, full life. At one time, she never thought she'd see her 30th birthday. Now 40 looks like a certainty, and turning 50, 60, or even 70 isn't unrealistic.

And life is good. "Things are under control," said Broecker, petting her black cat, Kona. And if there's a message in all this, it could be this, she said:

"We all need to take care of ourselves. Your health has to come first."

—By Kathryn McKenzie Nicols,
Reprinted with permission from the *Monterey Herald*, December 6, 2002

SEXUAL ASSAULT

What Is Sexual Assault?

- *Sexual assault is any type of sexual activity that is unwanted, by someone to whom you have not given your consent. A sexual assault may include the use of physical force, threats or intimidation. Sexual assault is a crime.*[5]

- *The term acquaintance rape will be defined as being subjected to unwanted sexual intercourse, oral sex, anal sex, or other sexual contact through the use of force or threat of force. Unsuccessful attempts are also subsumed within the term "rape." Sexual coercion is defined as unwanted sexual intercourse, or any other sexual contact subsequent to the use of menacing verbal pressure or misuse of authority (Koss, 1988).*[6]

- *Until recently, clear physical resistance was a requirement for a rape conviction in California. A 1990 amendment now defines rape as sexual intercourse "where it is accomplished against a person's will by means of force, violence, duress, menace, or fear of immediate and unlawful bodily injury." The important additions are "menace" and "duress," as they include consideration of verbal threats and implied threat of force (Harris, in Francis, 1996). The definition of "consent" has been expanded to mean "positive cooperation in act or attitude pursuant to an exercise of free will. A person must act freely and voluntarily and have knowledge of the nature of the act or transaction involved.*[7]

- *Date rape is forced or coerced sex between partners, dates, friends, friends of friends or general acquaintances. Date rape can be coerced both physically and emotionally—some emotional tactics include: threats to reputation, threats to "not like you", name calling, saying you "brought it on" or "really want it," threats to break up and threats to say you "did it" even if you didn't.*[8]

- *Date/acquaintance rape is forced, unwanted intercourse with a person you know. It is an act of humiliation, violence, and power.*[9]

Prevalence

- *One in four women surveyed was a victim of rape or attempted rape.*

- *An additional one in four women surveyed was touched sexually against her will or was a victim of sexual coercion.*

- *Eighty-four percent of those raped knew their attacker.*

- *Fifty-seven percent of those rapes happened while on dates.*

- *One in twelve male students surveyed had committed acts that met the legal definitions of rape or attempted rape.*

- *Eighty-four percent of those men who committed rape said that what they did was definitely not rape.*

- *Sixteen percent of the male students who committed rape and ten percent of those who attempted a rape took part in episodes involving more than one attacker.*

Responses of the Victim

- *Only 27 percent of those women whose sexual assault met the legal definition of rape thought of themselves as rape victims.*

- *42 percent of the rape victims did not tell anyone about their assaults.*

- *Only 5 percent of the rape victims reported the crime to the police.*

- *Only 5 percent of the rape victims sought help at rape-crisis centers.*

- *Whether they had acknowledged their experience as a rape or not, 30 percent of the women identified as rape victims contemplated suicide after the incident.*

- *82 percent of the victims said that the experience had permanently changed them.*[10]

"DISTORTION" by Daniela DiGregorio

Kevin

I am not proud of what I did, but it definitely wasn't rape. Pamela unquestionably consented and didn't take much convincing. I never led her to believe it was anything more than just sex—she is the one who convinced herself it was anything else.

The part I am ashamed of is just the lies and pressure that pushed me to come on to Pamela. I am a pretty good athlete and macho kind of guy. The guys at my school talk big and we like to top each other's stories—particularly about sex. I talked just as big as the next guy, but the problem was that I was a virgin. I don't know why exactly— I went out with a bunch of girls and we did a lot of stuff, but I just never felt comfortable pushing to go all the way. My folks are real strict and my dad always goes on about the sacredness of sex and marriage. I don't agree with him, but I could never completely forget about what he had said. Plus, I just never felt comfortable pushing a girl if she seemed uncomfortable or unsure.

I didn't know what was wrong with me and it started to feel like I wasn't a real guy or something. My locker-room stories began to seem fake and embarrassing. I was sure the other guys could see through my deception and I felt like a phony. In retrospect, I actually don't think that anyone really suspected anything, but I knew. I de-

Pamela

He didn't rape me. I consented and was dumb enough to believe the stuff he said and think he really cared about me. I feel ashamed and stupid. I don't know why I even did it and it certainly wasn't the way I thought I would lose my virginity. I think Kevin is a jerk, but what happened wasn't his fault. I guess I just romanticized the whole thing.

I don't get invited to many of the popular parties, so when a couple of girls said I was welcome to come, I was pretty excited. I am usually nervous around that group, but they seemed nice enough. I thought perhaps this was my big chance to be more accepted and spent a lot of time thinking about what to wear and what to say. I always get tongue-tied and say something stupid, but I was determined to just relax and encourage others to talk—people usually like to talk about themselves and would be flattered by my attention.

I had a couple of drinks as soon as I got to the party to relax myself and try to blend in. That helped and I felt a little more confident. After all, I *had* been invited to the party and what did I have to lose. When I saw Kevin, I was on a roll and went up to him and said something about the math assignment in a class we had together. Kevin is one of the most popular guys in the school, but he sometimes talked to me in math class and seemed like a nice

cided I needed to remedy the situation by having sex. But the thought still intimidated me—I didn't know why, and that was what pushed me more than anything else. There were even girls who came on to me, but I always lost my nerve. That sounds stupid, even to me, but it is the truth.

The night of the party, I had decided that it was time to confront this situation and just get it over with. I had a few drinks to screw up my courage, but I still panicked when I approached most of the girls. Then I saw Pamela. Pamela is a nice enough girl, but she is not very popular and worries a lot about what other people think of her. She is always trying to hang out with the more popular people and do things to make people like her. She is in my math class and I have seen how people make fun of her. I don't think that is cool, but she does kind of ask for it. I was always nice to her, but had never spent any time with her. When she smiled and tried to talk with me at the party, it seemed like the perfect solution. Pamela was anything but intimidating. She fairly begged for attention and I could tell that she would do just about anything I wanted her to do. She looked surprised when I started talking with her and got her a drink. I didn't want the others to think I was really with her, so I told her to meet me out at my car in ten minutes.

I know it was kind of scummy, but I swear she was very eager to please.

guy. He is very good looking and one of the best players on the football team. I didn't expect him to stay and talk, but he was really nice and seemed to actually want to spend some time with me. He got me another drink and suggested that we go out to his car where it wasn't so loud and we could really talk. I couldn't believe he really wanted *me* to go with him. I told a couple of girls that I was going with Kevin and would be back in a little while. I was sure they were a little jealous and could tell they were impressed. I just smiled, got my coat, and met Kevin out at his car. This party was turning out to be a dream.

When I got out to the car, Kevin was already there and suggested that we take a ride. I wasn't sure I should leave with him, but it sounded romantic—the full moon was out and it was a warm spring night. We drove to some point out near the ocean and Kevin started kissing me and touching me. I tried to slow things down and bring up some things to talk about, but he said he really liked me and wanted me. I could hardly believe it—Kevin wanted me?? It felt good to kiss him and, even though I was nervous, his rough hands felt strong and sure as they touched my breasts. I had never been touched like that before and I felt a strange combination of physical pleasure, surprise, and fear. I tried to act sure of myself, like I did this all the time. But when his hand reached in my underpants and started to touch me, I got scared. When I hoped for a good time at tonight's party, I

We drove out to this quiet place I know and we started making out. She kept wanting to talk, but I told her that she really turned me on and I couldn't stop wanting her. She was pleased and didn't do more than say a few times that she didn't know if she should do this. At one point, she started to cry and said she was a virgin and asked me to please be gentle. I felt kind of bad about that, but she didn't stop me. Hell, I was a virgin too, so what did it matter?

I didn't have anything to compare it with, but it was not great sex. I got it up and had an orgasm, but it felt pretty empty. At least it was over with. She started crying afterward and kept apologizing and asking if I still liked her. Shit, I didn't really like her much to start with, so that was a hard question to answer. I tried to comfort her and told her she was fine and it was good, etc., etc. Then she started acting like we were a couple or something, and asked when I would see her again. I just wanted to get her back to the party and get away. I told her that I would call her in a couple days, dropped her back at the party, and went home.

A few days later, she called me and asked if she had done something wrong and when could we get together. I felt bad, but I thought the best thing was to end it quickly and directly. I told her that while it was a great night, I didn't think it was a great idea to get together again. I could tell she was upset, but I had

never imagined this. I knew that many other girls would love to be out here in a car with Kevin, but I felt scared and confused.

I guess I started to cry and Kevin got mad at me. I finally told him I was a virgin and didn't know what to do. I said I thought things were moving too fast and maybe we should just talk for a while. He said he couldn't stop and he would be gentle—he told me I was beautiful and he couldn't control his passion for me. A guy had never talked that way to me before and I fell for it. I guess I didn't really think we would go all the way, but before I could say anything, he was inside of me. It hurt and scared me. He just kept saying, "I can't stop" and jerked in and out on top of me. I kept trying to remember how this was Kevin, one of the most popular boys in school, and he wanted *me.*

It didn't last very long and I just lay there crying quietly when he finished. He got mad and asked what was wrong with me. I apologized and just said I wasn't really thinking we would have sex. He assured me that it wasn't just sex and that he really cared for me. He said he had to get home, but would drop me off at the party and give me a call the next day. I tried to smile and convince myself that it really was exciting and good.

He didn't call all the next week and I began to wonder what had really happened. He seemed to always be in a hurry when I saw him at school, never promised her anything in the first place. She had her night with a big man on campus and I got what I was after. In fact, she probably got more out of it than I did. I'm not a virgin anymore, but I still don't feel particularly macho or proud of myself.

so I finally called him to find out what was wrong. He fumbled around for a little while, but then finally just came out and told me that it had been good sex, but that was all and he didn't want to see me again. I don't know what I was thinking that he might seriously like me or want to go out. I feel ashamed and stupid for even thinking he might be interested in me.

Art Work:

Jennifer JungEn
Shim
Emma Willard School

Hana Tuskamoto

Robyn Strumpf
Viewpoint School

Katie Mullet
Mercersburg
Academy

Daniela DiGregorio
Viewpoint
School

Notes

[1] *The Life and Times of Harvey Milk*, directed by Robert Epstein

[2] *Ibid.*

[3] From *Growing Up Sexually* by Samantha Stephens. *Casualties of Privilege: Essays on Prep Schools' Hidden Culture*, edited by Louis M. Crosier, Avocus Publishing, 1991.

[4] Carie Ford-Broeker. *Reach for Your Soul: A Journey Into Healing* Published by Writer's Showcase an imprint of iUniverse, Inc., 2002

[5] Sexual Assault Care Center, www.sacc.to

[6] *Perspectives on Acquaintance Rape* by David G. Curtis, Ph.D., B.C.E.T.S., *Clinical Psychologist* www.aaets.org

[7] *Ibid.*

[8] http://teenadvice.about.com/cs/daterape/

[9] www.surehelpline.org/RapeCrisisCenterEnglish

[10] *Perspectives on Acquaintance Rape* by David G. Curtis, Ph.D., B.C.E.T.S., *Clinical Psychologist* www.aaets.org.

"The very first thing I tell my new students on the first day of a workshop is that good writing is about telling the truth. We are a species that needs and wants to understand who we are. Sheep lice do not seem to share this longing, which is one reason they write so very little. But we do. We have so much we want to say and figure out."

—Anne Lamont from "Bird by Bird"

Chapter 6.

Writing Your Own Story

As Pawnee Elder, Uncle Frank Davis, said in his conversations in *Wisdom-keepers: Meetings with Native American Spiritual Elders*, our experiences are "like little scraps of paper in front of us along the way. We must pick up those pieces of scrap paper and put them in our pocket. Then one day, we will have enough scraps of paper to put together and see what they say."[1] Each of us is a distinct person with a unique path to walk. Even twins, who share the same genes and much of the same environment, experience and influence their lives in individual ways. Much of your own story is a personal discovery of what you share with others and what about your journey is uniquely yours.

Sigmund Freud, the founder of the field of psychology, theorized that the basic struggle of human existence is between our need to feel safe and connected to others on one hand and our desire to be unique and significant on the other. We don't want to stick out too far from our friends and family, but we don't want to be swallowed up by them either. Some people are more comfortable being safely close to the center of their group of family and friends, while others are more aloof or thrive on being on their own. In either case, each person is still a unique set of stories, uniquely told, and individually experienced.

Writing is a way of setting down your thoughts and experiences both for personal reflection and to share with others. In your stories, you attempt to communicate your experience in a way that helps someone else to understand who you are and how you think and feel. When you successfully do this, it documents your connection to the universal experience while also defining your uniqueness. In each of the stories in this book, there were probably feelings and reactions that you could quickly understand and relate to. There may have also been other experiences and feelings that were very foreign and perplexing, maybe even offensive or frightening. Empathy is your ability to understand and identify with another person's experience. Personal stories can help you to understand what another person was thinking and feeling in a situation—in part, helping you imagine how you might have responded in the same situation, and, in part, to help you understand why another person might behave so differently.

Writing is also a powerful opportunity to reflect on your own thoughts and feelings. The process of writing can help you understand yourself. Writing demands that you pay attention to the details of your life. Writing requires that you notice the decisions you have made, how they have affected you and others, and what you have learned from them. When you review what has happened and examine how and why you have reacted in a particular way, you are often better able to grasp the situation's significance. By stepping back from your day-to-day life, you gain objectivity and a sense of time and place. You can better appreciate how a particular experience fits into the larger plan of your life and has helped to shape your character and destiny. Without this type of reflection, you may overreact to something that will not matter in the larger scheme of things and miss the more subtle lessons that could change your life forever.

Personal writing can also access your unconscious thoughts and inner wisdom. You sometimes don't know what you really think until you start to write it down. You may not be aware of what you were thinking or feeling until you start to focus and pay attention. Something that seems obvious on first glance may look quite different when you try to explain it. Finding the right word may help identify a feeling. Explaining an action will raise your self-awareness. Writing about what has happened in your life can help you fit the patterns of your life together. Articulating a thought gives it form; putting that thought into writing can give it clarity and power.

Some people hate writing. Like frustrated artists, they can't get their thoughts and ideas into words on a page. Writing is a linear process— word by word, thought by thought. Some people are more holistic thinkers. They visualize the big picture and have difficulty breaking their experience down into distinct ideas. Drawing, painting, acting, singing, poetry, music, and speaking are less linear ways that people have used to communicate their human experience. There is great advantage to seeing the whole picture, recognizing the relationships and abstract concepts in an experience. There is also benefit in understanding the components that make up this picture. The effort to step back, examine a sequence of events, and look at the impact of specific actions and reactions can help you to learn from your experience and incorporate those lessons into your understanding and choices. If you find writing difficult, be patient and try to make writing a tool that works for you. Or find another means of expressing your experiences.

Initially, and perhaps entirely, this type of writing is for *you*. Put aside all the rules and insecurities you may have about your writing. There is time later for grammar and organization if you want to polish and share your stories. First, you must capture the details and meaning of your experience. *What happened? What did you feel and think? Why does this experience stand out in your life? How did it change you? Why is it important?* These are things that only you can know. No one else can judge what is significant or how you have experienced it. You may want to explain or explore your ideas, but they are uncontestably yours. There is no right or wrong way you should feel about your experiences, only the reality of what you actually do feel and think. Others may have opinions about your experience that actually shed light on something for you, but it is your perception that makes you who you are. Enjoy it and let it stand for itself. Only you can write your story.

Free Writing

The start of your story is to begin to remove the censors and external voices in your head so that you can express your own experience of your life. A journal can be a good way to practice writing whatever you think about, noting the things that happen in your day that have mattered to you. You might like to take note of the external things around you or focus more on what you are thinking and feeling. A journal should be a dialogue with yourself. Rant and rave. Ask yourself questions. Celebrate and complain. Think out loud on paper. Your journal should be your friend and confidant, not your judge or critic.

After years of schooling and essay writing, you may initially find it difficult to stop writing for someone else. There is nothing wrong with that, but it may censor your writing before you have fully discovered what you are actually thinking and feeling. If you stop to exclude anything that seems stupid or illogical, you will only be writing about who you think you should be, not who you are. It will be your manicured version of your experience, not your true experience. It may help to try to identify your censors, your imagined audience or critic. Who is reading over your shoulder? Is it a friend or parent or teacher or your idealized self? Forget all that for now. Write unconditionally. Let this be a private conversation. Don't worry about making sense or getting it right or justifying yourself.

The best way to start is just to start. Find a notebook and pen you like or set up a private folder on your computer and start writing. You might like to have a special time each day when you sit down and write, or carry a little notebook with you to record your reactions and thoughts on the spot. As questions or feelings come to you during the day, you may want to jot them down and come back to them later when you have private time to think about them. Do it *your* way. Just follow your thoughts without leading or critiquing them, like opening a present to see what is inside. Listen to yourself. Don't assume where you will end up. Don't push the river; it flows by itself. Just go along for the ride.

With free writing, the trick is to just keep writing whatever comes to your mind.

> *I don't really have anything to write about today . . . It has been a hectic day and I have just felt tired and overwhelmed. I hate Mondays because I always feel discouraged. The whole week spreads in front of me with all its demands, homework, stuff . . . I feel like I never have any time just for myself. It is so hard to keep up with everything—this is supposed to be the free time of my life . . . It doesn't feel free . . . It feels like everyone else owns it and tells me what to do. My dad tells me to enjoy it while I can because being an adult is full of stress and work . . . I can't tell if he is happy about that or not . . . at least he gets paid and has some choice about what he does . . . why am I doing all this work if it will just get me to all the stress and work my dad complains about . . . he doesn't have any idea what I have to deal with . . . he expects me to get all this stuff done, but then tells me to enjoy life while I am young . . . now exactly how am I supposed to do both? And what do I want to do? What would happen if I really did what I wanted to do? We've been reading Huck Finn and I can't even imagine just floating down a river taking life as it comes . . . I am supposed to keep making my life happen, like I have complete control over it. It scares me sometimes because I don't really feel in control and even when I do, I am not sure where I want to be going. That sign in the hallway at school—"If you don't know where you are going, you may end up some where else." Am I going where I want to go or where everyone else wants me to go? How am I supposed to know all this?*

Every time your writing stops, check what you are thinking and where your mind has drifted. Follow it—remember, you don't have to make sense or have an introduction, main idea, and conclusion. Just write what you are experiencing. You may be surprised where you end up and that can be fascinating. If you find that you can't stop writing for someone else, write about that. Who are you writing to and why are they intruding on your private dialogue? It may help to write an imaginary letter to them in your journal asking them to get out of your journal time. This letter is for you to understand why you are trying to please them; not to send to them. Even if they are a dominating personality, they are not really imposing themselves; *you* are putting them there. Remember, the critic or reader looking over your shoulder is of your own making; it is the way you judge or see yourself. You may model this judge after someone in your life that you want to please or impress, but it is still of your own creation. It may be your conscience or your expectations of yourself. It is not bad or insignificant; it may represent your goals and hopes for yourself. But it may limit your writing and self-awareness if you are constantly trying to edit what you write. Write first, edit later. Nobody will see your writing unless you want to share it with them.

One way to stimulate free writing is to ask yourself questions. *Why do you always let that girl bother you? What is bothering you? What do you need to do next? What do you really want to do? What are you afraid of? What would be best for you in the long run? What makes you feel good about yourself? What truly makes you happy?* It may seem a little odd at first—*who is talking and who is listening?*—but you will be surprised at how often you know the answers to these questions when you stop and really listen to yourself. Argue. Commiserate. Challenge yourself. When you are conflicted about something, take both sides and fight it out. Have an actual conversation with yourself.

I am so sick and tired of the way she treats me.

Well, stop complaining and break up with her then.

I don't want to break up with her. I love her. I like being with her; I just want her to understand my need to have time to myself. She thinks we should be together all the time. I have no time for my friends or just to be on my own.

Well then, tell her, stupid. You have to set some limits. You always back down and go along with whatever she wants to do.

Not always. And I do love her. She just doesn't understand what I am trying to say—she thinks it means I don't care about her or want to break up with her. I don't want her to think that.

Explain it to her and then it is up to her what she thinks. If she can't understand that you have a life of your own, she doesn't really respect you or understand you.

That's not fair. She respects me, but we have so little time after school and sports and stuff. I would like to have more time with her too—it is just that my spare time is so limited. If I spend it all with her, I have no time for the other things I care about.

Well maybe you need to cut back on all the stuff that you do so you have more time.

Like what? If I'm not at school, I'm at practice. If I'm not at practice, I have homework. And my folks want some time. And Roger is always complaining that I never spend any time with the guys anymore. And then Alicia starts crying and says I don't care about her like I used to. I hardly ever have time to just relax and play my guitar.

What do you really want?

I just want Alicia and Roger and my parents—and even my coach and teachers—to understand I can't do it all. There are only 24 hours in the day and I barely have control over any of them. I want to have time with Alicia without giving up everything else. I am tired of rushing around and never having any time to myself. I want to have fun and enjoy my high school time before it is gone and I am dealing with adult responsibilities.

What can you do about it?

Oh, I don't know. I guess I could drop debate club—it takes up a lot of time and I haven't really been enjoying it lately . . . maybe limit my time on the Internet—I know it eats up a lot of time. I guess I need to talk to Alicia about it and figure out a way to get some time to myself without her feeling bad.

Just tell her what you have said here. If she doesn't understand or agree, are you going to stand up for yourself?

I need to. As much as I like her, I am starting to resent her and she is right, I am distracted when we are together because I am thinking of all the things I can't do because I spend all my time with her.

Don't worry about being reasonable. Many of the things that keep you from accomplishing what you want to accomplish are not reasonable or logical at all—but they still influence your behavior. By writing and listening, you get everything on the table and can begin to understand and take charge of your life.

Some people find it fun and enlightening to keep a dream journal. Dreams are intriguing. Your brain sorts through your thoughts and problems while you are sleeping. Without the logic of daytime thought, your dreams can often uncover more unconscious feelings and questions. Dreams sometimes offer solutions or bring up questions that your conscious mind did not consider. There are different theories about dreams, but most psychologists believe that your dreams are the key to your unconscious thoughts.

Some people remember their dreams in great detail while others never remember dreaming at all. Everyone dreams, so it is a matter of contacting your dreams. This is actually easier than you might think. Start by instructing yourself to remember your dreams when you go to sleep at night; just say out loud to yourself: "I am going to remember my dreams." Remember, your brain is just a physical mechanism—you are its master. Keep a journal or pencil and paper next to your bedside table and write down your dream as soon as you awake. Remember, your dreams are not based in language. They are a series of images without words or daytime logic. Attempting to put your dreams into words may be illusive. Don't worry about the inconsistencies. Just write the dream down as you remember it. Some people prefer to speak their dreams into a tape recorder and later translate them into writing. Note your feelings when you wake up from a dream: happy, anxious, relieved, frightened, angry, sad. It may not be obvious right away that your feelings are attached to your dream, but they probably are.

You are the director and creator of your dreams. Everything in your dream reflects some part of yourself, so you can see the physical interaction between your different feelings and interests. You are not only the main character off on a journey, you are also everyone and everything you encounter, including the road. You can often gain more understanding of your dream by taking on each character and item in the dream and giving it an identity. *I am the road. I am hard and rocky. You are walking quickly over my surface, not paying attention to the rocks in your way. It is important that you stay on the road, but be careful of the rocks that are there to trip you up.* You may be very surprised at all the different parts of your experience you will find in your dreams and what they will tell you if you give them a voice. *I am a rock in the path. I am small and unobtrusive, but can easily trip you if you don't pay attention to me. You are watching off into the distance, when you should be careful to get around me without falling. I am not big, but I can hurt you if you trip over me.* What are the small things right now that you are not paying attention to in your quest for something in the future? Dreams are usually not premonitions, but do reflect some part of your mind that is playing a part in your experience. The rocks may not be important, but some part of you is worried about them and is afraid that you are not paying enough attention to them in the present moment.

Dreams are full of symbolism and allusions. You may be traveling down a road and come to an intersection—perhaps a decision you are facing. Often your dream will put the answer your unconscious mind favors on the right-hand side, wanting you to do the "right" thing. You may find certain recurring dreams show up when specific issues or concerns are in question—a childhood home when you are needing comfort or feeling lost, running in slow motion when you are feeling trapped, falling when you are feeling out of control. Classic dreams like taking an exam in a class you forgot to attend or appearing at some grand gathering without any clothes usually represent feelings of anxiety or vulnerability. Death in your dreams usually represents the end of something rather than an actual death.

Pay attention to your dreams. Ask yourself a question or ask your dreams to clarify something for you. This is one way of contacting your inner voice and better understanding your life. Weave your dreams into your stories. Use them to represent the important issues and characters in your life. Your dreams *are* your stories in their most primitive form.

Your Life Line

A good way to identify the important stories of your life is to create a life line. Take a large piece of paper and draw a line from one side to the other. This is your life. On one end, write your birthdate. On the other end, project a date for your death. This can be a story in itself—how do you imagine your death? How old will you be? What makes you pick this time and age?

On the line, proportionately between your birth and your death, put a mark for today—write the date and your age. How much of your life have you lived? How much of your life lies in front of you?

Take the space between your birth and today, and carefully mark the events that have been important in your life so far, the events that affected and changed you. Some of these may be typical benchmarks: a move, a death, or the birth of a sibling. Others might be external events that impacted your life: a war or hurricane or political event. Some might be particular to you, something that happened that changed you or your life even though it may not have even been noticed by anyone else—a certain afternoon when you almost had an accident, a person who said or did something to you that made a lasting impression, the particular way a teacher responded to you on your first day of school.

Only you can know what these events are. Take some time to think about your life. Allow memories to surface; you may not know why at first. Trust your instincts. You can have as many markers as you want, but try to narrow it down to ten at first in order to be selective and take note of the big stories in your life. Describe each marker in as much detail as possible: where you were; what your surroundings looked, felt, sounded, and smelled like. Recapture your memory of the event as accurately as possible—don't worry about the significance, just capture the time and place. Describe yourself and the people around you. Describe the surroundings. Put yourself back in time and remember what it felt like to be you. What were you excited about? What were you afraid of? What was confusing? What did you want? Who was there with you?

After you have captured the details of the story, think carefully. Why did you pick this particular time, of all the times in your life, to be a benchmark? What change did it create in you or your life? What was the message or lesson this experience taught you, positive or negative? How did this experience impact who and what you are today? How would your life have been different if this had never happened? Weave this insight into your story. Notice how it evolved, how you changed because of it.

Work with each of your benchmarks, one at a time. Begin to notice the connections between these marks. Explore the accounts of the other people in your stories. Ask your parents or friends about their experiences related to your own—either as a part of your story, or just a similar incident in their lives. How is their story different from yours? What is typical and atypical about your story? What difference does time and place make? If they are in your story, what role did their previous stories play in the outcome of your own? What did they bring to your story?

As you look at your life line, notice the changes in your character and mind-set. One girl remembered that she was four when her grandmother died. They had been very close and, for the first time, she understood that things did not last forever. She began memorizing everything around her in great detail in order to preserve the things she cared about. She developed an excellent, almost photographic, memory and this had strongly influenced her as a student and as a person. The grandmother's death had been important, but even more important was the resolution she made because of it. A young child might assume responsibility for something like a divorce or accident that an adult could easily understand was not his or her fault. It is that child's perception, however, that will shape his or her experience. Can you find things on your time line as a child that you may have misunderstood or interpreted? How have they affected you? How can you change that influence now?

Finding Your Voice

Through your writing and your stories, you will begin to find your own voice—your own answers to life's questions. Your voice will change with time and with the process of speaking. As you emerge as an adult, all the voices of your childhood, of your education, of your family will merge together and raise the questions you must answer.

- *What is important?*

- *What is the meaning and significance of my life?*

- *What do I care about? What makes me happy?*

- *How am I connected to others? In what ways am I forever alone?*

- *Where do I fit in my family? In my community? In the larger scheme of things?*

- *What experiences have shaped me? Who has strengthened and supported me? Who has undermined or devalued my sense of myself?*

- *What do I want to accomplish? What tools do I carry? What obstacles do I bring along as well?*

- *Who can I learn from? What do I need to know?*

- *What mistakes have I made? How can I make amends?*

- *What do I owe to others? What do I need from others?*

- *How can I understand and respect stories that are fundamentally different than my own?*

- *How will the life of others and the physical and political world at large intersect with my life?*

- *Who do I want to become? What qualities and achievements will make me proud of myself?*

You will live the answers as you live the questions. Your whole story is not what happens to you, but how you respond to what happens to you. Each day, each sadness, each celebration is a scrap of paper waiting to be saved and woven into your life story. *"If we do this all through life, we'll know when to pull out those scraps to read more of the message. The more we read, the more we'll learn the meaning of life. We can become wise—at least wiser than we were.*

"But if we never pick up those scraps of paper and never read them, we never become wiser. We'll keep wondering about life and never learn the Creator's instructions for us. Remember one thing . . . if we pick up all those scraps, we'll still be learning. Nobody ever learns all the answers."[2]

Chapter Questions for Journal Writing and Discussion

The following questions are designed to help you reflect on the stories in this book, perhaps for your own writing, understanding, or discussion. Some of the questions may help you think about the meaning and implications of the stories themselves; others suggest ways that you can compare and contrast these stories to your own life and feelings. You can come to understand yourself better both by identifying the thoughts and feelings that you share with others as well as those that are uniquely yours. As you come to understand the commonalities and differences in the human condition, your experience of life becomes larger. As you step out of your own comfort zone to imagine different realities and experiences, your respect and empathy for others will both instruct and connect. We are perhaps more alike than different, but our differences celebrate our unique contributions and relations. Like the individual instruments in an orchestra, we must know our own instrument *and* the part that we play in the larger composition so that we contribute a clear, distinct sound that both enhances and blends.

CHAPTER ONE:
QUESTING—COMING OF AGE IN THE WORLD

Self-Esteem *Page 00*

1. *Think about one time when you felt really good about yourself. What was going on that contributed to your positive self-esteem at that time? Think of another time when you felt really bad about yourself. What was going on this time? How much control did you have over these two situations?*

2. *Gloria Steinem struggled with the idea of whether or not people have control over many of the circumstances that determine their success and how they feel about themselves. How would you define the "internal center of power" that she came to believe is the center of self-esteem?*

3. *If you stand back and watch or remember yourself in different situations, what do you like or not like? How harshly do you judge yourself? Looking back, what do you wish you could say to yourself at those times?*

Adoption *Page 00*

1. *What does Kate mean by "ghost kingdoms"? Do you think that everyone has some ghosts in their life whether they have been adopted or not? What ghosts are a part of your family and your life?*

2. *What role do you think that nature and nurture have played in your life? If you were not adopted, how can you separate one from the other? If you are adopted, what parts of your life and personality can you not account for just from your environment?*

3. *What right do you think Kate has to know who her biological parents are? What rights do you think her biological parents have to keep their identity private? Do adoptive parents have any rights in this consideration? What do you think of underground search agents?*

4. *It took Kate almost four years and much procrastination to finally find her mother. What do you think she was afraid of? What would you have felt and done in her place? Why might a search not turn out as well as it did for Kate?*

To Thine Own Self Be True *Page 00*

1. *Describe one situation when you were at odds with a group you were a part of but went along with the group and did not speak up. Describe another situation where you did speak up. What made the difference? How did you feel in each situation?*

2. *What role do you think that race played in the relationship between Melinda and Tyrone—in the beginning and later on? How do you think this was different for Melinda than it was for Ty?*

3. *Melinda said that not backing down to her friends harassment "wasn't really a choice or heroic—it was the only thing I could do." Why did she feel that way? What do you think?*

4. *Why do you think Roger asked Melinda to the prom? What choices was he making? Why did he get involved? What choices were other friends making and why?*

5. *How do you think this incident changed Melinda? Tyrone? Roger?*

6. *This was Melinda's version of this relationship. What might it have been like from Tyrone's standpoint? How do you think it looked from Roger's perspective?*

Privilege and Entitlement *Page 00*

1. *After the terrorist attack on the United States in September of 2001, many Americans were shocked, hurt, and angry at the response from some of the rest of the world. In effect, some governments and individuals said, "Welcome to the real world. This is the type of violence and fear that most of the world lives with every day." How do you feel about the privilege, freedoms, and security that you enjoy as an American? What role does that place you in relation to the rest of the world?*

2. *How do political boundaries impose physical, economic, and social conditions on the land and people living in one place or another? How do neighboring countries affect each other—economically, environmentally, socially?*

3. *While working in the colonia, why did Luke's world of "carpets and cars and dishwashers and Starbucks" begin to seem imaginary and absurd?*

4. *Why do you think that the arrests of migrant workers decreased during the picking season and increased when pickers were no longer needed? What does this say about the realities of illegal immigrants?*

5. *Why was the Mexican teenager offended when Luke referred to the United States as "America"?*

6. *What do you think are the answers to the questions that Luke asks at the end of his story? How do you feel about your position and responsibility as a citizen of the United States? What do you think is the price of privilege?*

7. *What is your reaction to the idea of "affluenza"? How do you think that advertising and consumerism affect you and your friends? Your parents? Your community? The environment? The image of Americans in the world?*

8. *What changes in your life could you make to reduce consumption and waste? How easy would that be? What difference would it make?*

Violence *Page 00*

1. *How would you define a "hate crime"? How do you think it is different than any other crime?*

2. *Why do you think the police and school reports about Fred were so different than Fred's mother's story? What is the truth?*

3. *Why would someone like Fred continue to dress differently and behave in feminine ways if other students talked and made fun of him? Why would his behavior bother other people?*

4. *Students at Fred's high school said that he was openly harassed, but the school administration said that he was well adjusted and accepted at school. How does harassment escape the adults in a school? How can they make school a safe place if they don't know what is going on? What could teachers have done to protect Fred and others who are different?*

5. *It is students who bully, students who respond with violence, and students who know the underlying realities of school violence and harassment. What can students do to make schools safer and more accepting of differences? What is the responsibility of bystanders when harassment or bullying occurs? Could students have prevented Fred's violent death?*

6. *Seventy-five percent of the attackers in school shootings had been the target of serious bullying in their school. What kinds of bullying or harassment go on at your school? Do you think that violence or a shooting could ever break out at your school? Why or why not?*

7. *In what ways do you think the number of school shootings and international terrorist attacks have personally affected you and your friends? What powers do you have to protect yourself and the people you care about? How optimistic are you about the world's ability to resolve these conflicts?*

8. *Why do you think that some people respond to frustration and violence with violence and others do not?*

9. *"Before you know what kindness really is you must lose things . . ." What is Naomi Shihab saying in this poem? Think of an incident where this has been true in your life.*

Culture Shock *Page 00*

1. *Which parts of the American stereotype do you find to be true of yourself and the people around you? Are there any stereotypes that you think are mostly untrue or misunderstood? Which parts do you take pride in and which are a source of some cultural embarrassment?*

2. *As you read each of the "Americanisms," try to imagine a culture that is "un-American." How would life and relationships be different? What is hard to understand or appreciate about those differences? What might other cultures find difficult to understand or appreciate about ours? What things that Meiko noticed about America surprised you?*

3. *Have you ever been in a country or environment where you were the only one of your culture or nationality? What did you learn from that experience? What was difficult? What was exciting?*

4. *What are the things about your culture that are comforting and reassuring? What would you miss most?*

5. *How do people of a different culture appear to you? What cultural differences seem most strange and difficult to understand?*

6. *Meiko was becoming bicultural—able to understand and function in two cultures. She also felt that she no longer completely fit in either culture. What do you think are the advantages and disadvantages of being bicultural in today's world?*

Social Responsibility *Page 00*

1. *Phillip Graham states that in business and in life, we spend much of our time "getting by" without a genuine connection to the meaning and value of our lives. We make decisions based on expediency and social pressures rather than what we believe to be right and true. In what ways do you agree or disagree with this position? Think of a situation where you have had "some better sense of the meaning" of a situation and acted accordingly. How did your actions change and define who you are?*

2. *What do you think is a society's obligation to individuals who have been unfairly judged and punished? How do you think that Steven's life and attitude have been affected by spending almost fourteen years in jail for a crime he did not commit? How can or should he be compensated?*

3. *When you see something that violates your sense of fairness, what is your response or obligation? What is your response or obligation if it violates your own rights? What is your response or obligation if it violates the rights of others?*

4. *Albert Einstein said, "The evil in this world is not done only by those who commit it, but by those who stand back and watch it happen." As a citizen of any group, do you have an obligation to speak up if the group or government of that group behaves wrongly? If you are a member of a group that behaves badly, are you responsible for those actions if you do not actively protest or try to change them?*

5. *In what ways can you assert yourself in a situation that you believe is wrong or unfair?*

   - *A friend is shoplifting from a local market.*

   - *Someone at school is being physically harassed and bullied.*

   - *You have been unfairly accused of cheating on an exam.*

   - *A school policy discriminates against students who have afterschool jobs.*

   - *Local police unfairly restrict and harass teenagers.*

   - *A local business is illegally polluting the environment.*

   - *You feel strongly about pending legislation that is counter to your beliefs about abortion.*

   - *The shoes that you wear were in part produced by underpaid child labor in a third-world nation.*

   - *You disagree with an important national policy or action.*

   - *You are concerned about the number of children around the world who are malnourished and homeless while you have more than what you need.*

   - *AIDS is spreading rampantly in countries where individuals do not have the information or finances to prevent or treat it.*

- *Global warming and unrestricted pollutants threaten the continued existence of our planet.*

The Seach for Meaning *Page 00*

1. *What are the opinions of the people around you about what your "good life" should be? What do you think?*

2. *One of the absolute truths about life is that nothing stays the same; even from minute to minute, change is inherent in everything. What things are a part of your life now that you want to appreciate and preserve in some way? What things about yourself and your life will you grieve when they are past?*

3. *Saroya asks a lot of questions about life and her place in the larger scheme of things—her "personal engagement with the mystery of human experience." What questions do you have? How do you go about looking for the answers?*

4. *What are your beliefs and feelings about God and spirituality? How does this affect your choices and the way you live and view the world?*

5. *What role does ethics play in your choices and in the culture around you? Is cheating or dishonesty acceptable? How does it affect people's behavior and relationships? How do you feel about it?*

6. *How do you view death? How does that affect the way you live?*

7. *Saroya came up with a metaphor about light and a prism to help her conceptualize life and death. This belief guides her choices and the type of life she wants to lead. What guiding principle or belief do you hold that gives meaning and significance to your life?*

CHAPTER TWO: LIVING IN YOUR BODY

The Changing Body *Page 00*

1. *How much do you think appearance affects popularity and "coolness" at your school? How is it different for boys and for girls?*

2. *Physical development occurs at a different time and rate for everyone. Think about how your rate of growth has affected your confidence, status, and role in your social group.*

3. *Studies have shown that early and late maturing boys and girls actually are treated differently. Early maturing young people are often expected to be more mature and responsible than they really are and late maturing people may not be given as many opportunities to take on responsibilities as others. What do you think are the advantages and disadvantages of each? How do you think these influences might affect adult personality?*

Eating Disorders *Page 00*

1. *Why does Clara suggest that keeping her feelings to herself may have been a sign of trouble that set the stage for her eating disorder?*

2. *Confronted by eating disorders for the first time, Clara wondered why she was so desperate to be thin. What is the pressure on girls to be thin? Where does it come from? How pervasive is it in your school? What pressures do overweight students have to deal with?*

3. *Clara states that her ability to not eat gave her a sense of "control" in her life. Adolescence is a time of transition and change—new skills, new relationships, and new responsibilities. It is often difficult to feel competent and in control. Our world is also fast moving and overwhelming at times. How difficult is it to feel in control of your life? How do you react when you feel powerless in situations that affect your life? Is this more important to some people than others? What are some other ways that you see people coping with this kind of stress and powerlessness?*

4. *Why do you think that none of Clara's friends approached her about her weight loss and change in her eating?*

5. *Clara denied everything and brushed aside her adviser's concern, but seemed relieved that someone had noticed and confronted her. What do you think her adviser was thinking and feeling during this encounter? Why do you think he continued to stay involved and concerned after Clara brushed him off?*

6. *Why do you think that Clara's parents had not noticed this serious change in their "perfect" daughter's appearance and behavior? Who was expecting Clara to be "perfect"?*

7. *Clara says that in spite of the physical and emotional damage, she considers the time and opportunities lost during her struggle with anorexia to be the most detrimental of all. What did Clara lose?*

8. *Why do you think it is so difficult for friends to help someone with an eating disorder? What can you do when you see someone that you really care about doing something that you know is damaging and painful, but they push you away?*

Disabilities and Differences *Page 00*

1. *How much of your sense of personal identify depends on your body and on how you look? How do you think you would change if your appearance or physical abilities were different? What would remain the same?*

2. *Can you think of a time in your life when everything was normal and then suddenly something happened and "in less than twenty seconds" your life totally changed?*

3. *How do you think you personally might have responded to the kind of tragedy that Anne and her family faced? What personal strengths and weaknesses would affect your recovery? What skills or qualities would you need to develop?*

4. *How do you think Anne's life was different during adolescence than the one she imagined? What do you think she lost? What do you think she gained?*

5. *Anne's friends and family were an incredible source of support and strength for her. How do you think that her friend, Pam, would tell this story? How would her mother, father, or siblings?*

Dealing with Stress *Page 00*

1. *What is "perfectionism"? Rosalie is extreme, but do you know others who overwork and expect too much from themselves? Are there areas of your life where you expect yourself to be the best and never make mistakes?*

2. *Rosalie blames her obsessiveness on cursive writing. Can you remember an experience in early elementary school that has shaped your efforts and confidence as a student?*

3. *What is the physical, mental, and social price of perfectionism?*

4. *How do you think the awards and recognition that Rosalie gained as a child may have set her up? Do grades and awards affect how hard people work and how much they learn?*

5. *Making mistakes is a valuable part of learning. How can competition and fear of failure make it difficult to learn? Under what circumstances do you learn best?*

6. *How can you find the best balance between doing your best and not obsessing on your performance? What advice would you give yourself?*

Loss *Page 00*

1. *How has death touched you and your family? How are you included or excluded in family discussions or observations of death?*

2. *How do our culture and the media deal with death? How has that formed your impressions, fears, and expectations?*

3. *Greg is very disillusioned and angry with the medical profession. The doctors provided a target for his rage and sadness, but what did he want and need from the doctors that he didn't get?*

4. *Cancer is an exhausting roller coaster of hopes and disappointments as well as physical devastation. Greg says he would rather have a loved one murdered or hit by a car than slowly eaten away by cancer. Other people have said that as difficult as cancer is, at least you have the time to prepare and say good-bye to a loved one. Which would you prefer for yourself? For someone you love?*

5. *Anger is a very big part of loss and grief. In what ways do you think anger does or does not help us heal and accept our losses?*

6. *One philosophy is that you should forget about death and live as if you were going to live forever. Another point of view is that you should live every day as if you were going to die tomorrow. What do you think? How does the attitude you choose affect your choices and the way you live your life?*

Aging and Death *Page 00*

1. *How does our culture view aging? In what ways are old people respected and cherished? In what ways are they neglected and disregarded?*

2. *What is the role of old people in your life? How well do you know your grandparents and how do you feel about them?*

3. *What would your story about your grandmother or grandfather be like?*

4. *If any of your grandparents have died, what was that like for you?*

5. *What do you want to be like when you are old? How would you like your grandchildren to feel about you?*

6. *How do you feel about your own death? What do you hope to accomplish before that time? What story would you like your grandchildren to write?*

CHAPTER THREE: THE BRAIN AND THE MIND

Choosing Not to Use *Page 00*

1. *How do you think things are different for nonusers at your school than they are for Brandon? What are the unspoken assumptions about people who don't drink or use drugs?*

2. *What part do drinking or drugs play at a party? What would a party look like with no using at all?*

3. *Why do you think Brandon has chosen not to use? What are the reasons you or others give for using or not using?*

4. *What does Brandon mean by "peer pressure"? What choices are difficult to make at your school?*

Nicotine: A "Minor" Addiction *Page 00*

1. *WARNING: THE SURGEON GENERAL HAS DETERMINED THAT SMOKING IS HAZARDOUS TO YOUR HEALTH. And yet over 6,000 individuals try smoking for the first time every day—most of them under twenty years old. What factors would cause someone to start or continue smoking despite the warnings?*

2. *What is the "look" and promise that advertising gives about smoking? Since a large proportion of the cigarette market dies every year, tobacco companies must continually attract new customers. Studies have also shown that if an individual does not start smoking before age twenty, he or she is not likely to start at all, so much of tobacco marketing is aimed at teens. Do a survey of cigarette advertisements—what promises or techniques do they use that might appeal to teens?*

3. *Why do people continue to smoke even when their first experience is unpleasant?*

4. *Why was Leslie so convinced that she was not addicted? What is the difference between an alcohol or heroin addiction and a nicotine addiction? What makes it so hard to quit smoking?*

Addiction *Page 00*

1. *David Crosby told students at Beverly Hills High School in 1986 that he was just like them, privileged in many ways, but he had ended up in prison with a serious drug addiction. What factors do you think influence why one person never gets addicted and another runs into trouble? What factors do you think played into David's addiction?*

2. *"Enabling" is any behavior on the part of friends, family, or institutions that protects an addict or alcoholic from the consequences of his or her use—enabling them to avoid or deny the problems it is causing. What behaviors, relationships, or responses to David's drug use "enabled" him to continue?*

3. *David did not use drugs in high school probably because they were not as easily available to teenagers as they are today. Do you think he would have started using earlier if drugs had been more available? How do you think his life might have been different if he had started using in junior high or high school?*

4. *Crosby strongly believes that freebasing cocaine was the most damaging and addictive drug he became involved with. Physically and psychologically, why do you think this was true?*

5. *After his girlfriend, Christine, was killed in a car accident, David started using heroin to "medicate the pain." How is this different from "recreational" drug use? What other kinds of pain or discomfort might people use drugs to medicate?*

6. *How do you think that David's career and lifestyle made him especially vulnerable to excessive drug use? In what ways did that lifestyle also protect him from the consequences of his use? Was this an advantage or disadvantage?*

7. *Many friends thought that David and Jan were dragging each other down, but later Jan said that she didn't think that either of them would have made it alone. How do you think they helped and hurt each other?*

8. *After years of physical, financial, legal, professional, social, and personal pressures to quit, what do you think finally made the difference? Why did David and Jan stop?*

Growing Up in an Alcoholic Family *Page 00*

1. *Randy said that he was powerless over alcohol even though he had never had a single drink. How was this true? What efforts had he made to control it in the past?*

2. *Over half of the people in the U.S. have been strongly affected by alcohol—personally, family members, friends, accidents, or worries. What role has alcohol played in your life?*

3. *How was Randy "enabling" his mother's drinking? How do you "enable" friends or family members? Why is it so scary and difficult just to let people you love deal with the consequences of their drinking?*

4. *"Denial" is a tricky concept. If a person has a problem with alcohol, they will most likely say they don't. But if a person doesn't have a problem with alcohol, they will also say they don't. How can you tell the difference?*

5. *Alateen, Alanon, and Alcoholics Anonymous have been very successful programs for alcoholics and their families. From Randy's story, what do you think makes these programs work? What need do they fill?*

6. *Even families without an alcohol or drug problem have difficult times and sometimes respond to them in rigid ways that lock individuals into a pattern of behavior that protects them or the family—enabler, hero, scapegoat, lost child, or family pet. Can you see any of these roles in your family? In yourself?*

7. *How are you most likely to respond to problems in your family? Does that carry over to problems outside your family? How does it affect your personality, feelings, and behavior?*

8. *Think about your life as it is right now. How might the Serenity Prayer relate to the different areas of your life?*

Mania and Depression *Page 00*

1. *What do you think makes manic depression different than normal mood swings? What do you think is the difference between" being depressed" and "depression"?*

2. *"Control your own reactions to other people's annoyances, and you'll control the situation around you." Can you think of a time when this was difficult for you to do?*

3. *Why is it sometimes difficult to accept the need for medicine to help control a chronic mental or physical condition?*

4. *How would you react if a friend of yours told you that he had bipolar mood disorder? What would you be worried about or afraid of? What would help you understand? What do you think your friend would need from you?*

5. *Psychological disorders sometimes carry a sense of shame and weakness. They impact our feelings and the intimate sense of who we are. What kinds of support and information does each of us need to understand and accept our mental quirks and challenges?*

Hitting the Wall *Page 00*

1. *What events in your life have made you grow up quickly? In what ways have your parents and other adults tried to protect you? Have you ever felt invincible the way Eliza did before the accident?*

2. *How do you think Eliza's experience with Paul affected her mood and choices at the party? Can you think of times when your emotional state influenced your decisions and risks that you have taken?*

3. *Eliza struggled with the question of how much the beers she had had affected her ability to avoid the accident. Paul reassured her that she did the best she could have done. What do you think?*

4. *Eliza said that the worst part of the accident was its finality—"no excuses, no second chances, no going back." What did she mean? Has there been anything irreversible in your life that has changed everything?*

CHAPTER FOUR: THE QUEST FOR CONNECTIONS

Popularity *Page 00*

1. What does "cool" mean? What do you think about Joe's observations about coolness?

2. What makes someone or something cool at your school? Do you think there are any qualities or behaviors that are universally and forever cool?

3. How do you think the media and advertising influence what is cool or desirable in our culture?

4. Joe believes that the pressure to be cool decreases with age. What evidence do you see that either supports or contradicts this claim? Do you ever see adults being influenced by a desire to be cool?

5. What do you think are the advantages and disadvantages of being either cool or uncool?

Gender *Page 00*

1. How do you think that gender expectations have changed since your mother and father were growing up? What do you see as the advantages and disadvantages of these changes for you?

2. Think of ways that gender and race interact to create unique advantages and disadvantages for individuals. How is being a white woman different from being a black woman? What different roles and pressures might Latino and white men face? What gender expectations might conflict with various cultural expectations or status?

3. What challenges or struggles have previous generations faced which have made it easier for you? What rights or freedoms related to gender do you take for granted?

4. Katherine Graham became the editor of the Washington Post when her husband died and few women held editorial positions. She said that the things that got in her way more than anything else were insecurity and the exaggerated desire to please of women in her generation. Have you seen that tendency in older women? In what ways has this changed or persisted for young women today?

5. Joe Marshall believes that much of the violence and crime of inner-city black males stems from the unrealized loss of history and racial pride. How does he make that connection?

6. Malcolm X was feared and defamed by most white Americans during his lifetime. Many black males in this culture live with both the power and confines of being a symbol of fear. How does race and gender collide for young black men? How is your gender identity affected by your race?

Racial and Ethnic Differences *Page 00*

1. Why was Carol never aware of her race before she moved to Cleveland? Even though she didn't think about being white, how do you think her race had affected her life and identity up until then?

2. *If you read Carol's story substituting black for white and white for black, how do you think the story would have been different?*

3. *What do you think that Jose has lost and gained by going to the private school? In what ways do you think it will or will not be worth the compromise?*

4. *Think of a time when friends have been making fun of something that you care about. What were the pressures to speak up or to stay silent? How did you feel if you said something—or if you didn't? How did people react? How did it affect your feelings and relationships with them?*

5. *What part of your ethnic and personal identity is genetic and what part is based on the way you are raised? In what ways do you think being racially Korean has and will affect Tiffany's life and identity?*

6. *How does appearance affect the way we think about other people? How do you think that your appearance has affected the way you think about yourself?*

7. *Do children and adults respond to race and economic differences in different ways? Do you think that people instinctively prefer people like themselves or that racial prejudices are subtly and not so subtly taught?*

8. *Why do you think that Salvador and Pepe stopped being friends with Billy? How could the three of them have avoided the pressures on their friendship?*

9. *Discrimination or reverse discrimination is used to manipulate the diversity of a group—either to reduce or increase diversity. For many years, racial, ethnic, religious, and gender groups were simply excluded from certain organizations. In some cases, this meant they were also excluded from opportunities to develop the skills, education, and confidence needed to even qualify for those organizations, so that when the formal barriers were dropped, they were still at a big disadvantage. Affirmative action or quotas are sometimes set as a temporary adjustment to help level the playing field. Discrimination, reverse discrimination, affirmative action, and quotas are all about groups, not individuals. How have these social policies affected you? Be sure to consider the subtle advantages and disadvantages that you have inherited.*

10. *In returning to his hometown, Lorenzo realized that his history and family were an integral part of who he was. What do you know about your family and cultural history? In what ways do you think that this has affected who you are?*

11. *What are "the Borderlands" and how does one "be a crossroad"?*

Friendship *Page 00*

1. *What is your reaction to Richard Cohen's article about male friendship? Which men's reactions best reflect your experience?*

2. *Many of the men reacting to the article refer to their relationships with their fathers. How do you think that father-son relationships affect male friendships and relationships?*

3. *How do you think that the UCLA study of gender responses to stress might explain the way men and women form friendships?*

4. *What role do friends play in your life? What do they add, both positive and negative?*

Outsiders, Bullies, and Bystanders *Page 00*

1. *Why do you think that some people get along easily with others and other people seem awkward and left out? Can you remember a time when you felt each way? What makes the difference?*

2. *What do you think makes some people bully other people? Can you remember a time when you were a bully or part of a group that was being mean to someone? How does someone get drawn in to this kind of situation?*

3. *Bobby Kennedy once said "If you are not part of the solution, you are part of the problem." Have you ever been in a bystander when someone was being unfairly treated or bullied? What were your options? What were the consequences of acting or remaining silent?*

All Kinds of Families *Page 00*

1. *Kyra defines her family as "anyone, related by blood or not, who shows up to engage in a relationship of love and support . . ." How would you define your family?*

2. *Many children's family relationships today are shaped by changes in their parent's relationships—divorce, death, remarriage, stepfamilies. How do you think these changes affect the relationships within a family?*

3. *Today's families may include nontraditional family members and patterns of interaction, including important changes in where a child lives, who takes care of her, finances, and how individuals relate to each other. What advantages and disadvantages do you see in these nontraditional family patterns?*

4. *Kyra looks at her paternal grandparents as they celebrate their fifty-fourth wedding anniversary and shares her fantasy that she will marry one true love forever. How do you think that modern family patterns have affected young people's ideas and expectations about marriage and families?*

CHAPTER FIVE:
SEXUAL QUANDARIES AND QUESTIONS

Family vs. Peer Values *Page 00*

1. *How do you think that your world and sexual realities are different than the way that your parents grew up? How well do they understand your experience and how well do you understand where they are coming from?*

2. *Mercedes clearly loves and respects her family. Her new school and friends have become increasingly important to her and she finds herself balancing between two very different worlds. Describe the advantages and disadvantages of living in both worlds.*

3. *What do you do when your friends and activities violate the rules and values of your family? How much of your peer life do you keep secret from your family? How much*

of your family life do you share with your friends? Which parts are genuinely "you"?

4. As adults, most people's values and behavior closely adhere to the values and behaviors of their parents. Which family values do you think you will keep and which do you think you will change? How do you think you will raise your children?

5. How do your parents' values and attitudes about sex affect your sexuality? How much of your sexual feelings and behavior are you comfortable sharing with them?

6. Why did Mercedes want her mother's blessing in her decision to have sex with David? Why did her mother refuse to give it? What do you think Mercedes will or should do now?

Coming Out *Page 00*

1. What pressures and feelings do you think that Harvey Milk experienced between age fourteen when he realized he was gay and age thirty when he finally "came out" as a gay man? What factors do you think might have influenced his decision to stay in the closet or come out?

2. Why do you think that certain places like the Castro district in San Francisco have attracted gay people? Why do some gay individuals participate in Gay Pride parades and activities? Why do you think that some people find this offensive?

3. Why did Harvey Milk feel that it was important to young people for gay individuals to come out, openly run for office, and be recognized in their public and personal roles?

4. What attitudes and experiences do you think that Supervisor Dan White might have had that made him so uncomfortable with homosexuality? Why do you think some people are strongly opposed to gay rights and accepting homosexuals as teachers and other professionals?

5. What would it be like to come out as a gay person in your school? In your family? In your community?

6. Why do you think Joey hid his feelings for so many years? What did he gain by coming out?

7. What is hardest for you to understand about someone being gay?

Abstinence and Virginity *Page 00*

1. Why do you think Ramona decided to remain a virgin? Do you think her position would be realistic and reasonable at your school? What do you think about her decision?

2. What factors have you considered in deciding how sexually active you want to be? List pros and cons that you have considered in your thinking.

3. Ramona asserts that there are big differences in the ways that boys and girls think about and experience sex. What do you think?

4. *Have you had an open conversation with your parents about your sexual choices? What are your parents' attitudes about your sexuality? How realistic are they about your sex life and pressures?*

5. *How would you define virginity? Is "oral sex" sex?*

6. *Ramona has set some pretty clear standards for when and why she will have sex. What are yours?*

Male Sexuality *Page 00*

1. *What is the stereotype of male sexuality that is common at your school? What pressures or assumptions does this stereotype put on boys? On girls? On male/female relationships? Where does this model for male sexuality come from?*

2. *"I think most of the big talk that guys do is to impress other guys, not girls." What does Brett mean by this? Do you agree? Do girls do the same thing with girls?*

3. *How does the question of homosexuality affect male sexuality? Do you think girls have the same concerns or influences? Why or why not?*

4. *Brett thinks that girls are just as influenced by male stereotypes as guys and contribute to the pressures. How does this affect male/female relationships?*

5. *What do you think is an honest and realistic description of male sexuality? How is it different than female sexuality?*

6. *What does Brett mean by his last sentence: "As long as guys or girls are defined by this superficial sexual mythology, it's not sex; it's just masturbation"?*

Pregnancy *Page 00*

1. *"Passion was more powerful than logic." What factors do you think influence whether or not people use a reliable method of birth control on a regular basis? In what ways can parents or schools provide effective education?*

2. *How do you think Samantha's friends and peers felt about her continuing in school while she was pregnant? What reactions and feelings do you think her parents and teachers may have had? What would you have done? How do you think that students and teachers at your school would react to a pregnant student?*

3. *What do you think would be the hardest adjustments for you if you were pregnant during your senior year? How would all this be different if you were a boy who had gotten a girl pregnant?*

4. *How do you think Samantha felt about putting her baby up for adoption? What things might she have considered in making this decision? How do you think she might think and feel about this baby as she goes through her life?*

Abortion *Page 00*

1. *Why do you think that Melissa found it difficult to write about her abortion?*

2. *How do you feel about Melissa and Mike's sexual relationship? Were they truly responsible? How realistically and maturely do you think they handled this pregnancy?*

3. *Melissa found that facing a real-life decision about abortion was much more complicated than either pro-life or pro-choice opinions. What unforeseen factors do you think made this decision so difficult?*

4. *What do you think Mike was feeling and thinking throughout this whole experience? What role do men have in the decision to have an abortion?*

5. *How would this story have been different if Melissa and Mike had disagreed about what to do about this pregnancy? What if Mike had wanted to keep and raise the baby, but Melissa didn't? What if Mike thought an abortion was the only sensible choice, but Melissa decided to go on and have the baby on her own?*

6. *Why do you think many teens are reluctant to talk with their parents when they become pregnant? Would you talk with your mother or father? How do you think they would react?*

7. *Melissa never talks about giving birth and putting the baby up for adoption. How do you think that option fit into her decision to have an abortion? What factors do you think a person should consider in making this kind of decision?*

8. *How do you think this experience changed Melissa? Mike? What impact do you think it had on their relationship and future relationships?*

AIDS *Page 00*

1. *How was Carie coping with the pain and mortality her husband, Scott, was facing? Why was it so difficult for her to accept the fact that he was really dying? Why did they both keep insisting that he was going to "make it"?*

2. *Scott was infected with HIV by sharing a needle to inject cocaine during a party in high school before he went into rehab and stopped using drugs and alcohol. Carie was infected with HIV by having barrier-free sex with Scott before either of them knew he was HIV positive. These mistakes came at a high price. How could either of them have been protected?*

3. *How scary is it to be tested for HIV? What do you think was going through the minds of the "normal, healthy" looking people in the waiting room when Carie was waiting for her test results? How would you have reacted to Carie's news?*

4. *Why is it so difficult for people to accept the real possibility of AIDS or other sexually transmitted diseases? Why do people continue to take the risk?*

5. *Carie has chosen an alternative path for dealing with HIV. In addition to some medical help, what factors do you think are keeping her healthy? How can you use that message in your life?*

Sexual Assault *Page 00*

1. *Both Kevin and Pamela say that what happened was not rape. What do you think? How would you define what happened?*

2. *What responsibility did each of them have for what happened? What pressures were each of them dealing with?*

3. *How common do you think it is in your school for people to have sex for purely social or ulterior reasons? How can you tell if someone is being honest and sincere with you?*

4. *What do you think will be the long-term effects of this experience on Pamela? Kevin? What advice or recommendations would you give to each of them?*

Notes

[1] Steve Wall and Harvey Arden. *Wisdomkeepers: Meetings with Native American Spiritual Elders.* (The Earthsong Collection) Beyond Words Publishing, 1990 Berkeley, CA. Publishers Group West (800) 788-3123

[2] *Ibid.*